012

D0571984

May, Simon.
Windows 8 for tablets :
plain & simple
c2012 WITHDRAWN
33305226368482
mh   03/19/13

 Microsoft

Windows 8 for Tablets
Plain & Simple

Simon May

Published with the authorization of Microsoft Corporation by:
O'Reilly Media, Inc.
1005 Gravenstein Highway North
Sebastopol, California 95472

Copyright © 2012 Fakeurl Ltd.

All rights reserved. No part of the contents of this book may be reproduced or transmitted in any form or by any means without the written permission of the publisher.

ISBN: 978-0-7356-7083-9

1 2 3 4 5 6 7 8 9 TI 7 6 5 4 3 2

Printed and bound in Canada.

Microsoft Press books are available through booksellers and distributors worldwide. If you need support related to this book, email Microsoft Press Book Support at mspinput@microsoft.com. Please tell us what you think of this book at http://www.microsoft.com/learning/booksurvey.

Microsoft and the trademarks listed at *http://www.microsoft.com/about/legal/en/us/IntellectualProperty/Trademarks/EN-US.aspx* are trademarks of the Microsoft group of companies. All other marks are property of their respective owners.

The example companies, organizations, products, domain names, email addresses, logos, people, places, and events depicted herein are fictitious. No association with any real company, organization, product, domain name, email address, logo, person, place, or event is intended or should be inferred.

This book expresses the author's views and opinions. The information contained in this book is provided without any express, statutory, or implied warranties. Neither the authors, O'Reilly Media, Inc., Microsoft Corporation, nor its resellers, or distributors will be held liable for any damages caused or alleged to be caused either directly or indirectly by this book.

Acquisitions and Developmental Editor: Kenyon Brown
Production Editor: Kristen Borg
Editorial Production: Octal Publishing, Inc.
Interior Composition: Lisa Greenfield
Technical Reviewer: Katherine Murray
Indexer: Ron Strauss
Cover Design: Twist Creative • Seattle
Cover Composition: Zyg Group
Illustrator: Rebecca Demarest

Contents

About This Book   1

Exploring Your New Tablet   9

What do you think of this book? We want to hear from you!

Microsoft is interested in hearing your feedback so we can continually improve our books and learning resources for you. To participate in a brief online survey, please visit:

www.microsoft.com/learning/booksurvey/

Interacting with Windows 8   47

Customizing Windows 8   79

Using Apps   221

Connecting Email 241

Connecting to Social Networks 261

Enjoying Videos and Music 275

Connecting Cloud Storage with SkyDrive — 291

Working with Photos — 313

14 Keeping Files Organized 333

15 Connecting Your Tablet to TV and Display Devices 355

16 Connecting Printers and Devices 365

What do you think of this book? We want to hear from you!

Microsoft is interested in hearing your feedback so we can continually improve our books and learning
resources for you. To participate in a brief online survey, please visit:

www.microsoft.com/learning/booksurvey/

Acknowledgments

To Donna: Thank you for your support, I couldn't have done this again without you.
To baby May: Welcome.

I'd like to thank Helen Codling for the many introductions and support; Kenyon Brown for seeing potential and making this book happen; Katherine Murray for her expert technical review; Kristen Borg and the team who masterfully took the book through production; and finally thanks to Matt, Dan, Andrew, and Alex.

1 About This Book

This book is for people who have a Windows 8–based tablet and aren't quite sure how to do everything with it. Windows 8 makes your tablet very intuitive and very easy to use with touch, but you'll want a guide to help you get the most from it; that's why you have this book in your hand. Sure, you'll want to spend time with your tablet, getting used it and learning what it can do, but this book will help you cut down that time by showing you the quickest, easiest, and most memorable ways to complete a task.

Windows 8–based tablets aren't just about getting a job done. (Sure, they're brilliant at that!) They're also about having fun, checking your emails, catching up with friends, surfing the web. This book assumes that you'll be using touch to navigate Windows 8; however, where it makes sense, we expand on that so that you can also use a keyboard and mouse, which is still great for programs like Microsoft Excel.

A Quick Overview

Do you have the time to decode a book about your tablet? No, I thought not. When you want to do something on your tablet that you're not familiar with, you want learn how to do it quickly and easily. That's why we've built this book to be at-a-glance, quick to understand, with absolutely no knowledge of binary and hexadecimal math required! We get right to the point; every task is laid out in a simple-to-follow, step-based approach, showing you where to tap on the screen to make something happen.

I've written this book in plain English, with plenty of tips and cross references to other parts of the book so that you can easily work out what you're doing. You'll find that many things work in many places in Windows 8—for example, gestures like pinch to zoom work in many places throughout your Windows 8–based tablet. I've tried to highlight those so that you can get used to using touch. Occasionally, you'll spot a caution box; they are there to prompt you to think twice before doing something that, potentially, you cannot undo.

In Section 2, you'll learn how to get up and running with your tablet and learn how to find the Start screen at any time, how to open the desktop and desktop apps, lock and unlock your tablet, and where to find basic settings.

In Section 3, you'll learn how to use touch and touch gestures to navigate your tablet. We'll also take a look at how to use the on-screen keyboard and how you can connect a traditional keyboard and mouse to your tablet. Windows 8 can recognize your handwriting, too, so we'll look at how you switch from using a keyboard to writing by hand. We'll also explore some of the sensors that help Windows adapt to current situations, such as ensuring that the screen is oriented the right way.

In Section 4, you'll learn to customize Windows 8 to your needs, from the basics such as changing colors and backgrounds, to working with notifications and syncing your settings across computers.

In Section 5, you'll learn to connect your tablet to networks and to the Internet by using Wi-Fi or mobile broadband. When connected, you'll learn to share files and media by using HomeGroup, and you'll also learn how to get disconnected with Airplane mode.

In Section 6, you'll learn how to keep yourself and other users of your tablet, such as your kids, safe with the built-in anti-malware features of your Windows 8–based tablet. This section also teaches you about keeping your tablet up to date with updates from Microsoft, and if you have kids, you'll want to learn about the simple yet advanced features in Family Safety.

In Section 7, you'll learn how to browse the Internet with the built-in Internet Explorer web browser, using touch and on the desktop. You will gain an understanding of managing downloads and how to keep yourself safe online with Internet Explorer's built-in privacy features, such as InPrivate browsing and Tracking Protection.

In Section 8, you'll be introduced to apps in Windows 8 and learn how to download apps from the Windows Store and how to install desktop apps. You'll also learn how to have two apps running on screen at the same time and how to change settings within apps.

In Section 9, you'll learn to connect your Windows 8–based tablet to your email and how to do some basic tasks such as reading, writing, and organizing your emails. We'll also look at how to do some basic calendaring by using the Calendar app.

In Section 10, we will connect your social network accounts to your Microsoft Account and you'll learn how to find people, post status messages, and "like" your friends' social media updates.

In Section 11, you'll learn how to watch videos and listen to music on your Windows 8–based tablet by using the Music and Video apps. These apps are also connected to music and video stores, and you'll learn how to rent and buy new music and videos—and you can bring your existing collection along, as well.

In Section 12, you'll learn how to connect your tablet to the cloud and how to use cloud storage, in the form of your free SkyDrive account, to store your files. Storing files in the cloud means that you can securely access them anywhere, even without your tablet, which means that you don't fill up your tablet too quickly. We'll also look at using your SkyDrive with Microsoft Office to create and share documents with friends and coworkers.

In Section 13, you'll learn about using the Photos app on your tablet to view and share photos that are stored on your device, in the cloud, or on another cloud-connected computer. You'll also learn how to manage photos from the desktop.

In Section 14, you'll learn how to organize content such as videos, documents, and music on your tablet and how you can share those files with other home computers by using the Windows 8 HomeGroup feature.

In Section 15, you'll learn to show your videos, music, and photos on a big screen, by using technology such as PlayTo, with which you can send your media over your home network. You'll also learn how to connect to TVs and monitors by using cables or by using wireless display technology from Intel.

In Section 16, you'll learn how to connect devices that extend the functionality of your tablet, such as USB printers, and you'll learn how to use printers to print from any app that supports printing.

In Section 17, you'll learn how to use troubleshooters that are built into your Windows 8–based tablet to resolve common problems. Action Center is the place to understand the health of your tablet, and you'll learn to interpret what it's saying and take steps to resolve any potential problems Windows encounters. Backup, Recovery, Resetting, and Refreshing your tablet are also covered, and you'll learn the right time to use each option.

Tip

There's no need to read this book in order; simply jump to the appropriate section when you find yourself wanting some help.

What's New in Windows 8

A better title for this section might be "what isn't new in Windows 8"! Much has changed in Windows with this release from Microsoft; we have a new "style" of apps that consume the whole screen and don't distract you with notifications that pop up here, there and everywhere. This new style of immersive app lets you focus on what you're doing and maximizes all the space on screen for doing just that. The controls for using your tablet are almost always invisible and activated with a subtle but natural swipe this way or that—it can take a few minutes to get used to, but it will feel natural in no time.

It's not just the look of apps that has changed; along with this simplification comes an easier approach to obtaining new applications. Previous versions of Windows required you to get hold of the installation media for a program on either some physical media such as a CD or DVD, or to download it from a random web page. Windows 8 introduces the Windows Store which you can use in addition to these other installation methods, which makes it far easier to acquire any app you can dream of. The Windows Store is where any developer can place an app that they have built (after Microsoft have vetted that the app works and matches security requirements). This means that not only is there a single place to go to get the latest apps but that you can trust that the apps that are there won't go stealing your data or crashing your tablet.

Your Windows 8 tablet also takes a simplified approach to doing some everyday tasks such as connecting to networks. In previous versions if you wanted to use wireless broadband (3G/4G or LTE, for example) you had to install some software to make it all work. Now, that's changed and connecting to this type of network is almost identical to connecting to your home Wi-Fi.

Your tablet runs on batteries, and Windows 8 makes that much more efficient, too. Apps will shut themselves down when they aren't being used and will be very judicious about using the hardware in your tablet to also save battery life. Tablets are of course far more casual devices than desktop or laptop computers; you will likely want to pick it up for 5 minutes, check your mail, and put it down again. Microsoft recognizes this and has made simple things such as startup times much, much, much faster—typically taking less than 7 seconds from when you press power button to start up on many tablets.

The clever use of "wake up" on your tablet is also a huge improvement in Windows 8. Every hour or so your tablet will silently wake momentarily and update selected apps such as Mail. When you next return to your tablet your email will magically be updated with the latest messages you've received. One huge advantage your Windows 8 tablet has over other tablets is that it has a desktop that is built for really productive apps such as Microsoft Office. In fact, your tablet might well come with Microsoft Office preinstalled, and you'll find that it still runs on the desktop—which massively reduces your learning curve.

A Few Assumptions

This book is based on what I think you need to know about Windows 8 on a tablet, which means that everything is explained with touch in mind. If you're trying to use this book with a Windows 8 computer with a mouse and keyboard, you'll probably do just fine; just read *tap* as *click* and *tap and hold* as *right-click*. This book also assumes that you've used a computer before because so many people have at one time or other; however, it doesn't assume that you're an expert.

One major assumption in this book is that you have a Windows 8 tablet in front of you while you're reading this, and by that I mean that your tablet has Windows 8 installed. This book doesn't tell you how to do that. I also don't walk through the initial setup of a Windows 8 tablet, because Microsoft has created a very simple, self-explanatory wizard that does that for you when you turn it on for the first time. The book assumes that you've run through this process and to some extent expects that you've set up a Microsoft Account in the process. There are ways to use your tablet without a Microsoft Account, and I point some out, but I recommend that you embrace the account as you embrace your tablet—the experience is far better that way.

This book is also not aiming to make you a proficient Windows 8 business user; primarily, it's aimed at your personal use of Windows 8 tablets. As a result, we don't explain how to join a business network (domain) and how to link your Microsoft Account to your domain account. However, much of what is in this book is relevant in this situation because people are now commonly taking their own devices into the office to maintain their productivity. What you can and can't do in such circumstances is at the control and behest of your employer; my advice is to follow their counsel and ask your IT department or specialist before you do anything!

Access to the Internet is also assumed. The tablet is designed to be connected to the Internet as often as possible, if not continuously. If you are using your tablet in a completely disconnected way, parts of this book will not be for you, but some of it still will be useful. Internet access speed is largely irrelevant, too, but your tablet is highly unlikely to have come with a modem, so this book assumes that your Internet access is snappy.

The Big Non-Assumption

This book does not assume that you have a specific tablet other than that it runs Windows 8; this book doesn't care who the manufacturer is or whose logo is on the device. As a result, there are times when I will say "consult the manual," often because the exact location of your USB ports or what your tablet is capable of are beyond the scope of this book.

A Final Word

This book addresses the following basic goals:

- **Get you started with Windows 8**   A book that went into detail about every single detail of Windows 8, doing every single possible task would be very long, very heavy, and ultimately very advanced. This book aims to get you doing most things quickly.

- **Help you learn to learn**   Apps make the features and functionality of Windows 8 on your tablet infinitely extendable. As you read, try to keep an eye on what you're doing generally, not just on getting the task done; you'll find that things translate throughout Windows 8 very easily. For example, when you zoom in on a picture, you do that to see more detail, and when you zoom into a list of people in the People app, you also do that to see more detail. This gesture is repeated throughout Windows 8 and Windows 8 apps.

- **Have fun**   You didn't buy your tablet to be bored, did you? I'm sure you didn't. You'll find that the techniques in this book will get you moving quickly and that they lead you to exploring more; please do.

- **Stay safe**   There are online threats for both adults and kids, and it's the intention of this book that you can circumvent these threats. Watch out for cautions, read the safety sections, and always make a backup.

2

Exploring Your New Tablet

In this section of the book, we will come to grips with the shiny new Windows 8–based tablet device you have in your hands. The all-new, beautiful, fast and fluid look of Windows 8 is stunning, but you might need some help finding your way at the start. We will be exploring how you interact with Windows 8 to find information at a glance and to locate apps that focus on things you want to do. There are common ways to do things such as accessing the Start screen and changing settings, searching, shaping apps, and connecting devices by using Windows 8 charms. This chapter will show you how to perform these tasks.

Discovering apps in Windows 8 can be far more than just touching a tile on the desktop; you will also learn how to search for apps in this section so that you can discover some of the hidden gems available on your tablet. We will also take a look at the desktop, the space reserved for traditional applications, which helps deliver the no-compromise promise of your Windows 8–based tablet. You'll also find out how to customize the Start screen and how to switch between running apps and the desktop on your device. Of course, there will be times when you want to put your device down for a while, so we will be taking a tour of how you can sleep, restart, hibernate, and shut down your device.

Using the Start Screen

After unlocking your device, the first screen you see in Windows 8 is the Start screen. From here you can launch any app that you have installed on your device, access the desktop, access settings, and connect to other devices. The Start screen is made up of a number of *tiles*, which you use to launch apps as well as display information pertaining to those applications. Navigation of the screen is done just like everything else on your device—by using your fingers. And many more apps are available to you, in addition to what you see on the initial page of your Start screen.

Explore the Start Screen

1 Tap to open an app. This "live" tile represents information from an application (Weather, in this case).

2 Tap to reveal options to change the account picture of the current user or to sign out of or lock the device.

3 Tap the Desktop tile to display the desktop. This tile always shows a thumbnail of the desktop wallpaper.

4 To open the Maps app, tap its small app tile.

Pan the Start Screen

5 Touch and slide your finger left or right to navigate the Start screen. The Start screen sticks to your finger, but you can "flick" left or right to move rapidly.

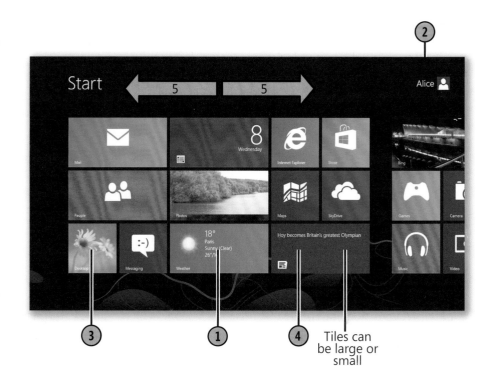

Tiles can be large or small

Tip

Not all tiles are "live"; some tiles, especially small tiles, are static and don't update with new information or pictures. These tiles display an icon. Similarly, tiles can be large or small, but only large tiles can be live.

Viewing More Apps

The apps you see on the Start screen have been *pinned* there, and there are more apps on your tablet than you see on the Start screen alone. To access all of the apps installed on your tablet, go to the All Apps screen.

The Start screen will grow to fit as many apps tiles as you have pinned to it, so you can pan left and right to view them all or you can zoom out to quickly move from one point to another.

View More Apps

① Place two fingers (thumb and forefinger) on the screen and pinch together to zoom in. You can control the zoom by how much you close the gap between your two fingers.

② Zoom out by placing two fingers on the screen and widening the gap between your fingers.

③ Tap the area near a group of tiles to instantly zoom in to that tile group.

Tip

It doesn't matter how hard you try; it is impossible to start an app when zoomed out.

④ Swipe downward from the top of the screen or upward from the bottom of the screen up to reveal the Apps Bar.

⑤ Tap All Apps to access all the apps installed on your tablet, not just the ones pinned to your Start screen.

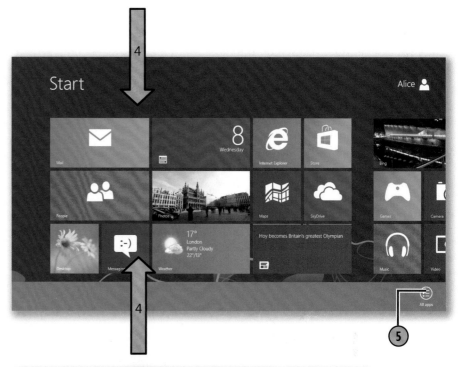

Try This!

Zoom out to categorize apps alphabetically and by app groups.

Understanding and Using Tiles

In Windows 8, tiles are used to launch all apps from the Start screen, but they are also invaluable as a way to quickly find information. For example, the Mail app will show you a short excerpt from your most recent emails and the number of unread messages that are currently in your inboxes, and the Calendar app will show your next upcoming appointment. This quick view into apps can be instantly insightful but can also become overwhelming with many rapidly changing live tiles.

Thankfully, you can selectively turn live tile updates on and off on a per-app basis.

Not all apps use a live tile; some have a static symbol that represents their purpose—Internet Explorer 10, for example. App tiles can come in two sizes, small and large, and a mix of the two will help you maintain a balance between fast access to apps and information awareness.

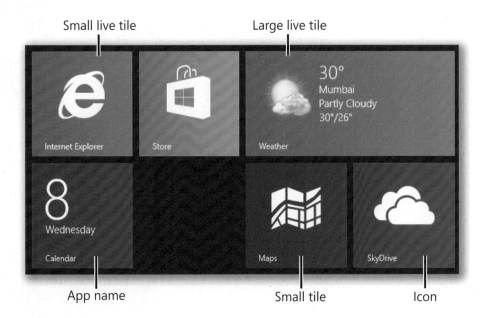

Use Tile Options

(1) Touch and swipe down slightly on an app tile to reveal the app bar at the bottom of the screen.

(2) Tap to remove the tile from the Start screen; don't worry if you do this accidentally because there will also be a tile in the All Apps screen.

(3) Tap to remove the app from your device. When you do this, the app and possibly its data will be unavailable.

(4) Tap to shrink the tile to half its size (available only on large tiles). For small tiles, the option is to make them larger.

(5) Tap to prevent the tile from receiving live updates and, therefore, showing information from within the app.

App bar with app tile options

More Tile Options

You might find that you need to unpin more than one tile at a time to quickly clear up your Start screen. You can do this by selecting multiple tiles. Tiles are also available for desktop apps, and they have alternate options for starting an app, such as in administrator mode or in a new window.

Select Multiple Tiles

① Add tiles to a selection by touching a tile and swiping down a little. Repeat for each tile to add to the selection.

② Tap if you want to remove all the selected tiles from the Start screen all at once.

③ Deselect all items in the selection.

④ Remove a single item from a selection by touching the tile and swiping down a little, the same method as selecting the tile.

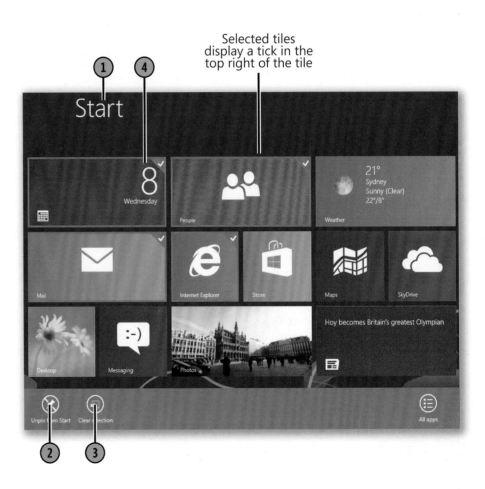

Selected tiles display a tick in the top right of the tile

Options for Desktop Apps

① Tap to remove the tile from the Start screen.

② Tap to add an icon to the taskbar visible only on the desktop; use this as a way to quickly open the app from the desktop.

③ Tap to uninstall the app from your tablet—to complete this process, you'll be taken to the Control Panel.

④ Tap to open the application in a new window on the desktop, even if an existing copy of the app is already open.

⑤ Tap to run the app with Administrator credentials. Most apps in Windows 8 run with User credentials, so they are less likely to inadvertently damage the system. Selecting Run As Administrator gives the app the ability to do almost anything it wants to your tablet.

⑥ Tap to open the location of the app's program files in a desktop File Explorer window.

See Also

For more information on uninstalling desktop applications, see page 239.

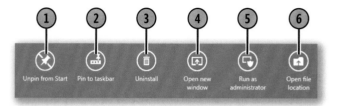

Arranging Programs

The default arrangement of tiles on the Start screen helps you to see what Windows 8 can do for you, but it doesn't really make things personal. You can move tiles around on the Start screen to your liking, creating groupings of items that are meaningful to you. Groups can also be named, and you can order the tiles within a group to help you gather more information at a glance.

Move a Tile to a New Group

Transparent bar represents a place to create a new group

① Tap and hold a tile, swipe down slightly, and then move to where you would like to create the new group. A transparent bar appears, indicating the location of the new group.

② When you get to where you want the group to be, lift your finger to release the tile and create the group.

Try This!

Using one finger, start to move a tile to a new location. Then, using a finger on your other hand, swipe left or right. You'll find that the tile you're moving stays still but the rest of the Start screen moves, allowing you to more quickly place tiles where you want them!

Name a Group

 1 Zoom out.

2 Tap, hold, and swipe down a group to select it. Notice the check mark that appears when it is selected.

3 Tap Name Group to display the dialog box in which you can enter a name for your group.

4 Enter the name.

5 Tap the Name button to finish.

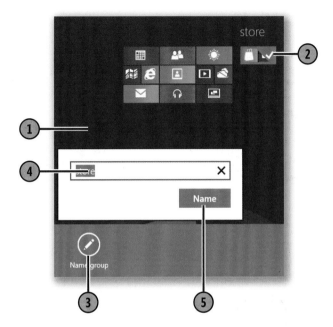

Tip ✓

If you want to remove the name of a group, follow the above procedure—but when prompted for the name, just delete what's in the box.

Move a Tile Within a Group

1. Tap and hold a tile and then swipe down slightly.

2. Drag to where you would like to place the tile within the group.

3. When the tile is in the location where you want it to stay, lift your finger.

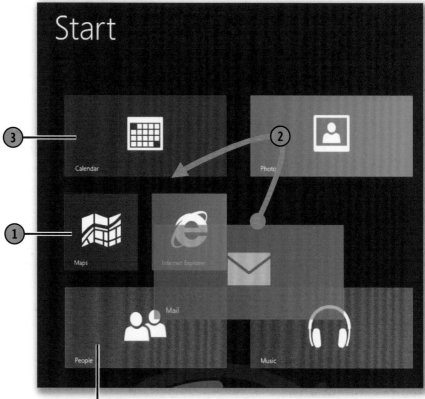

Tiles move to make space for the tile you wish to rearrange

Discovering Charms

Charms are a new addition to Windows 8. They provide easy access to settings and tools you use regularly. They are available anywhere in Windows 8, be it an app, the desktop, the Start screen, or a webpage, and you can use them to quickly accomplish common tasks, including the following:

- Use the Search charm to quickly find anything on your tablet. You can search for apps, settings or files, and you can search within the information stored and offered by many apps on your tablet. For example, typing coffee into search and tapping Internet Explorer performs a search on your chosen Internet search engine.

- The Share charm provides instant access to ways by which you can share the content you are currently looking at with friends, whether via email or with any of the social networks to which your tablet is connected.

- The Start charm is the route for instant access to the Start screen.

- Use the Devices charm to connect your tablet to other devices such as secondary displays or network media devices.

- The Settings charm quickly accesses commonly used settings, such as volume, brightness, and available wireless networks. Notifications can also be disabled and enabled here, and the power state of your device can be managed, as well. With a couple of extra taps, the Settings charm also provides access to more advanced settings for your device.

Search

Share

Start

Devices

Settings

Tip

Keyboard and mouse users can also access the charms by moving the mouse pointer to the upper-right or lower-right corners of the screen. The charms will fade in.

Tip

The Windows logo key+C can also be used from a keyboard to display the charms.

 **See Also**

See page 24 for more information about changing settings.

Show Charms

① From the right edge of the Start screen, swipe inward to display the charms.

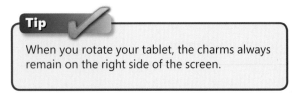

Tip

When you rotate your tablet, the charms always remain on the right side of the screen.

Hide Charms

1. Repeat the same gesture, swiping from the right edge of the Start screen to hide the charms.

2. Alternatively, swipe toward the right to hide the charms.

3. Alternatively, tap the screen to hide the charms; be sure to do this in an inactive area of the screen.

Tip

If you need to know the current date and time, remaining battery life, or connectivity signal strength, this information is displayed whenever the charms are displayed.

Exploring Settings

The Settings charm provides quick access to a number of key options that you might need to be able to change quickly. The menu is contextual, meaning that different options are displayed depending on the app you have open. Settings is also the gateway to the deeper configuration options of Control Panel.

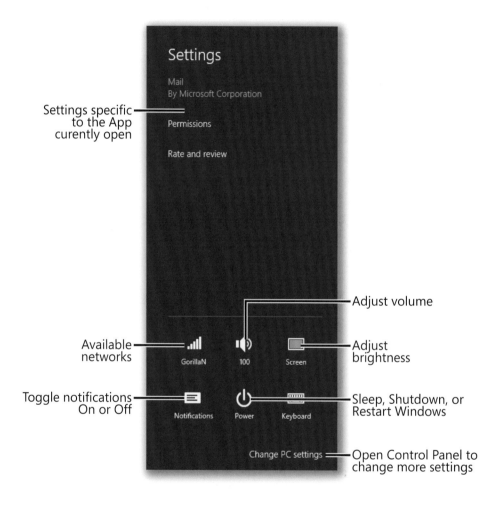

Settings specific to the App curently open

Adjust volume

Available networks

Adjust brightness

Toggle notifications On or Off

Sleep, Shutdown, or Restart Windows

Open Control Panel to change more settings

See Also

Read "Connecting to Wi-Fi" on page 126 for information about how to connect to networks from the Settings menu.

Adjust Volume and Screen Brightness

① Display the charms and then tap the Volume icon.

② When the slider appears, touch it and drag up or down to increase or decrease volume. A number indicating the percentage volume appears, too.

③ When done, lift your finger and tap the screen elsewhere.

This same process is used to adjust screen brightness.

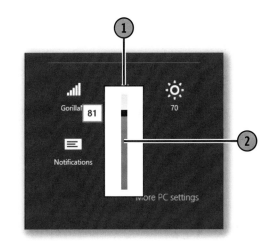

Tip

You can still use the volume buttons on your tablet to control volume; they work in conjunction with these volume settings.

Try This!

Mute your sound. On the Settings menu, tap the volume icon, and then at the top of the slider, tap the speaker icon—a small X will appear and the volume will be muted.

Searching Your Device

Search in Windows 8 is an immensely pow-
erful and efficient way of getting around
your device and finding information.
Windows 8 apps provide search in the
same place, from the charms, which makes
finding information easier than ever before.

Search from the Start Screen

1. Type in anything you want to find
   on your device; results will start to
   appear as you type and will narrow as
   you complete words.

2. Select a category to see results from
   that category.

3. Tap an app to search from within that
   app.

4. Tap a result to open an app, setting,
   or file returned by the search.

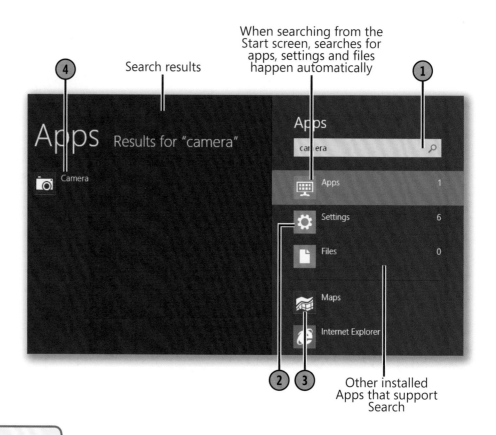

When searching from the
Start screen, searches for
apps, settings and files
happen automatically

Search results

Apps   Results for "camera"

Camera

Apps

camera

Apps   1

Settings   6

Files   0

Maps

Internet Explorer

Other installed
Apps that support
Search

Try This!

To find files that include your name, type your name into
the Search box and tap Files. Windows will search all files
on your tablet for any that contain your name. Tap a result
to open the file.

Search from Within an App

(1) Type the name of the item you want to search for. Tapping the X clears the entry.

(2) Select a search result to open that item.

(3) Tap an alternative app in which to search.

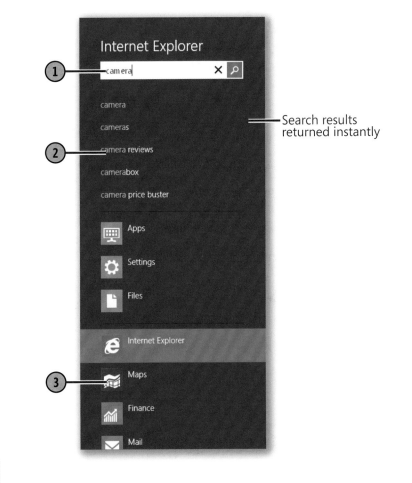

Search results returned instantly

 Try This!

Type your favorite vacation destination into the Search bar and tap Internet Explorer to get results from the web. Then, tap the Maps app to get a map of the location, or tap the Finance app to get the latest exchange rate to local currency.

Tip

It's possible to search within a different app from any app with search capability, so you can be researching things to do on the weekend in Internet Explorer and then search for the location in the Maps app.

Navigating PC Settings

PC Settings is the primary location for changing and customizing your device. From here, you can change your wallpaper, lock screen and account images, set up new users, change passwords, control privacy and search settings, and configure a whole host of other options. The PC Settings page can be accessed by tapping the Settings charm and then tapping the More PC Settings option.

Setting	Description
Personalize	• Change the lock screen wallpaper and the information displayed on the lock screen. The applications that can run in the background to update lock screen notifications are also controlled here. • Customize the background color and pattern on the Start screen. • Select an account picture.
Users	• Change the type of account (local, synced with a Microsoft Account, or a Domain account). • Change the account password of the current account, or select a short PIN for rapid entry or a picture password. • Add extra users to the device.
Notifications	• Control which applications are allowed to make use of notifications to let you know when they have something to announce.
Search	• Decide whether Windows can save your search history and control apps that can use search as well as delete your search history to keep it more private.
Share	• Allow or block apps from appearing in the Share charm menu.
General	• Adjust the time zone and enable and disable the ability to switch quickly between apps • Adjust how the on-screen keyboard completes words, what it auto-capitalizes, and the text it suggests. • Turn the system-wide, built-in spelling checker on or off and control how it highlights errors. • Change the language your device uses for keyboard layouts and on-screen text. • Refresh your device without losing your personal files. • Wipe everything on your device by performing a reset. • Change the startup settings for your device to boot from something special such as a CD, DVD, or USB key, or to restore from a saved image of your device.
Privacy	• Control whether apps are allowed to use your location, name, or account picture or to send information about your app usage. You can also view the Microsoft privacy statement here.

Setting	Description
Devices	• View and add devices connected to your tablet over the network, such as printers, media servers, or your Xbox 360. • Control whether Windows can download additional device drivers over metered connections, such as 3G/4G, HSPA, LTE, or Mobile Broadband.
Wireless	• Turn on or off the wireless networking in your device. • Enable Airplane mode so that you can use your device while in flight.
Ease of Access	• Apply high-contrast screen setting, make text bigger, cursors thicker, or notifications longer to make the screen easier to read. • Turn browsing modes (caret) on or off to enable screen readers. • Enable Windows Narrator to explain what's on the screen.
Sync your settings	• Allow settings to sync to your Microsoft Account to enable a near identical experience from multiple devices. • Configure sync settings such as backgrounds, lock screens, themes, taskbars, Ease-of-Access preferences, languages, app settings, browser settings, mouse settings, and accounts for websites and social networks. • Control whether Windows syncs these settings over metered connections , such as 3G/4G, HSPA, LTE, or Mobile Broadband.
HomeGroup	• Enable sharing with other computers in your home and with media devices such as network-capable TVs. • View the HomeGroup password so that you can allow others to join.
Windows Update	• Check for and select Windows Updates to keep your device up to date and to fix problems with your device.

See Also

Read "Change Desktop Wallpapers for a Theme" on page 88 for more information about how to change wallpapers and where those wallpapers can come from.

See Also

Read "Sharing Files and Media with HomeGroup" on page 138 for more information on setting up and connecting homegroups.

Change Between PC Settings Categories and Options

(1) Swipe up or down to reveal additional settings categories not shown on the initial screen.

(2) Swipe up or down to reveal additional options that do not fit on a single screen.

(3) Tap a category to select and display the options in the right pane.

(4) Tap a setting tab to display more setting options.

Setting categories panel   Setting options panel

Understanding Types of Setting Controls

Select one of
multiple options.
Tap the current option
to produce a popup
with alternative
options

Toggle switches to turn
a setting On or Off

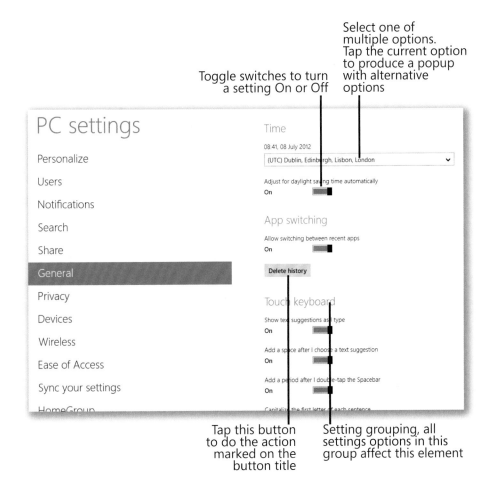

Tap this button
to do the action
marked on the
button title

Setting grouping, all
settings options in this
group affect this element

Viewing More Settings in Control Panel

Although many settings have been made available through the PC Settings app, there are more settings that can be controlled on your device. They are located in the same place they traditionally have been, inside the Control Panel. You can display the Control Panel by swiping up from the bottom of the Start screen and tapping All Apps. The Control Panel is viewed from the desktop and provides a task-based and category-based approach to changing settings.

View Settings

① Tap a category title to view all the settings that can be changed within that category, or select a task to go directly to the settings for the detailed task.

The View By drop-down can be used to show all items within Control Panel

Search can be used to find a specific setting

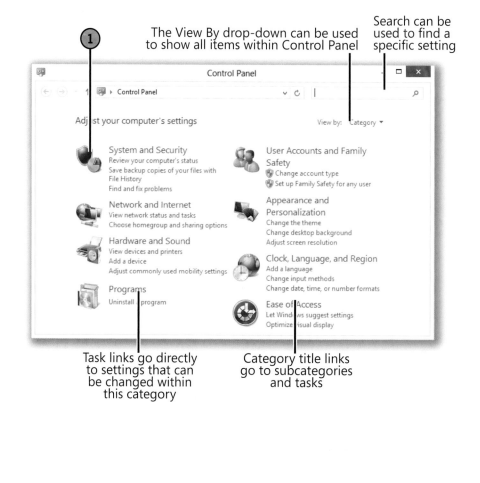

Task links go directly to settings that can be changed within this category

Category title links go to subcategories and tasks

Tip

A quick way to get from the desktop to the Control Panel is to click the Settings charm.

Exploring the Desktop

Windows 8 provides a no-compromise approach by incorporating a desktop you are probably already familiar with, allowing apps that worked in Windows 7 to continue working through the desktop. The desktop is accessed from the Desktop tile on the Start screen. The Desktop tile is also personalized with your wallpaper, so you can select a personal photo to reflect your personality.

The desktop itself, as typified by the wallpaper

Desktop shortcuts used to launch desktop apps

Application jump list revealing quick access to common app features or tasks

A running desktop application

Apps pinned to the taskbar

Running apps, distinguishable from pinned apps by the order around the icon

The taskbar

Launch the onscreen keyboard—hidden by default on the desktop

Current date and time

Notification area icons, can be turned on and off

Tip

There are many elements to the desktop, and more than just your fingers might be required to perform some tasks. Luckily, the desktop is also designed to work with a keyboard and mouse, just as it always has in Windows.

Start Desktop Apps

1 On the Start screen, tap an icon for a desktop app to open that app on the desktop.

2 Access jump lists by touching an icon on the taskbar and swiping up without removing your finger.

3 Tap your choice of action.

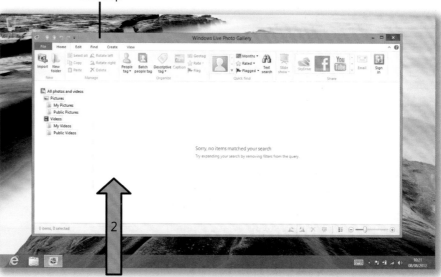

Apps that launch on the desktop also appear on the Start screen; however they don't appear with an interactive tile, making them easy to distinguish from Windows 8 apps

Desktop App (Microsoft Windows Live Photo Gallery) running on the desktop

Close, Maximize, and Minimize Desktop Apps

1 Tap to close the application.

2 When an app is windowed maximize the application to take up the whole desktop, when already maximized, restores the application to a windowed application.

3 Minimize the application to the taskbar, removing the window from view.

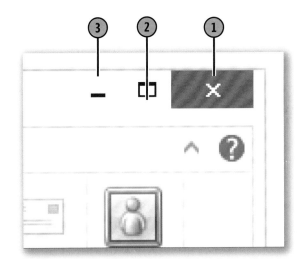

Tip ✓

You can also "snap" desktop apps to the left and right or to full screen. Tap the title bar of the app and drag to the left edge of the desktop to "snap" to the left half of the screen. Tap the title bar of the app and drag to the right edge of the desktop to "snap" to the right half of the screen. Or, tap the title bar of the app and drag to the top edge of the desktop to "snap" the app into full screen. Snapping is really useful when comparing the contents of two app windows.

Switching Between Apps

Windows 8 is capable of running many different apps at once, and switching between them is done with a simple, fluid movement. When desktop apps are running at the same time, switching to a desktop app is achieved by first selecting the desktop and then selecting the desktop app.

Cycle Through Apps

① From the left edge of the screen, swipe inward from the left side of the screen to bring up the last-viewed app.

Try This!

To view two apps at the same time, swipe to the right, hold, and then go a little further. You'll see the current app "pop backward" and a border appear around it. While still holding the switched app, move your finger left and hold about half an inch from the left edge. You'll see your main app move slightly right; when you lift your finger, the app you're switching to will move into a space to the left of your original app.

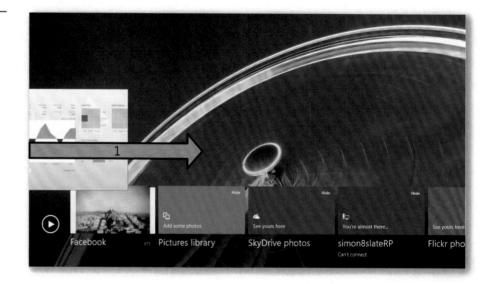

Select from Running Apps

① Repeat the previous gesture for cycling through apps by swiping from the left side of the screen, stopping part way, and swiping back off, left of the screen, all without removing a finger from the screen.

② Select the app you want to view by tapping the thumbnail preview.

Tip ✓

This is also an alternative way to return to the Start screen (select the Start screen thumbnail).

Tip ✓

Keyboard shortcuts can make this much quicker if you have a keyboard attached. There are alternatives too; pressing Windows logo key+Tab to select from thumbnails, as above. Use Alt+Tab to switch between the Start screen and desktop apps.

Setting Passwords, PINs, and Picture Passwords

Given all the information you store on your tablet and the accounts and clouds it can access, one of your priorities will be keeping it secure. Windows 8 introduces two new ways to unlock your tablet, PIN (Personal Identification Numbers) and Picture Passwords. Both provide a more convenient and secure way to unlock your tablet than typing in a traditional password. Which you use is up to you (and your administrator, if you have one). Go to PC Settings to select the method you want to use.

Change Your Password

1. Open PC Settings by tapping More PC Settings from the Settings panel.

2. Select the Users category to change user account settings.

3. Tap Change Your Password to start the password change process.

Caution

Changing the password for a Microsoft Account (usually your Hotmail address) will change your password everywhere, so the next time you try to log in to a Live service such as Hotmail, you will need to use your new password.

Enter your existing password.

 Tap Next.

 Enter a new password.

 Repeat the password entry to ensure that it's correct.

 Enter a hint to help you remember your password if you forget it.

 Tap Next to complete the process, and then tap Finish at the confirmation screen.

Set a Picture Password

① Tap Users to select user account properties.

② Tap Create A Picture Password.

You will be asked to enter the current text password to proceed.

③ Tap to browse for a picture to use as a picture password.

Tip

You will need to pay attention to how the lines are redrawn by Windows, too. Generally, your pattern will be fine, but occasionally Windows gets it a little wrong.

Select the picture to use as a picture password.

 Tap Open to view a larger version of the picture and to confirm it or to change it.

 Tap to confirm this picture.

 Follow the on-screen instructions to draw a pattern on the screen that you will repeat to unlock the device. You can use either circles or lines drawn in specific directions, and dots.

Select a location on your device where pictures are stored

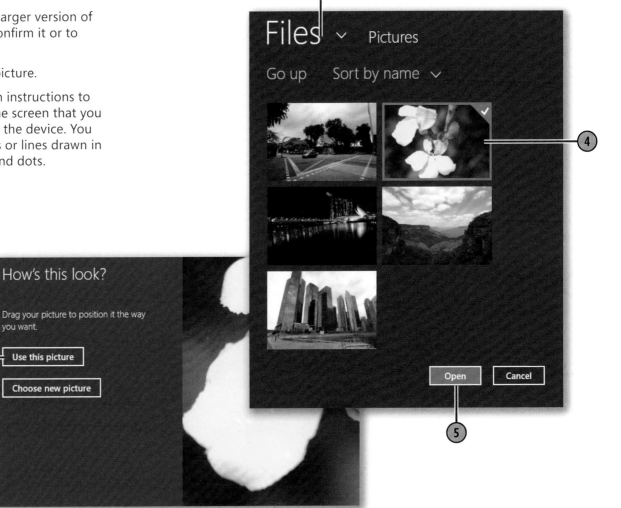

Files ∨   Pictures

Go up   Sort by name ∨

4

How's this look?

Drag your picture to position it the way you want.

Use this picture

Choose new picture

6

Open   Cancel

5

Set a PIN

(1) Tap Users to make changes to the current user account.

(2) Tap the Create A PIN button to begin the PIN setting process. When prompted, confirm your current text password.

(3) Enter a four-digit number as your new PIN code.

(4) Confirm the exact same four-digit number.

(5) Tap Finish to set the PIN number. From this point, you will be able to log on with just this PIN.

Tip

Make your PIN easy to remember but not easy to guess, just like your ATM card PIN. Try to avoid obvious numbers such as birthdays.

Caution

A four-digit PIN is easier to guess than a 19-character password that's a combination of letters and numbers. If you are using a corporate device or one connected to Microsoft Exchange for email, your administrator might require more stringent security.

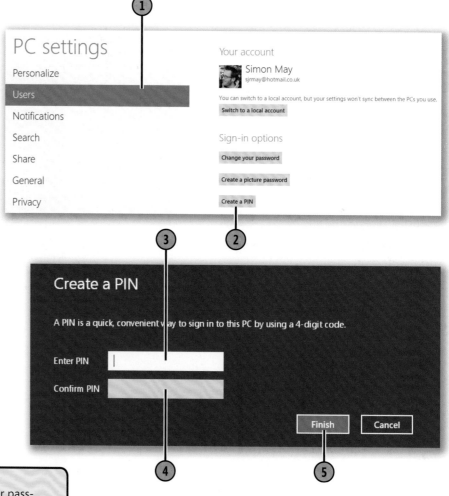

PC settings

Personalize

Users

Notifications

Search

Share

General

Privacy

Your account

Simon May
sjrmay@hotmail.co.uk

You can switch to a local account, but your settings won't sync between the PCs you use.

Switch to a local account

Sign-in options

Change your password

Create a picture password

Create a PIN

Create a PIN

A PIN is a quick, convenient way to sign in to this PC by using a 4-digit code.

Enter PIN

Confirm PIN

Finish   Cancel

Locking and Unlocking Your Device

Locking your tablet is one way to ensure that information stays safe, and if you're in a managed environment, it's something your administrator might require and enforce.

① Tap the name of the currently logged-on user to open a dialog box with account options.

② To lock the screen, tap Lock and require the entry of a password, PIN, or picture password to continue. Alternatively, tap Sign Out to switch to a different account.

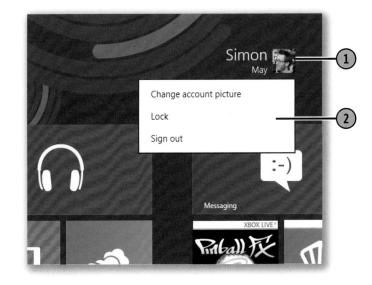

Tip ✔

If you already have other users set up on your device, you will see them listed on this pop-up and you can quickly switch to one of those accounts by tapping it.

Unlock or Log On to Your Device

(1) Touch anywhere on screen and slide up to reveal the unlock screen.

(2) Enter a password or PIN in the text entry box, as requested.

(3) You can tap the Go button to unlock, but the device will unlock automatically without you needing to do this as soon as the password or PIN is correct.

(4) Tap the Sign-In Options link to reveal options to change to a different sign-in type, either password, PIN, or picture password.

(5) Tap the key icon to switch to signing in with a text password number.

(6) Tap the keypad icon to switch to signing in with a PIN number.

(7) Tap the picture icon to switch to signing in with a picture password and then complete the required gestures over the picture.

Sleeping, Restarting, and Shutting Down Your Tablet

Windows 8 includes the ability to very rapidly turn your tablet device on from either a totally shut down state or from a sleep state. The difference between the two is that in sleep, the device wakes periodically for brief moments to update your information from the cloud. It's because of this that your emails, weather, and calendar will be up to date as soon as you log on.

Sleep, Shut Down, or Restart Your Device

(1) Display the charms, and then tap the Settings charm.

(2) Tap Power to open the power options dialog box.

(3) Select Sleep, Shut Down, or Restart, depending on your choice of action.

Tip

You can also just push the Power button on your tablet to send it to sleep.

3

Interacting with Windows 8

There are many ways to interact with Windows 8 on your tablet; the first is obviously touch, where there are some hidden gems in the form of gestures. Gestures help to get things done in Windows 8, aiding navigation and control on your device.

Other input methods, such as keyboard and mouse, still work brilliantly. For example, this book was written using a Windows 8–based tablet, but writing a book is not something I'd want to do purely using the on-screen keyboard—great though it is. If you need to enter lots of text to write long emails or be accurate with the mouse when editing a photo, you'll want to make use of more traditional input methods by connecting a mouse and keyboard. If you're a keyboard warrior, adept at the fast-paced language of keyboard shortcuts, this section will show you some new and popular keyboard shortcuts.

Most of us are comfortable with handwriting, and while our lettering might be illegible to some, Windows 8 can use handwriting recognition to transform your handwriting into typed letters. In this section, we will see how Windows automatically recognizes your handwriting.

Using Touch

Throughout Windows 8, there is a language of gestures by which you can get things done. Many of them were introduced in Section 2, "Exploring Your New Tablet," which explains how to navigate and manage the settings on your tablet; however, they are also used in many other places.

Tap to Do Something

① Tap any item on the screen to perform the action, like starting an app or clicking a button.

Tap any item on screen to perform the action, like starting an app, clicking a button

Scroll by Dragging

① Tap and drag anywhere to scroll in the direction you move your finger. Moving to the left reveals more to the right, and vice versa. The same is true for scrolling up and down.

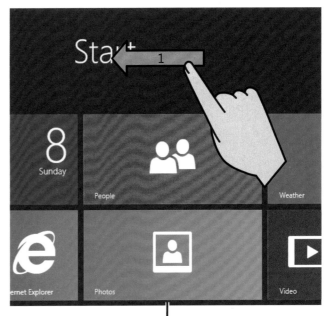

This scrollbar tells you where you are scrolling

Tip

Scrolling can also be achieved with a flick. Imagine holding a penny against a table with one finger and then flicking to the left or right to send it flying. Now use the same gesture to control your device; don't send your tablet flying though, just the items on the screen.

Zoom In or Out with a Pinch

① To zoom in to a list or a picture, place two fingers together and then move them apart. To zoom out, place two fingers apart and then move them together.

Tip

It's not just pictures and lists that can be zoomed. Windows 8 uses "semantic zoom," with which you can zoom in on information. Imagine a hierarchical list, much like this book: sections have topics, and topics have tasks—each a parent and a child. In an app organized in such a way, zooming out from a task would reveal the topic and the section. Many magazine apps are structured like this.

Turn by Rotating Fingers

1 To rotate objects on screen, such as photos or shapes in an app, place two fingers on the screen and pivot one about the other. Imagine using a compass to draw a circle; replicate that movement with your fingers.

Using Touch on the Desktop

Touch is also available on the desktop in Windows 8, but if you're familiar with using the desktop with a mouse in a previous version of Windows, some things will be different. With a mouse, you can left-click or right click to bring up different options. However, the screen cannot tell the difference between your left and right hand, so an alternative is needed.

Press and Hold for Options

1. Press anywhere on the desktop, and do not remove your finger. A box will grow around your finger. When it stops growing, remove your finger to reveal the options menu.

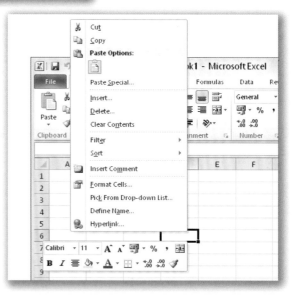

See Also

Use the Pen and Touch settings described on page 74-75 to adjust the timings to suit your style. You can also adjust how far you can move your finger while completing this action; if you move your finger too far, the action will be canceled.

Using On-Screen Keyboards

Windows 8 includes different on-screen keyboards that work better under different circumstances, depending on your own preferences. If you like to hold your tablet in one hand and tap the keys with the other, the default style will suit you—likewise if you like to put your tablet down to type on it. A second keyboard layout allows you to type with just your thumbs while holding the device in both hands—it's easier than it sounds!

Use the up arrow keys for upper case but tap and hold to select Caps Lock

Tap the &123 button to access the numeric and symbols keyboard

Tap the smiley button to access the extensive emoticons keyboard

Use these cursor keys to move left and right through text

Tip ✓

Both the numeric and symbols and the emoticon keyboards include multiple pages of symbols. Use the left and right arrows on the keyboards to page through the emoticons.

Tip ✓

If you need even more emoticons, use the balloon, pizza, airplane, weather, exclamation, and basic smiley buttons to select additional pages of emoticons.

Select Thumb or Full Keyboard

 Tap the keyboard symbol, which is the button located in the lower-right corner on the current keyboard.

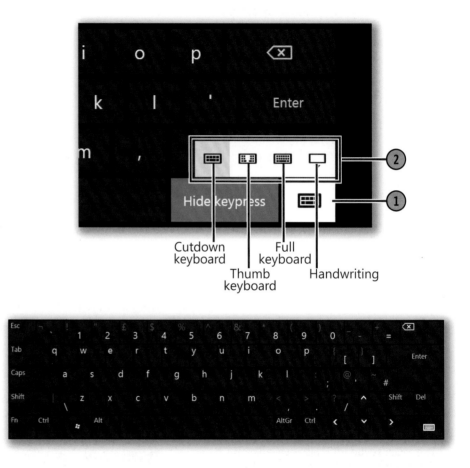 Select one of the alternate keyboards, thumb or full, or alternatively, select handwriting recognition.

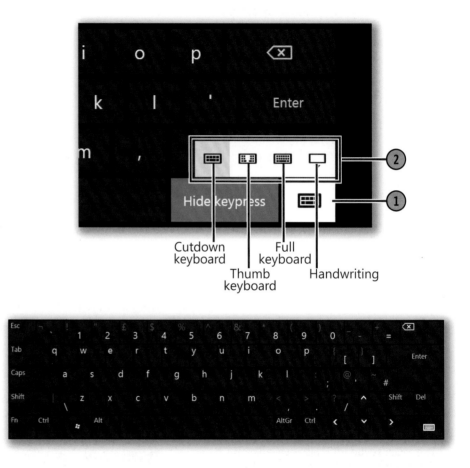

Cutdown keyboard
Full keyboard
Thumb keyboard
Handwriting

Tip

On the desktop, dock the keyboard by tapping the dock icon to the left of the X that closes the keyboard.

Change Touch Keyboard Settings

1 In PC Settings, tap the General category.

2 Scroll down until the Touch keyboard settings are available.

3 Turn settings on or off by tapping toggle switches.

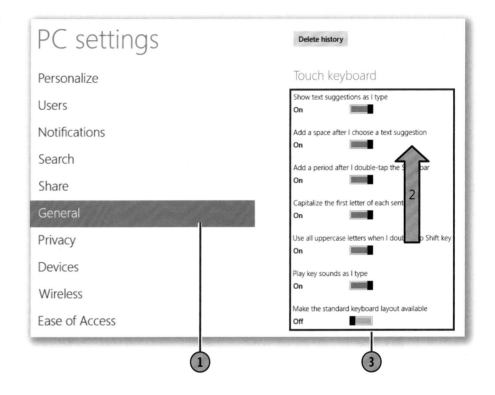

Tip

The touch keyboard is also available on the desktop via an icon on the taskbar. If the icon is not visible, right-click the taskbar (or tap and hold), select Properties, and then on the Toolbars tab, select Touch Keyboard and click OK.

Connecting a Keyboard and Mouse

Even though you might be totally happy with touch, sometimes you might need to enter more significant amounts of text, or sometimes the accuracy of a mouse over a finger might be preferable. For those reasons, Windows 8 is still a great experience when you attach a keyboard and/or a mouse.

The way you attach a mouse or keyboard varies depending on the type of connection the mouse or keyboard uses. Generally, you attach mice and keyboards by using either USB or Bluetooth. USB keyboards and mice can be either wired or wireless. With wireless, there is usually a "dongle" that transmits a wireless signal between your device and your keyboard or mouse. Bluetooth keyboards and mice connect to the Bluetooth connection built in to your tablet.

Usually, when you plug in a keyboard or mouse, your tablet will recognize them and they'll just work. Some keyboards and mice require the installation of additional "drivers." These are small software programs that work wth Windows 8 to let it know how to work with a particular device and whether there are any extended features of the keyboard or mouse, such as extra keys or buttons. Often these will download automatically from Windows Update, but sometimes you will need to download the driver from the manufacturer's website or install it from the CD that came with the keyboard or mouse.

Connect a USB Keyboard or Mouse

(1) To connect a USB keyboard or mouse, simply plug in the USB dongle. Windows 8 detects the device, and the Device Setup pop-up window might appear to indicate installation progress.

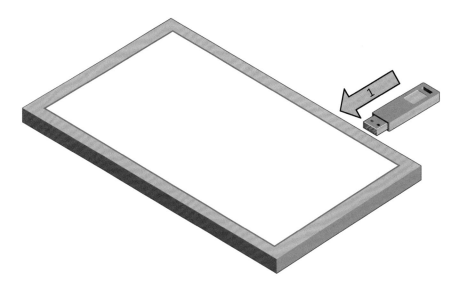

Device Setup

Installing USB Multimedia Wireless Kit

Please wait while Setup installs necessary files on your system. This may take several minutes.

Close

Connect a Bluetooth Keyboard or Mouse

(1) In the Settings pane, tap the More PC Settings link and then tap the Devices category.

(2) Tap the command to Add A Device to instruct the tablet to start searching for devices; any devices that can be connected to your tablet will be displayed.

(2)

PC settings

Personalize

Users

Notifications

Search

Share

General

Privacy

Devices

Wireless

Ease of Access

Sync your settings

HomeGroup

Devices

Add a device

DMA2200 (j7jrmhtvrl10)
Offline

GIBBON: home:

Jawbone

Journal Note Writer
Ready

Kitchen

Logitech Media Server [monkey]
Offline

Microsoft XPS Document Writer
Ready

Microsoft® Nano Transceiver v1.0

MONKEY
Offline

MONKEY: media center:

(1)

Tip ✔

Ensure that your keyboard or mouse is in "pairing" or "discovery mode" prior to trying to find it! This is different for every Bluetooth keyboard or mouse, so check your keyboard or mouse manual or search on the Internet to find out how.

3 From the list of available devices, select the keyboard or mouse you want to connect.

4 When pairing a Bluetooth device (creating a unique relationship between your tablet and the device), you will be given a passcode to enter into the keyboard. If you are connecting a mouse, you will be prompted to enter a passcode that is hard-coded into the mouse; this should be listed in the documentation for the mouse.

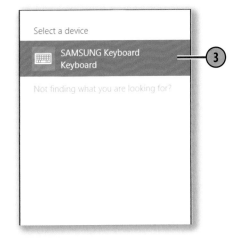

Tip

Most Bluetooth mice use a standard passcode of 0000 or 1234. Try these if you are unable to find the code in the documentation for your mouse. An alternative is to search the Internet for the code; most are documented on the manufacturer's website.

Changing Keyboard Settings

The way your keyboard responds to your key presses can make a great deal of difference to your typing experience, but there are a few things you can change. All settings for the non-touch keyboards for your tablet are accessible from the Control Panel and appear on the desktop.

Change Character Repeat Settings

① Search for "keyboard" by using the Search charm with Settings selected.

② Tap the Keyboard item to open the Keyboard Properties dialog box.

③ Use the slider to adjust the delay between repeated keys. A longer delay will result in fewer repeats; a shorter delay results in more.

④ Control the repeat rate, which is the time between one repeat and the next.

⑤ Use the text entry box to test the repeat rate, and then repeat steps 3 and 4 of this procedure to get to a comfortable point.

⑥ Tap OK to confirm the changes and close the dialog. Tap Apply to confirm the changes or tap Cancel to abandon the changes and close the dialog.

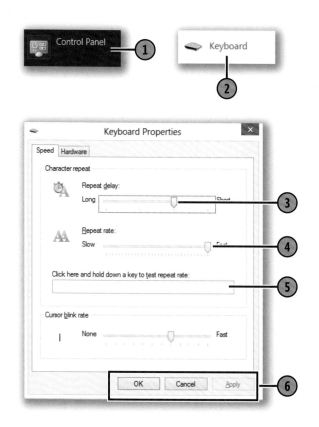

Check Keyboard Status

(1) Tap the Hardware tab.

(2) View the Device status and connection location of your keyboard. This is the place to look if for some reason your tablet is not responding to your keyboard.

(3) Tap Properties to view detailed information about your keyboard. Tap OK to close the Properties dialog box.

(4) Tap OK to confirm any changes and close the dialog. Tap Apply to confirm the changes or tap Cancel to abandon the changes and close the dialog box.

Tip ✓

It's possible to have multiple keyboards connected to your tablet at the same time; they will all be listed in this same dialog box.

Tip ✓

If you have a keyboard with extra functions, such as customizable buttons for browsing or photo editing, you will see extra tabs in the Keyboard Properties dialog box.

Keyboard Properties

Speed | Hardware

Devices:

Name	Type
Standard PS/2 Keyboard	Keyboards

Device Properties

Manufacturer: (Standard keyboards)

Location: plugged into keyboard port

Device status: This device is working properly.

Properties

OK | Cancel | Apply

Changing Mouse Properties

There are many configurable options for the mouse you've attached to your device, and they will vary depending on the number of buttons and other additions to your mouse. All set-tings are changed in the same way, from the Mouse item in the Control Panel. Changing these options can be especially useful if you struggle with mouse movement.

Set Mouse Properties

1 Tap the Search charm, type **mouse** into the search box, and then tap Set-tings to search just within settings.

2 Tap the Mouse icon.

③ Select the tab for the type of settings you want to change.

④ Make the changes desired, such as changing the double-click speed by moving the slider.

⑤ Tap Apply to make the change but keep the Mouse Properties dialog box open; tap OK to save the changes and close the dialog or tap Cancel to abandon the changes and close the dialog box.

Set Mouse Buttons for Left-Handed Use

⑥ Select the Switch Primary and Secondary Buttons check box to swap the left and right mouse buttons.

Make Clicking Easier

⑦ Drag the slider left to increase the time between mouse button presses to perform a double-click; drag the slider right to shorten the time between clicks.

⑧ Turn on ClickLock to change the behavior of drag and drop or drag and to group mouse actions so that you don't need to keep the mouse button depressed while dragging.

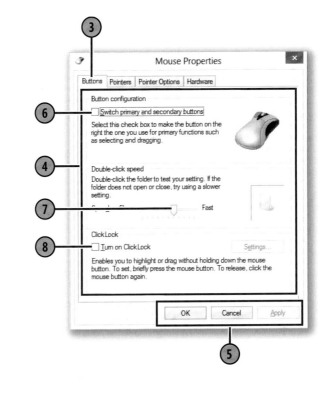

Set Pointer Styles

1 Tap the Pointers tab.

2 Select the pointer style scheme on the drop-down list.

3 Customize each individual pointer in the scheme by tapping the pointer style you want to change.

4 Tap Browse to select a different icon for the selected pointer. The pointer must already be on your device.

5 Scroll through the Browse dialog.

6 Tap the pointer style you want to use.

7 Tap Open.

8 Optionally, tap Use Default to revert the icon to the default for the select scheme.

9 Tap OK to confirm the changes and close the dialog box. Tap Apply to confirm the changes or tap Cancel to abandon the changes and close the dialog box.

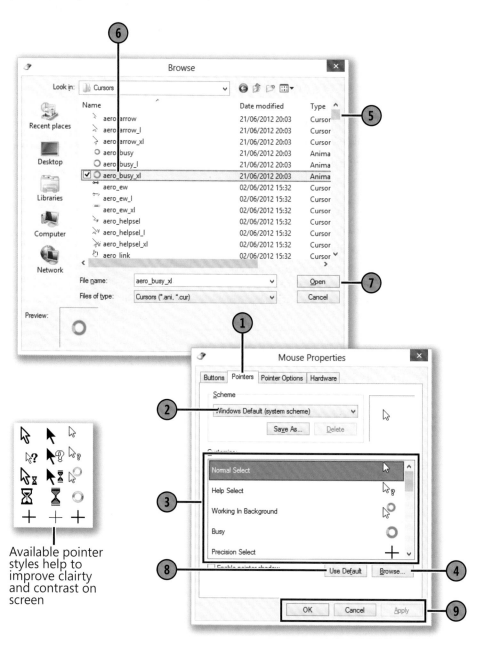

Available pointer styles help to improve clairty and contrast on screen

Control Pointer Motion and Visibility

① Tap the Pointer Options tab.

② Select the options you require to adjust the motion and control to the way you feel most comfortable; use the slider to control the speed of the mouse movement.

③ Tap OK to confirm the changes and close the dialog box. Tap Apply to confirm the changes or tap Cancel to abandon the changes and close the dialog box.

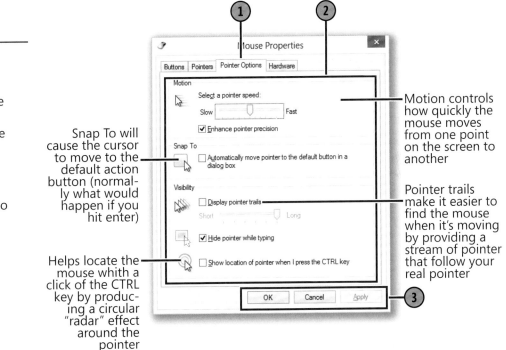

Snap To will cause the cursor to move to the default action button (normally what would happen if you hit enter)

Helps locate the mouse whith a click of the CTRL key by producing a circular "radar" effect around the pointer

Motion controls how quickly the mouse moves from one point on the screen to another

Pointer trails make it easier to find the mouse when it's moving by providing a stream of pointer that follow your real pointer

Using Handwriting Recognition

Windows 8 also allows you to enter text by using handwriting recognition, which is surprisingly accurate. You can use either a special pen or your finger.

Enter Text by Using Handwriting

1. Tap into any place you want to enter text in an app.

2. At the lower-right corner of the touch keyboard, select the icon to change keyboards.

3. Select the handwriting icon.

4. Select the on-screen area to enter text.

5. Using an input pen, enter text as you would if you were using a sheet of paper. Windows will recognize your handwriting and attempt to identify the correct word.

6. Tap the Insert button to enter the text in the selected place. If no handwriting is entered, Insert reveals an additional input panel including tab, space, and enter.

> **Tip**
>
> You can correct text by using strikethrough to delete words, a vertical line to split two incorrectly joined words, an open loop to join two incorrectly split words, or by tapping next to a letter to insert.

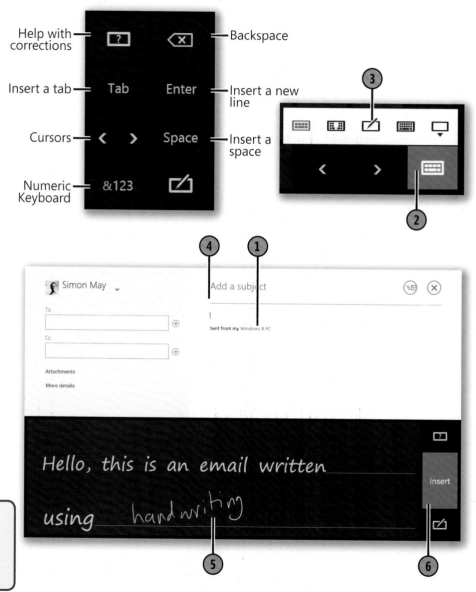

Help with corrections — Backspace

Insert a tab — Tab · Enter — Insert a new line

Cursors — ‹ › Space — Insert a space

Numeric Keyboard — &123

Navigating with Keyboard and Mouse

With a keyboard and/or a mouse connected to your tablet, you can navigate around simply and easily. However, you might find that it's not entirely obvious where to go to find items. You might expect that replacing your mouse pointer with a finger would work, but there are more appropriate ways to do things such as switching between apps.

Find App Menus

① Hold the mouse pointer over an area of the screen.

② Right-click (click the right mouse button) to open the App Bar, just as if you'd swiped the top or bottom of the screen.

The top left corner of the screen reveals access to the last active app. Dragging down reveals access to other open apps and allows you to bring those apps to the fore.

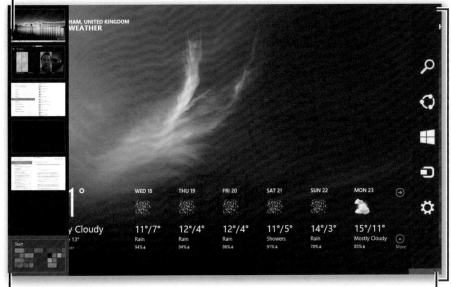

The bottom left allows access to the Start screen from within any app

The top right and bottom right corners of the screen allow access to the charms with the mouse in any app

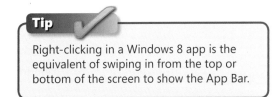

Tip

Right-clicking in a Windows 8 app is the equivalent of swiping in from the top or bottom of the screen to show the App Bar.

Using Keyboard Shortcuts for Everyday Tasks

When using a keyboard, it's often fastest to work using a variety of keyboard shortcuts. To use a keyboard shortcut, just follow the formula from left to right. For example, to complete Ctrl+Alt+Del, you can press Ctrl, and while keeping it pressed, press Alt, and while keeping these two pressed, press Del. When you press Del, the last key, the action will occur. There is no need to try to press all the keys simultaneously.

Shortcut	Action
Windows logo key+C	View charms
Windows logo key+D	Show the desktop
Windows logo key+E	Open File Explorer
Windows logo key+F	Go to Files in Search charm
Windows logo key+G	Cycle through desktop gadgets
Windows logo key+H	Access the Share charm
Windows logo key+I	Access the Settings charm
Windows logo key+J	Switch focus between snapped and larger apps
Windows logo key+K	Access the Devices charm
Windows logo key+L	Switch user or lock computer
Windows logo key+M	Minimize all windows on the desktop
Windows logo key+O	Lock the screen orientation
Windows logo key+P	Second screen options
Windows logo key+Q	Access the Search charm
Windows logo key+R	Run a command
Windows logo key+T	Cycle through taskbar items on the desktop
Windows logo key+V	Cycle through notifications
Windows logo key+W	Search for settings

Shortcut	Action
Windows logo key+X	Quick access to power user commands
Windows logo key+Z	Open the Apps Bar
Windows logo key++	Access the magnifier to zoom in
Windows logo key+-	Zoom out if already zoomed in
Windows logo key+<left arrow>	Snap desktop window left
Windows logo key+<right arrow>	Snap desktop window right
Windows logo key+<up arrow>	Maximize desktop window
Windows logo key+<down arrow>	Restore or minimize desktop window
F1	Help
F2	Rename item
F3	Search
F5	Refresh
Alt+Enter	Properties (note that an item such as a file must be selected).
Alt+Tab	Switch to next app
Ctrl+Alt+Del	Quick access to Task Manager to solve problems (always works if the device is unresponsive)
Ctrl+V	Paste
Ctrl+C	Copy
Ctrl+X	Cut
Ctrl+Z (or Alt+Backspace)	Undo

Switch Between Apps by Using the Keyboard: Windows Logo Key+Tab

① Press and hold the Windows logo key, and tap the Tab key once to reveal an app switching menu to the left of the display.

② Tap the Tab key to select each open app in turn; the white border indicates the selected app. When you release the Windows logo key, the app will become active.

Try This!

Tap the Windows button on your tablet twice in rapid succession; it will also show the app switcher.

Tip

To change apps quickly, just press the Windows logo key+Tab. There is no need to wait for the menu to appear. This is the same as swiping from the left edge of the display.

Switch Between Apps by Using the Keyboard: Alt+Tab

① Press and hold down the Alt key and then press the Tab key once to reveal an app switching menu in the center of the display.

② Press the Tab key to select each open app in turn; the white border indicates the selected app. When you release the Windows logo key, the app will become active.

All desktop apps and Windows 8 apps are available from this method of app switching

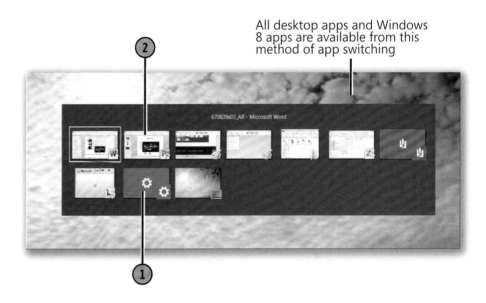

Changing Pen and Touch Settings

Windows 8–based tablets aren't just about using touch; many have the ability to accurately read the input from special pens that are packaged with the tablet or available as an add on. Pen recognition is more than enough to read your handwriting and can prove very accurate when used for precise tasks such as editing photos. Pens combine characteristics from touch, such as swiping to open the charms, and characteristics from mice. The Pen And Touch dialog controls the speed at which actions that simulate an equivalent mouse action, such as double-clicking, occur for both the pen and your finger when using touch on the desktop. Pen and touch settings are available from Control Panel.

Change Pen Interaction with the Desktop

1. Tap the Search charm, search for "pen" within Settings, and Tap Pen And Touch.

Tip

If you are finding it hard to double click with a pen, you are probably not tapping quickly enough. Rather than adjust yourself, adjust the time between taps to be greater.

(2) Select the action to change based on the pen action (left) and the equivalent mouse action (right).

(3) Tap or click the Settings button to access the settings for the selected action.

(4) Select or clear the check box as preferred to enable or disable the setting. This is the "master switch," and if not selected, the action will be unavailable on the desktop in any application.

(5) Control the speed of the action. If you double-tap very quickly, set this to the far left; if you find it difficult to double-tap quickly, set it further to the right.

(6) Change the length of time between taps and the distance your pen can move between taps.

(7) Test the new settings by interacting with the picture.

(8) Tap OK to accept the changes or tap Cancel to abandon them.

(9) Tap Apply to make changes and to continue making changes. Tap OK to make changes and close the dialog or tap Cancel to abandon all changes.

Settings map the use of the pen to the use of the mouse

Pen and Touch

Pen Options | Flicks | Touch

Pen actions
Use the pen to interact with items on the screen. You can adjust the settings for each pen action.

Pen action	Equivalent mouse action
Single-tap	Single-click
Double-tap	Double-click
Press and hold	Right-click

Settings...

Pen buttons
☑ Use the pen button as a right-click equivalent
☑ Use the top of the pen to erase ink (where available)

OK | Cancel | Apply

Press and Hold Settings

☑ Enable press and hold for right-clicking

Speed
You can change the amount of time you must press and hold before you can perform a right-click equivalent.

Speed: Short

Duration
You can change the amount of time during press and hold to perform a right-click action.

Duration: Short

Test settings
To test your settings, press and hold the graphic. The graphic changes when you perform press and hold successfully.

OK | Cancel

Change What Pen Buttons Do

1 Within the Pen And Touch dialog box, select the Use The Pen Button As A Right-Click Equivalent check box to use the button found on the side of the pen to perform a right-click of the mouse. To complete this action, press the button on the pen and tap the screen.

2 Select the Use The Top Of The Pen To Erase Ink (Where Available) check box to use the pen as an eraser, just as you would with a normal pencil. Note that not all pens support this.

3 Tap OK to accept the changes and close the dialog box. Tap Apply to accept the changes and continue working or tap Cancel to abandon the changes.

Change Touch Interaction with the Desktop

1 In the Pen And Touch dialog box, select the mouse equivalent action you need to alter.

2 Tap or click the Settings button to access the actions settings.

3 Adjust the speed of the action; if you find tapping easy, move the slider to the right.

4 Adjust the distance between taps or the length of the tap.

5 Test the action by interacting with the image.

6 Tap or click OK to accept the changes or tap Cancel to abandon them.

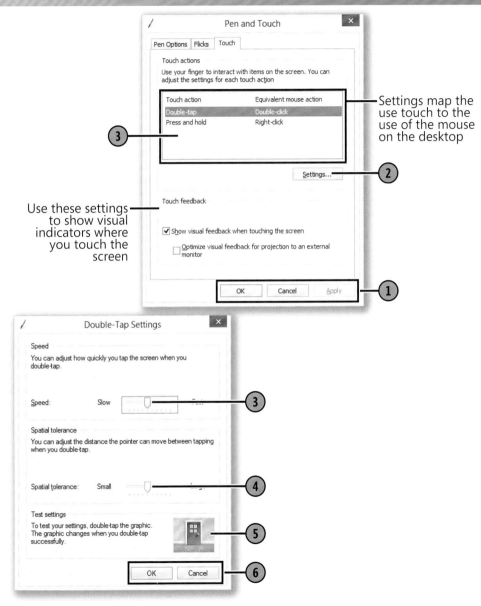

Settings map the use touch to the use of the mouse on the desktop

Use these settings to show visual indicators where you touch the screen

Working with Sensors

Your tablet includes a number of sensors by which it can automatically respond to your surroundings or the way in which you use your device. Almost all Windows 8–based tablets include rotation sensors to automatically reorient the screen, so that you can work in landscape or portrait, and GPS sensors by which apps can provide meaningful information about your location. You might choose to turn these on or off if you have concerns about your location being monitored or if automatic screen rotation annoys you.

Turn Screen Rotation On or Off

1 On the Apps screen, tap the Control Panel icon.

2 Tap the Display icon from the Control Panel.

3 On the quick actions menu, under Control Panel Home, select Adjust Resolution.

4 Enable screen rotation by selecting the Allow The Screen To Auto-Rotate check box. Disabling auto-rotate will even stop rotation using hardware buttons.

5 Tap OK, Apply, or Cancel when you've completed your changes.

> **Tip** ✓
>
> Most Windows 8–based tablets have a hardware button that lets you toggle rotation on and off and is more convenient than accessing the Control Panel. Consult your device manual for more information.

Turn Location Awareness On or Off

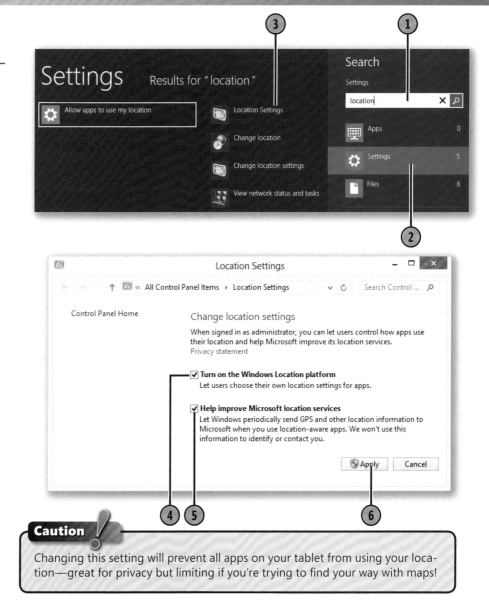

1. Tap the Search charm, and then type **location** into the Search box.

2. Tap Settings to search for settings on your tablet.

3. Tap the Location Settings icon in the results area

4. To enable use of the GPS within applications, ensure that the Turn On The Windows Location Platform check box is selected. Clearing this check box prevents apps from using location.

5. Decide whether to allow Microsoft to use location information to help improve products and apps.

6. Select Apply to save settings or Cancel to abandon changes. Note that Administrator access is required on your tablet to change location settings.

Tip

The settings within apps that use your location allow you to turn the use of location on or off for that particular app, or you can do this for every app on your tablet from PC Settings > Privacy.

Caution

Changing this setting will prevent all apps on your tablet from using your location—great for privacy but limiting if you're trying to find your way with maps!

4

Customizing Windows 8

Your tablet is going to become a very personal device to you; something with all your information on it; something you'll probably feel lost without. As a result, you will want to personalize your experience and customize the way in which Windows 8 works for you. In this section, we will explore ways to make your device uniquely yours, such as how you can make the first thing you see when you turn your tablet on (the lock screen) a picture that you love. We'll look at changing colors to match your mood or personality.

You probably have access to more than one computer; perhaps your tablet, a laptop, or a desktop, perhaps one at home and one at work. A new feature for Windows 8 is the ability to use your Microsoft Account to seamlessly synchronize your devices so that when you change the lock screen picture on one device, it changes on all of them.

Windows is sold all over the world, so there's a pretty good chance that you might need to change the default language to match that of your native tongue. Your tablet is capable of switching between any languages you have installed, for both input and for display. This section explores setting up a second language, changing defaults, and making Windows 8 more comfortable for you to use.

Personalizing Windows

Your Windows 8–based tablet will be a very personal device for you, containing all your emails, your family photos, your documents, and things you hold dear. You will want to personalize it, to make it your own, and Windows provides many ways to do just that, from the image you see when you turn the device on, to the color and tone of the Start screen, to the picture you want used throughout Windows.

All these settings can be changed from More PC Settings, which you can access on the Settings pane.

Personalize the Lock Screen

1. In PC Settings, tap Personalize.

2. Tap Browse to select a picture to use for the lock screen.

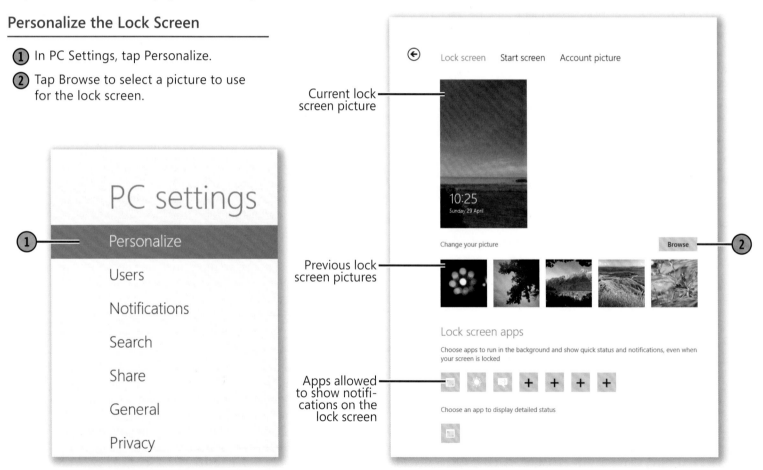

Current lock screen picture

Previous lock screen pictures

Apps allowed to show notifications on the lock screen

(3) Tap Files and then browse to the location where your pictures are stored.

(4) Pictures can be on your tablet, your network, or within any apps on your device; apps such as Pictures link to your SkyDrive, Facebook, and Flickr accounts. Tap the desired location.

(5) Tap the picture to use as a lock screen.

(6) Tap Choose Picture to set the picture as your lock screen.

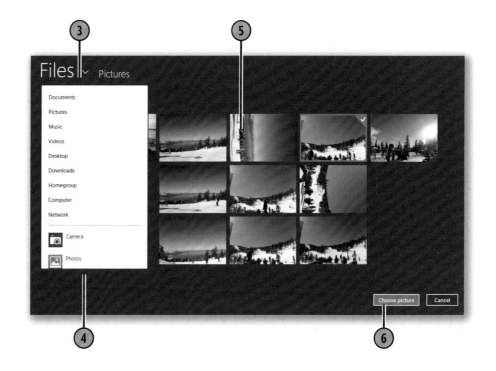

Personalize the Start Screen

(1) In PC Settings, tap the Personalize category.

(2) Tap the Start Screen tab.

(3) Select a background pattern from those available.

(4) Tap a color scheme for the Start screen.

Accent colors will be chosen automatically for you, and a preview will be made available. Changes are reflected immediately upon selection.

(1)

(2)

Preview area to reflect changes

PC settings

Personalize

Users

Notifications

Search

Share

General

Privacy

Devices

Wireless

Lock screen   Start screen   Account picture

(3)

(4)

Tip ✓

If you share your tablet with someone else, then setting your Start screen customizations to be different from theirs can instantly make you aware of who is currently logged on.

Personalize Your Account Picture

1. In PC Settings, tap Personalize.

2. Select Account Picture.

3. Tap Browse to locate a picture on your tablet or in the cloud.

4. Select the location where the picture you want to use is stored.

5. Tap to select the picture you want to use as your account picture.

6. Tap Choose Image to make the change.

Tip

You can choose apps as well as locations that might be storing your pictures. If you do this, you can select pictures stored in any cloud services connected to your tablet. For example, use the Photos app to select any picture on your SkyDrive, Facebook, or Flickr accounts, if you have them.

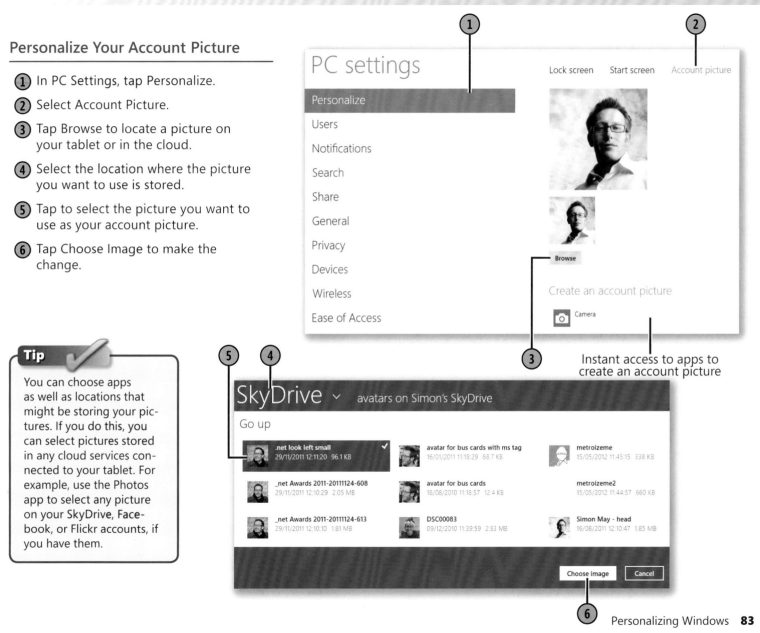

PC settings

Lock screen   Start screen   Account picture

Personalize

Users

Notifications

Search

Share

General

Privacy

Devices

Wireless

Ease of Access

Browse

Create an account picture

Camera

Instant access to apps to create an account picture

SkyDrive ˅   avatars on Simon's SkyDrive

Go up

.net look left small
29/11/2011 12:11:20   96.1 KB

_net Awards 2011-20111124-608
29/11/2011 12:10:29   2.05 MB

_net Awards 2011-20111124-613
29/11/2011 12:10:10   1.81 MB

avatar for bus cards with ms tag
16/01/2011 11:18:29   68.7 KB

avatar for bus cards
18/08/2010 11:18:57   12.4 KB

DSC00083
09/12/2010 11:39:59   2.83 MB

metroizeme
15/05/2012 11:45:15   338 KB

metroizeme2
15/05/2012 11:44:57   660 KB

Simon May - head
16/08/2011 12:10:47   1.85 MB

Choose image   Cancel

Personalizing the Desktop

The no-compromises experience of Windows 8 means that you might well spend time using desktop applications, and there is much to personalize about this experience, too. The desktop wallpaper or the color of Windows can be customized to your exact liking, or you might decide to use a theme based on your favorite game. All settings for the desktop are personalized from the Control Panel and are stored in a theme.

Open Desktop Personalization

1 Tap and hold a blank area of the desktop.

2 On the options list that appears, tap Personalize.

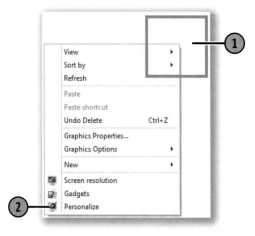

Tip

Desktop personalization settings are also available from the Control Panel or by typing **Personalization** into the Search box.

③ Select a theme to use.

④ Tap Desktop Background to set a specific picture or group of pictures as the desktop background.

⑤ Tap Window Color to change the color and transparency of windows..

Tip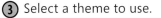

You'll notice a theme called "Synced Theme." This theme follows you across different Windows 8 devices.

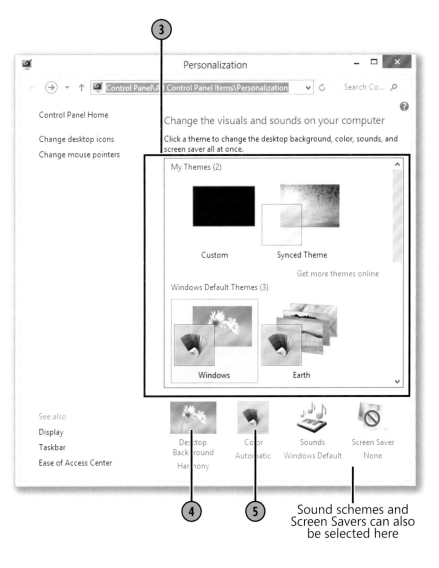

Sound schemes and Screen Savers can also be selected here

Get More Themes Online

1. Tap the Get More Themes Online link.

2. From the Microsoft website that appears in your browser, select the Download link for the theme you want to use.

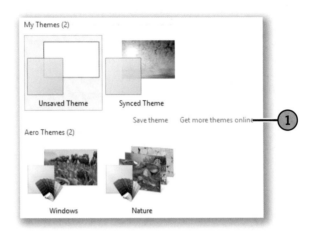

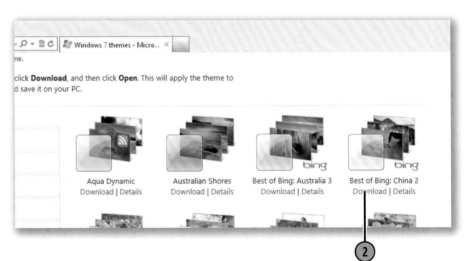

③ From the confirmation dialog box that appears, tap Open.

④ If the theme is live and can be updated by its creator, you will be asked to confirm that you want to subscribe to the RSS feed. Select Download Attachments.

⑤ The theme appears in the My Themes area; tap the theme to select it.

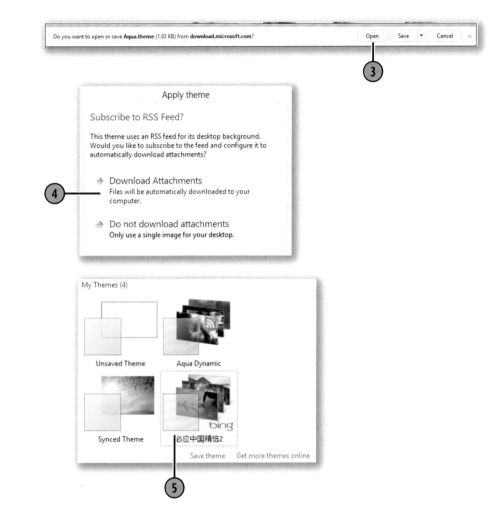

Do you want to open or save **Aqua.theme** (1.83 KB) from **download.microsoft.com**?   Open   Save ▼   Cancel   ×

Apply theme

Subscribe to RSS Feed?

This theme uses an RSS feed for its desktop background. Would you like to subscribe to the feed and configure it to automatically download attachments?

→ Download Attachments
Files will be automatically downloaded to your computer.

→ Do not download attachments
Only use a single image for your desktop.

My Themes (4)

Unsaved Theme   Aqua Dynamic

Synced Theme   必应中国精选2

Save theme   Get more themes online

Change Desktop Wallpapers for a Theme

① In the Personalization window, tap Desktop Background.

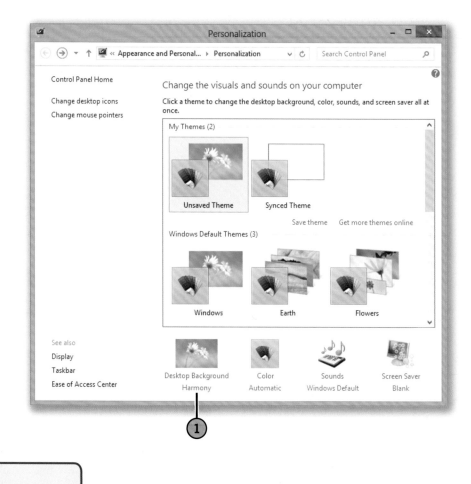

Tip

If you don't want to have a picture as wallpaper, you can also use solid colors. Simply select Solid Colors from the Picture Location drop-down menu.

② Browse for a folder containing pictures to use as wallpapers or select from pre-defined locations.

When you tap Browse, a folder list opens. Tap a folder to select it. If it contains sub-folders, they will expand. Tap OK when the folder you want is selected.

③ In the Desktop Background window, select a picture to use as wallpaper by selecting the check box in the upper-left corner of the thumbnail; it is possible to select multiple pictures and have the wallpaper change through each selected picture.

④ Select how the wallpaper will be displayed: scaled to fill the screen, centrally with a border, stretched, tiled, or fitted to the most accommodating length.

⑤ Select how long to wait between changes of the picture.

⑥ Tap Shuffle to have the wallpapers shuffle and change randomly. Otherwise, they will be changed in the order in which they are selected.

⑦ Changing wallpaper can impact battery life. Select the When Using Battery Power, Pause The Slide Show To Save Power check box to prevent wallpaper changes from consuming battery power.

⑧ Tap Save Changes to save your theme or tap Cancel to abandon changes.

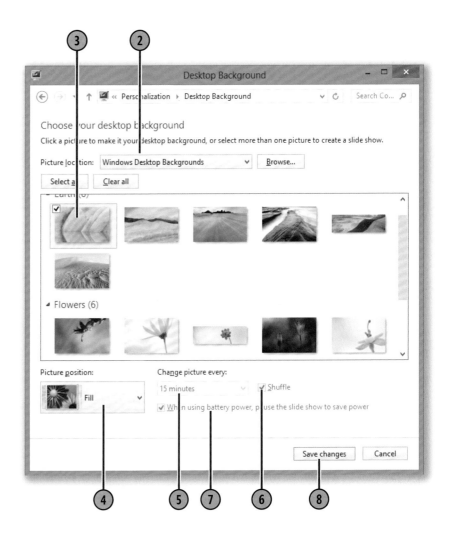

Change Window Colors for a Theme

① In the Personalize window, tap Color.

② Tap a predefined color palette for your window borders and taskbar.

③ Select the check box to enable transparent window borders and taskbar.

This check box might not appear if the theme doesn't support transparency.

④ Move the slider to the right to make colors more intense and vibrant and to the left to make them less so.

As you do, you will see this reflected in the taskbar and window borders currently on the desktop.

⑤ Select the Show Color Mixer option to reveal the Hue, Saturation and Brightness controls; select Hide Color Mixer if you don't want to use them.

⑥ Adjust Hue, Saturation and Brightness to come up with the perfect color for your desktop.

⑦ Tap Save Changes to save the new colors or tap Cancel to abandon them.

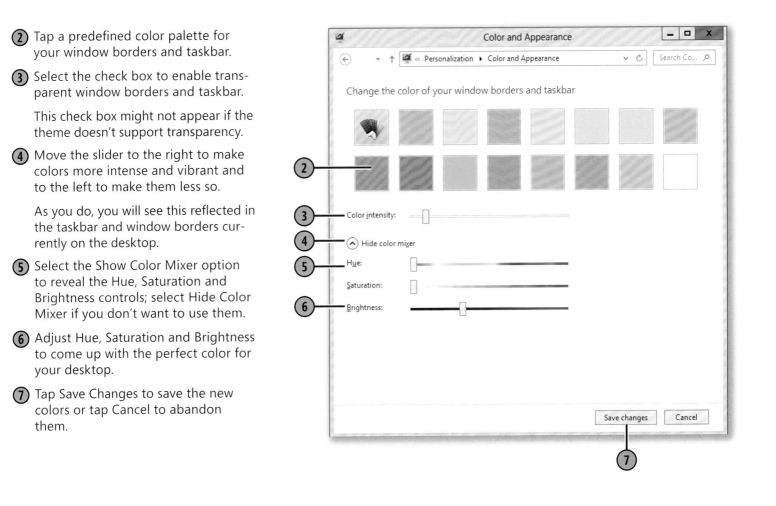

Syncing Settings Across Multiple Devices

Windows 8 includes the built-in capability to sync your settings with the cloud so that if you use more than one device, everything is set up just as you want it, on every device you use. It's possible to control which settings are synced from the More PC Settings link, which you can access on the Settings pane.

Enable Syncing of Settings Across Multiple Devices

 Tap the Sync Your Settings category.

② You will first need to confirm the device can be synced by authorizing it in your Microsoft Account. Click the Confirm This PC link; a browser window opens in which you can do this.

PC settings

Search

Share

General

Privacy

Devices

Wireless

Ease of Access

Sync your settings

HomeGroup

Windows Update

To help protect your personal info, w
trusted.

② ——— Confirm this PC   ① ——— Sync your settings

Sync your settings

Sync settings on this PC

On

Settings to sync

(3) Tap Next to confirm your email address

(4) Tap OK.

To complete the process, you'll now need to check your designated email account where you'll find a message from Microsoft asking you to confirm that you really want to add this computer. This is done for security, since you wouldn't want just anyone syncing computers to your account.

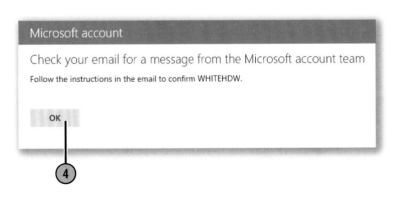

Microsoft account

Overview
    Edit Name
    Update email
    Personal info
    Password
    Security info
    Close account
Notifications
Permissions
Billing

Confirm WHITEHDW as a trusted PC

Use your existing security info to help us make sure this is you. How can we contact you?

[Next] [Cancel]

(3)

Microsoft account

Check your email for a message from the Microsoft account team

Follow the instructions in the email to confirm WHITEHDW.

OK

(4)

Change Sync Settings

1 In PC Settings, tap Sync Your Settings.

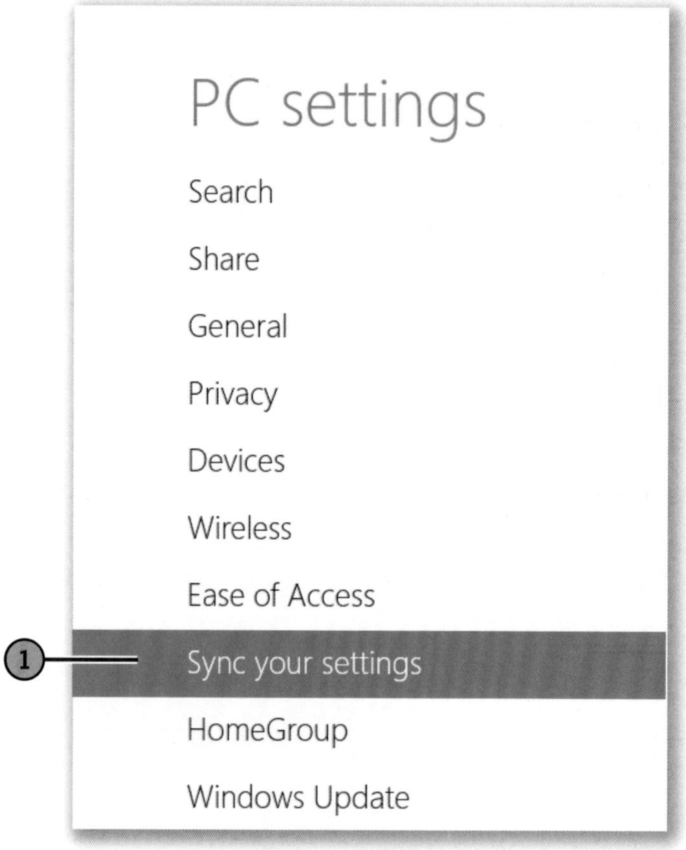

PC settings

Search

Share

General

Privacy

Devices

Wireless

Ease of Access

Sync your settings

HomeGroup

Windows Update

② To turn on syncing of any settings, ensure that Sync Settings On This PC is On.

③ You can choose to sync many settings, depending on how much of your experience you want to follow you from device to device. All settings marked On will by synced. Any changed setting is applied immediate effect.

④ Syncing is enabled by default under Metered Internet Connections— these are connections that Windows believes cost you on a pay-per-use basis, such as mobile broadband (3G/4G/LTE connections), but it is disabled by default when roaming.

Sync your settings

Sync settings on this PC
② On

Settings to sync

Personalize
Colors, background, lock screen, and your account picture
③ On

Desktop personalization
Themes, taskbar, high contrast, and more
On

Passwords
Sign-in info for some apps, websites, networks, and HomeGroup
On

Ease of Access
Narrator, Magnifier, and more
On

Language preferences
Keyboards, other input methods, display language, and more
On

App settings
Certain app settings and purchases made in an app
On

Browser
Settings and info like history and favorites
On

Other Windows settings
Windows Explorer, mouse, and more
On

Sync over metered connections

Sync settings over metered connections
On

Sync settings over metered connections even when I'm roaming
④ Off

Changing Language and Regional Settings

Windows 8 is available in many different languages and with many different regional settings to make your tablet more natural for you. For example, if you live in the United Kingdom, there is now a language pack that replaces Z's with S's and words like "Favorite" with "Favourite." Of course, regional settings also control preferences such as currency denomination. Multiple people can sign in to a Windows tablet and have different language settings. Most language Settings are found in the Control Panel, but some are also available from More PC Settings, which you can access in the Settings pane.

Add and Remove Languages

① In the Control Panel, tap the Language icon.

② Tap Add A Language.

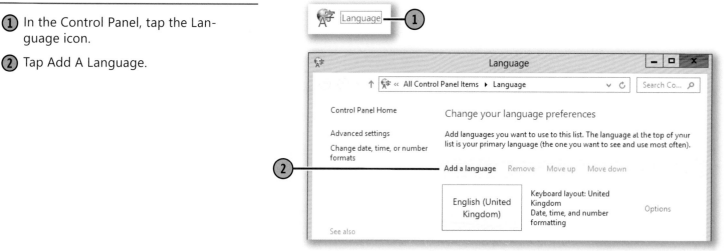

Tip ✓

Your language settings will roam with you from device to device, so if you log on to any other Windows 8 computer, your language settings should be the same as those on your tablet.

(3) In the extensive list of languages that appears, find the language you want to add.

Note that language variations such as English are grouped together.

(4) Tap Add to add the language.

(5) Order languages such that the most preferred is at the top.

(6) Remove any extra languages. Note that there must be a minimum of one language.

Change Advanced Language Settings

(1) In the Control Panel Language settings, tap Advanced Settings.

(2) On the drop-down menu that appears, tap to use either the language list that you have defined previously or US English as the Windows display language. This can be useful if there are no languages in the language list that you can read.

(3) On the drop-down menu that appears, tap to use either the language list that you have defined previously or US English as your input language. This can be useful if there are no languages in the list that are available on your keyboard.

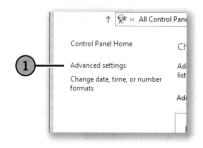

Tip ✓

It's easy to switch between different languages. Tap the keyboard icon on the Settings charm and select one of your available configured languages.

(4) Select the Let Me Set A Different Input Method For Each App Window check box to use different languages in each app on your desktop.

This is very handy if you need to enter text in a specific app, such as chatting in a different language.

(5) Select the Use The Desktop Language Bar When It's Available check box to be able to change languages by using a button on the taskbar.

The Options link helps to control the language bar.

(6) Automatic learning can help with handwriting recognition but it requires data to be sent to Microsoft's cloud for processing. If you have privacy concerns, you can turn the feature off.

(7) Tap Restore Defaults to go back to your tablet's original state, with the same language settings you had when you first unpacked your tablet.

Normally, all settings will use the language lists, and other settings will be disabled, with the exception of automatic learning.

(8) Tap Save to save the settings and close the Advanced Settings dialog box, or tap Cancel to leave settings unaltered.

Advanced settings

All Control Panel Items ▸ Language ▸ Advanced settings   Search Co... 🔎

Advanced settings

Override for Windows display language

If you want to use a display language that's different than the one determined by the order of your language list, choose it here.

(2) Use language list (recommended)

Apply language settings to the welcome screen, system accounts, and new user accounts

Override for default input method

If you want to use an input method that's different than the first one in your language list, choose it here.

(3) Use language list (recommended)

Switching input methods

(4) ☐ Let me set a different input method for each app window

(5) ☐ Use the desktop language bar when it's available   Options

Change language bar hot keys

Personalization data

This data is only used to improve handwriting recognition and text prediction results for languages without IMEs on this PC. No info is sent to Microsoft. Privacy statement

(6) ● Use automatic learning (recommended)

○ Don't use automatic learning and delete all previously collected data

Language for web content

☐ Don't let websites access my language list. The language of my date, time, and number formatting will be used instead.

(7) Restore defaults

Save   Cancel (8)

Change Date, Time, or Number Formats

① In the Control Panel Language settings, in the Action pane on the left, tap the Change Date, Time Or Number Formats link.

② Select the Format convention you'd like to use as the basis for your regional formats.

③ Customize the individual settings for the date and time.

④ If the settings are not detailed enough for you, it's possible to explore further settings by which you can make customizations, such as changing the symbols for currency, decimal points, or the measurement system.

⑤ Tap OK to save the changes and close the dialog box. Tap Apply to save the changes and keep the window open or tap Cancel to abandon changes.

Tip

Using the Additional Settings button, it's possible to take fine grain control over date, time, currency, and number settings. As a result, you can mix and match localizations—for example, an Englishman in New York might like to use date convention of the United Kingdom (dd/mm/yy) with the "$" symbol for currency.

Change Location

1 Tap the Location tab.

2 Select the location in which you reside.

3 Tap OK to save settings and close the dialog box. Tap Apply to save settings and continue to make changes or tap Cancel to abandon any changes.

Tip

Location settings can control some of the Windows features that are available in your region, so if there isn't a Windows Store in your region, you might need to change this setting to a region that has the capabilities you require. You might also have to do the same with your Microsoft Account.

Change the Welcome Screen Language Settings

① In Region dialog box, tap the Administrative tab.

② Tap the Copy Settings button. Note that administrative privileges are required.

③ Select to copy settings to the Welcome screen.

④ Tap OK.

⑤ Tap the OK button to copy the current language and region settings to the Welcome screen.

Working with Notifications

Apps on your Windows 8–based tablet are constantly doing things in the background to ensure that your information is up to date. The Email app is constantly checking to see whether there are new emails for you from your contacts; the messaging app is ready to receive chat messages from Facebook friends; and your favorite e-reader is just waiting to download the latest best-seller. There are multiple ways that apps will let you know what's happening, from icons on the lock screen to icons on the taskbar. Settings for these are controlled in different locations, from the PC Settings screen and, for desktop notifications, from the Control Panel.

Upcoming calendar appointment

App notification icons

Notifications appear as a pop-up window in the upper-right corner of your tablet's screen

Control Notifications

(1) In PC Settings, tap Notifications.

(2) Toggle app notifications on or off globally.

(3) Toggle app notifications on only the lock screen.

(4) Toggle if you want sounds to be played with notifications.

(5) Toggle particular apps that can provide notifications.

Most apps that can provide notifications install with this feature enabled. If you don't like an app or feel it's too chatty (messaging can be), turn it off here.

PC settings

Personalize

Users

Notifications

Search

Share

General

Privacy

Devices

Notifications

Show app notifications
On

Show app notifications on the lock screen
On

Play notification sounds
On

Show notifications from these apps

e	Internet Explorer	On	
:-)	Messaging	On	

Try This!

When you don't want to receive notifications for a short time, tap the Settings charm and then tap Notifications. From here, you can select to hide notifications for a period of 1 hour to 8 hours.

Control Desktop Notifications

(1) In the Control Panel, tap Notification Area Icons.

(2) In the drop-down menu, for each Notification Area icon, select the behavior you desire.

(3) When the icons are configured as you'd like, tap OK to save the settings and close the dialog box or tap Cancel to abandon the changes.

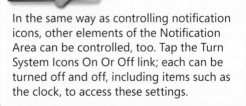

Tip ✓

In the same way as controlling notification icons, other elements of the Notification Area can be controlled, too. Tap the Turn System Icons On Or Off link; each can be turned off and off, including items such as the clock, to access these settings.

(1) Notification Area Icons

Notifications will only show up when Windows has something to tell you

Icons and notifications are invisible

Causes icons to be ever present and notifications to appear as required

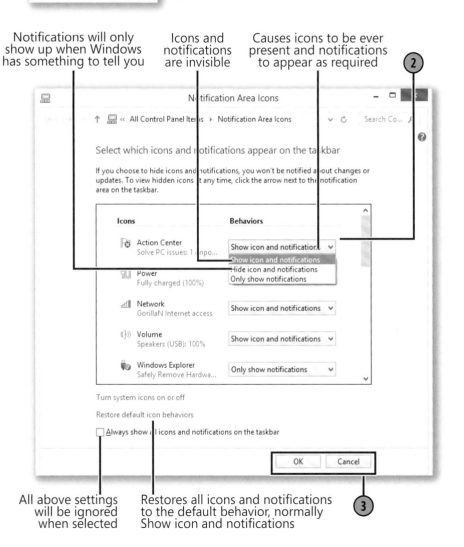

All above settings will be ignored when selected

Restores all icons and notifications to the default behavior, normally Show icon and notifications

Improving Ease of Access

Many people find using a computer to be challenging due to physical conditions that can impede some ways of using a device. This is even true of tablets. However, Windows 8 implements some excellent controls that can make your tablet easier to use, if you need to. Some features, such as voice control, are also useful if you just want to occasionally rest your typing fingers.

High contrast makes all on-screen elements far clearer by changing color schemes to emphasize critical elements

Enable Ease of Access Features

(1) In the Settings panel, tap the More PC Settings link, and then in PC Settings, tap Ease Of Access.

(2) Toggle to display a system-wide high-contrast color scheme; changes are applied instantly. Tap a second time to turn the setting off.

(3) Toggle to increase the size of all on-screen elements; changes applied instantly.

(4) Toggle the shortcut key combination for starting the narrator, the magnifier, and the on-screen keyboard.

This can also be achieved by using the hardware buttons (Volume Up and the Windows button, for example) on your tablet, not just on an attached keyboard.

(5) Change the duration for which notifications are shown; if you read slowly, this can be invaluable.

(6) Change the thickness of the cursor when entering text into boxes in applications to make the cursor easier to see.

PC settings

Search

Share

General

Privacy

Devices

Wireless

Ease of Access

Sync your settings

Ease of Access

High contrast
Off

Make everything on your screen bigger
Off

Your display doesn't support this setting.

Pressing Windows + Volume Up will turn on
Narrator

Show notifications for
5 seconds

Cursor thickness
1

Use the Computer Without a Display

① From the Control Panel, select Ease Of Access to open the Ease Of Access Center.

② Tap Use The Computer Without A Display.

③ Select the check box to have the Narrator read out on-screen prompts or text within an application.

④ Select to have the Narrator explain what is happening in videos. This is only available for videos that support this feature.

⑤ Tap the Set Up Text To Speech link to control settings such as the voice used for narration and the speed at which the narrator talks.

⑥ Unnecessary animations can cause a delay when the narrator is speaking while the animation completes. Select this to turn off designated box speeds narration.

⑦ When notifications appear on screen, they might not remain long enough for the narrator to explain them and for you to respond; increase the length of time here, if required.

⑧ Tap OK to save the changes and close the dialog box. Tap Apply to save changes but remain in the Ease Of Access Center or tap Cancel to abandon changes.

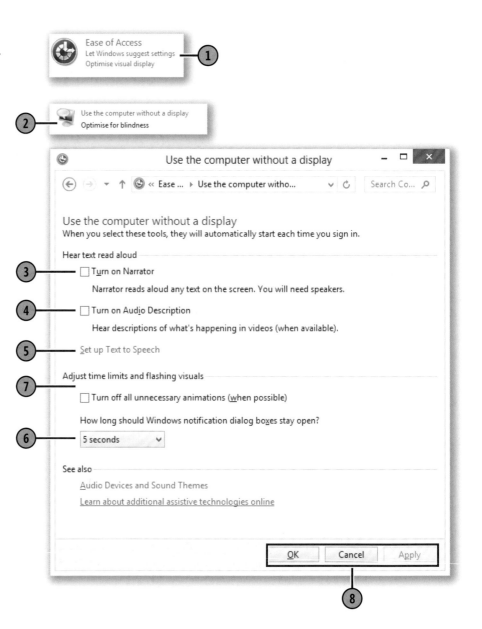

Make Your Tablet Easier to See

① In the Ease Of Access Center, tap the task labeled Make The Computer Easier To See.

② Select to enable a key combination that will displays a high-contrast screen theme and control the notifications when entering that theme.

③ Select Turn On Narrator and Turn On Audio Description to have on-screen items read to you by the Windows Narrator.

④ Tap the Change The Size Of Text And Icons link to quickly adjust display settings that increase the size of screen elements and title bar, menu, message, and other on-screen text sizes.

⑤ Select this check box to enable a magnifier that you can use just like a magnifying glass to temporarily increase the size of areas of the screen.

⑥ Tap the link to quickly access desktop personalization settings to change how windows appear.

⑦ Adjust how thick the cursor is on screen; making it thicker can make it clearer.

⑧ Disable animations that can take time and be visually distracting.

⑨ Remove background images that can make reading text or other elements hard.

⑩ Tap OK to save settings, tap Apply to save settings but keep the window open, or tap Cancel to abandon changes.

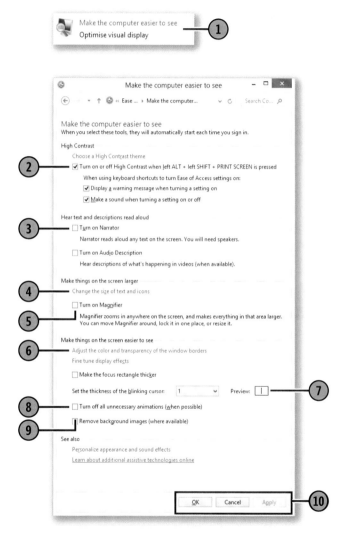

Use Your Tablet Without Touch, a Mouse, or Keyboard

1. In the Ease Of Access Center, tap Use The Computer Without A Mouse Or Keyboard.

2. Select the Use On-Screen Keyboard check box to enable all desktop applications to use the on-screen keyboard. This keyboard will mirror any input on a physical keyboard.

3. Tap the Use Speech Recognition link to begin training your computer to understand your voice. This is the ideal way to begin using your computer without touch, keyboard, or mouse, but it takes time to train. The training process is simple thanks to extensive wizards that help familiarize you with using your voice for control.

4. Tap OK to save settings, tap Apply to save settings but keep the window open, or tap Cancel to abandon changes.

Caution

The on-screen keyboard available within Ease Of Access is different from the touch keyboard on your tablet. While it is still touch friendly, there are many more keys and the keys are significantly smaller. It does, however, provide visual feedback by highlighting keys when using a physical keyboard.

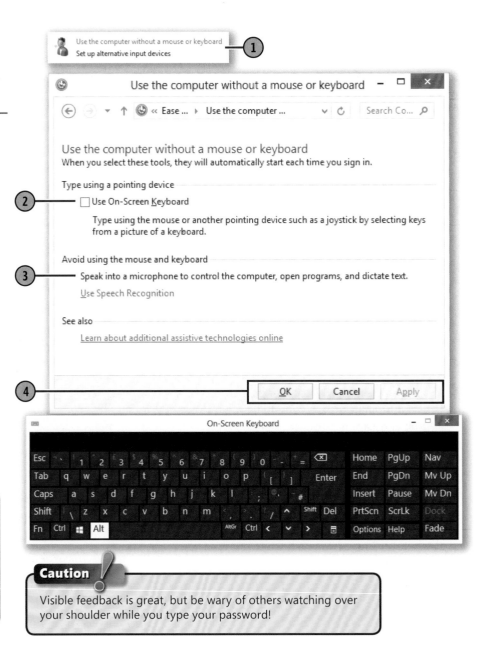

Caution

Visible feedback is great, but be wary of others watching over your shoulder while you type your password!

Setting Default Programs

You can use program defaults to determine which specific program will automatically open specific types of files, perform tasks, or start automatically when media such a USB keys are inserted into your tablet. You can configure this from the Control Panel either by selecting the types of files a program will open by default or by selecting the program that will open by default when you want to open a file.

Set Programs for Specific Tasks

(1) In the Control Panel, tap Default Programs and then tap Set Program Access And Computer Defaults

(2) If you want to use a profile that by default uses only Microsoft software, select the Microsoft Windows option.

(3) If you want to use a profile that by default uses non-Microsoft software if installed, select this option.

(4) Select Custom to create a profile that you manage.

(5) For each type of program—web browser, email program, media player, instant messaging program, Java virtual machine, and so on—select whether to use your current application or the Microsoft default.

(6) Select this check box to determine whether you want to totally disable the Microsoft default application to the extent that it is unavailable on your tablet.

(7) Tap OK to save settings and close the dialog box, or tap Cancel to abandon any changes.

Set a Program as the Default for Files It Can Open

1. In the Control Panel, tap Default Programs and then tap Set Your Default Programs.

2. Select the application for which you want to change the defaults.

3. To quickly set the program as the default for opening all the file types for which it is capable, tap Set This Program As Default.

4. Tap Choose Defaults For This Program to select the individual files types that the application is capable of opening.

5. Only file types that the program can open will be listed. Select the check box each file type to associate with the program.

6. If you want to select all the file types available, select the Select All check box; this is the same as performing step 3.

7. Tap Save to commit the changes or tap Cancel to abandon them.

8. Tap OK to close the dialog box.

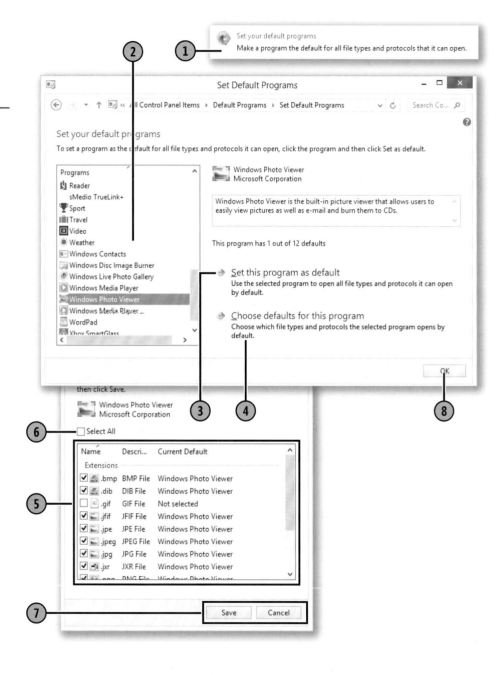

Set Which Program Opens Specific Files

1. In the Control Panel, tap Default Programs and then tap Associate A File Type Or Protocol With A Program.

2. Select the check box for the specific file type or protocol on which to work

3. Tap the Change Program button.

4. On the pop-up menu, tap the program that you want to set as the default.

5. If the program you want to be default for this file type or protocol isn't listed, tap More Options.

6. Tap Look For An App On The Web to search by using the Microsoft site for apps that are known to open this type of file or protocol.

7. Tap Look For An App In The Store to find an app from the Microsoft Store that can be used to open this type of file or protocol.

8. Tap Look For Another App On This PC to browse to the location of the program files for the app with which you'd like to open this type of file or protocol.

9. Tap Close to complete the changes.

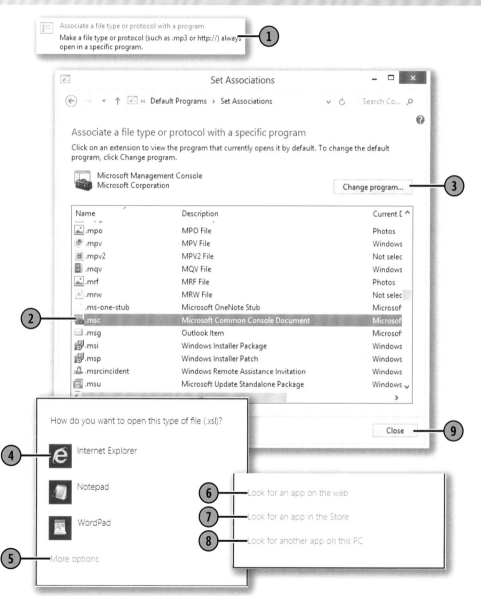

Change What Happens When Specific Media Is Inserted

(1) In the Control Panel, tap Default Programs and then tap Change AutoPlay Settings.

(2) Select the Use AutoPlay For All Media And Devices check box to be less detailed with your setting. AutoPlay will be used in all cases when media is inserted, even if no action is defined in advance.

(3) For each type of removable device or media, select from the following actions to perform: Take No Action, Open Folder To View Files (File Explorer), or Ask Me Every Time.

(4) If there are different types of content that are regularly associated with a specific type of device or media, settings can be more detailed, including opening a particular program that can use the content.

(5) Scroll down to explore all options.

(6) Tap Save to keep the changes or tap Cancel to abandon them.

Tip

You can also define what happens with a specific device, such as your camera or personal music device, when it is inserted. Plug in the device before trying to set things up; otherwise, it will not appear in the list.

Changing Power Consumption

Your tablet will consume power constantly. Even when it is in sleep mode, some power will be consumed. When in sleep mode, your tablet will wake momentarily to update apps that are allowed to run in the background, such as email, so that they contain the latest information when you next power on.

Ensuring that you're using the most efficient power schemes, depending on the tasks you're doing, will give you optimal performance and battery life. It's also useful to have control over security and what happens when you eventually run out of battery.

Choose the Optimal Power Plan

(1) In the Control Panel, tap Power Options.

(2) Select a predefined power plan that best meets your needs.

The Balanced plan attempts to balance performance with battery life; Power Saver attempts to save as much energy as possible and is far more aggressive at restricting performance to save energy.

(3) Tap the Change Plan Settings link to either view the plan's details or to change the settings in a power plan.

(4) Expand this section to show other power plans on this device.

High performance is defined by default and will attempt to favor better performance at the expense of energy efficiency. Custom plans are also shown here.

Create a Custom Power Plan

1. In the Control Panel, tap Power Options, and then in the Action pane, tap the Create A Power Plan link.

2. Select a power plan on which to base your new power plan.

3. Enter a meaningful name for the plan.

4. Tap Next to begin customizing the plan.

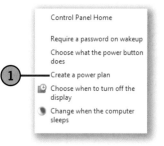

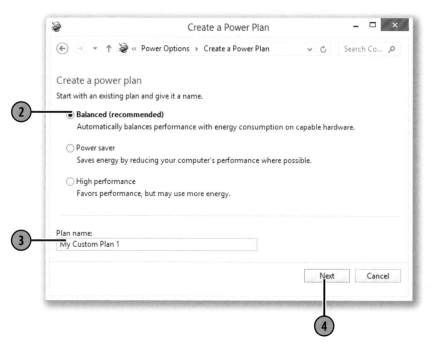

⑤ Select the length of time after which to dim the display, turn the display off, and put the computer to sleep, as well as the level of screen brightness for the plan.

⑥ Tap Create to save the plan.

⑦ If you'd like to configure further options after the plan is created, tap the Change Plan Settings link next to your new plan.

⑧ Tap the Change Advanced Power Settings link to change very detailed aspects, such as which USB devices to power down when in sleep mode.

⑨ Tap Save Changes to save the changes to your power plan.

Edit Plan Settings

« Power Options ▸ Edit Plan Settings   Search Co...

Change settings for the plan: My Custom Plan 1

Choose the sleep and display settings that you want your computer to use.

	On battery	Plugged in
Dim the display:	2 minutes	5 minutes
Turn off the display:	5 minutes	10 minutes
Put the computer to sleep:	15 minutes	30 minutes
Adjust plan brightness:		

Create   Cancel

Plans shown on the battery meter

Change advanced power settings

Save changes   Cancel

Require a Password When Your Tablet Wakes

(1) In the Control Panel, tap Power Options, and then in the Action pane, tap the Require A Password On Wakeup link

(2) To avoid accidental changes, most settings are unavailable. Tap the Change Settings That Are Currently Unavailable link to enable access to the settings.

Note that you will need administrative access.

(3) If you want to enable a password, select the Require A Password (Recommended) check box. This is the default setting.

(4) If you want to disable passwords, select the Don't Require A Password check box. This will prevent passwords on startup.

(5) Tap Save Changes to save and close the window.

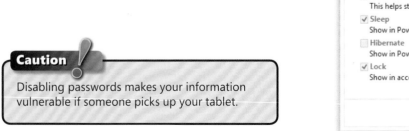

Caution

Disabling passwords makes your information vulnerable if someone picks up your tablet.

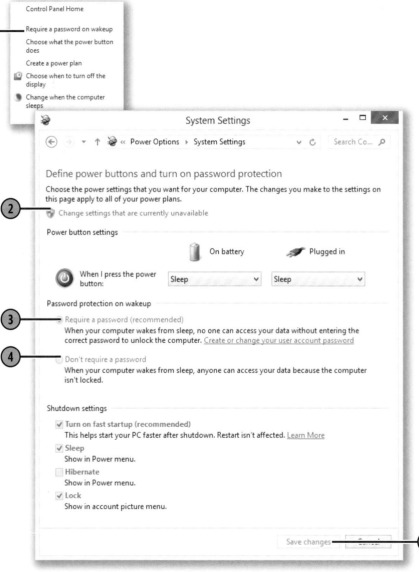

Control Panel Home

Require a password on wakeup

Choose what the power button does

Create a power plan

Choose when to turn off the display

Change when the computer sleeps

System Settings

⊛ « Power Options ▸ System Settings   ✓ C   Search Co... 🔎

Define power buttons and turn on password protection

Choose the power settings that you want for your computer. The changes you make to the settings on this page apply to all of your power plans.

💼 Change settings that are currently unavailable

Power button settings

	🔋 On battery	🏍 Plugged in
When I press the power button:	Sleep	Sleep

Password protection on wakeup

○ Require a password (recommended)
When your computer wakes from sleep, no one can access your data without entering the correct password to unlock the computer. Create or change your user account password

○ Don't require a password
When your computer wakes from sleep, anyone can access your data because the computer isn't locked.

Shutdown settings

☑ Turn on fast startup (recommended)
This helps start your PC faster after shutdown. Restart isn't affected. Learn More

☑ Sleep
Show in Power menu.

☐ Hibernate
Show in Power menu.

☑ Lock
Show in account picture menu.

Save changes   Cancel

Change Power Buttons and Behavior

(1) In the Control Panel, tap Power Options, and then in the Action pane, tap the Require A Password On Wakeup link.

(2) Most settings are unavailable to avoid accidental changes. Tap the Change Settings That Are Currently Unavailable link to enable access to the settings. Note that you will need administrative access.

(3) Configure whether you want your tablet to sleep or shut down when you press the power button.

(4) Select this check box to enable your computer to boot more quickly if it shuts down.

(5) Select the Sleep check box if you would like to have quick access to put your tablet to sleep from the Settings pane. You can also do this by tapping the hardware button, which is unaffected by this setting.

(6) Select the Hibernate check box to enable an entry in the Settings pane that will allow you to quickly hibernate (save settings and shut down) your tablet.

(7) Select the Lock check box to have a Lock item appear on your Account Picture menu.

(8) Tap Save Changes to save the changes and close the dialog box.

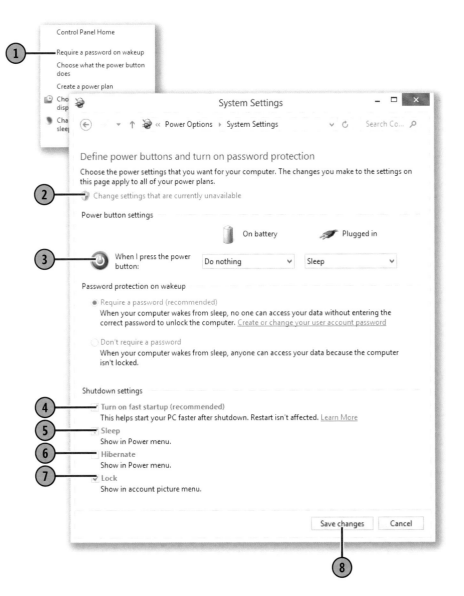

Connecting to Wi-Fi, the Internet, and Bluetooth

5

Your tablet is a very mobile device; you'll be able to take it with you almost anywhere you go. If you're sitting in the back of the car on a long journey watching movies or if you want to play the latest games or view photos you've just taken with your digital camera, you could probably live without connecting to the Internet. Otherwise, most of the time, you probably want to be online.

We live in a very connected world, and your tablet is no exception. Access to the Internet is probably almost as important to you as air.

Windows 8–based tablets commonly use either a wireless (Wi-Fi) or mobile broadband (3G/4G/LTE) network to get you online. In this section, we'll look at how your tablet connects to those types of networks and how Windows helps manage networks. Of course, your tablet can also talk to Bluetooth devices, such as headsets and speakers, and can even network with other devices, so we'll take a look at those settings too.

Sharing media and files with other devices is also a must, and Windows helps here, too, with HomeGroup and profile syncing.

Connecting to Wi-Fi

You won't want to use your tablet in isolation forever. The most common way to connect to the Internet is to connect to a Wi-Fi network. Your tablet will connect to most Wi-Fi networks, provided that you have the right information, such as a PIN, password, or access to a special button on the router. If you

have a business tablet, your administrator might have set it up already. When set up, Windows remembers all Wi-Fi networks you've connected to and will attempt to reconnect automatically, so you will need to know how to manage them to, for example, change passwords.

Connect to a Wi-Fi Network

① From the right edge of the screen, swipe inward and then tap the Settings charm. In the Settings panel, select the networking icon.

Note that the icon changes if your tablet is connected to a network already, but it's always the upper-left icon.

② Tap the name of the network you want to join.

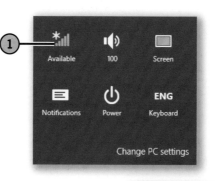

> **Tip** ✓
>
> Most home Wi-Fi networks will just need you to enter a PIN or password (security key) that you already know. If you're in a public place, you might not need to enter a password to connect but you could be presented with a webpage requiring a logon.

③ Select the Connect Automatically check box to have Windows remember the network and join it automatically in the future.

④ Tap Connect to connect to the network.

⑤ You will probably be asked for a network security key of some type. It can be a number or text and might be written on the router. If you're in a public Wi-Fi hot spot, you might need to ask for the password.

⑥ Tap Next to complete the connection.

Change a Wi-Fi Network Security Key

① From the right edge of the screen, swipe inward and then tap the Settings charm. In the Settings panel, tap the network icon.

If you're connected, it will have the name and signal strength of your current Wi-Fi network.

② Tap and hold the network for which you want to change the security key.

③ Tap the View Connection Properties menu item. The desktop will appear.

④ In the Wireless Network Properties dialog box, you can change settings for the current network. Change the password to match your Wi-Fi network password; you might need to tap the keyboard icon on the taskbar to reveal a keyboard.

⑤ Tap OK to save the changes.

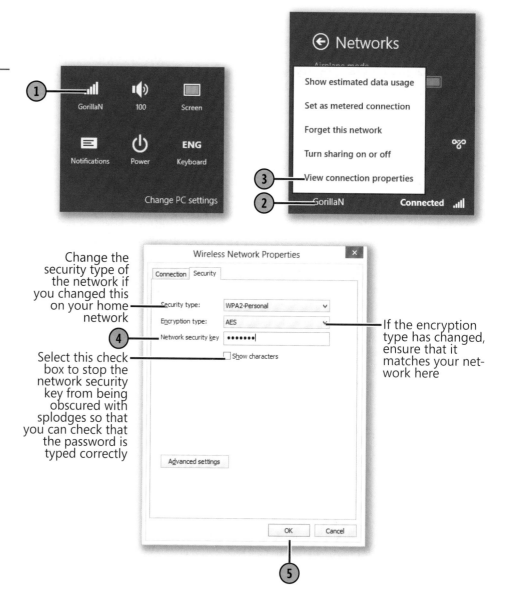

Change the security type of the network if you changed this on your home network

Select this check box to stop the network security key from being obscured with splodges so that you can check that the password is typed correctly

If the encryption type has changed, ensure that it matches your network here

Remove a Wi-Fi Network

1. In the Settings panel, tap the network icon. If you're connected, it will have the name and signal strength of your current Wi-Fi network.

2. Tap and hold the network you want the tablet to forget.

3. Tap Forget This Network.

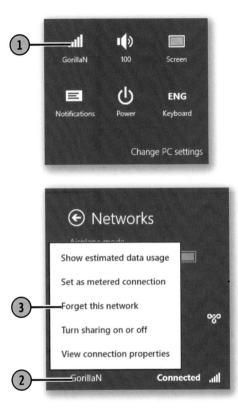

Tip

Forgetting networks is an easy way to reset the password security details again, which is especially useful if you change the password on your Wi-Fi network.

Disconnect a Wi-Fi Network

① In the Settings panel, tap the network icon. If you're connected, it will have the name and signal strength of your current Wi-Fi network.

② Tap the name of the network from which to disconnect.

③ Tap the Disconnect button.

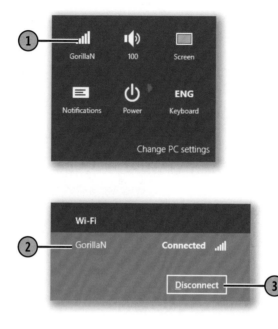

Connecting Your Tablet to Mobile Broadband

Tablet devices can be taken with you anywhere, but often you'll find that you don't have access to a Wi-Fi network. Luckily, Windows 8 has built-in mobile broadband capabilities, meaning that as long as you have a cell signal, you will probably be able to access a mobile cellular network for mobile broadband. Of course, many of these types of connections have limits on the amount of data that you're allowed to transfer in a month; sometimes the limit is enforced by the cellular carrier, but often it isn't. Even though the limits aren't enforced, you can still incur additional charges for going over your allotted limit. Windows 8 has built in "metering" controls to help you to avoid crossing those limits.

Your tablet will need to be equipped with a cellular radio and SIM card slot, or you will need to insert a USB mobile broadband dongle to access mobile broadband. Consult your device manual for details.

Connect to Mobile Broadband

1. In the Settings panel, select the network icon. If you are currently connected to a wireless network, it will show the signal strength and name of the network.

2. Select the Connect Automatically check box to have your tablet always connect to the network when the cellular signal of your carrier is available and better than any available Wi-Fi network.

3. Select the Roam Automatically check box to have Windows attempt to connect to a cellular network with which your carrier has a roaming agreement. This is normally used when traveling.

4. Tap the Connect button to connect to the network.

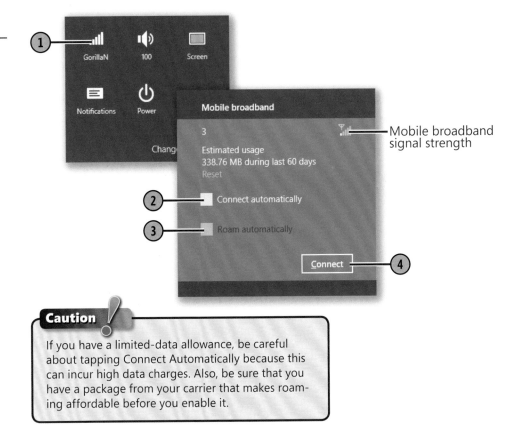

Mobile broadband signal strength

Caution

If you have a limited-data allowance, be careful about tapping Connect Automatically because this can incur high data charges. Also, be sure that you have a package from your carrier that makes roaming affordable before you enable it.

Disconnect Mobile Broadband

① In the Settings panel, select the network icon. If you are currently connected to a wireless network, it will show the signal strength and name of the network.

② Tap the Disconnect button to drop the connection to your cellular carrier.

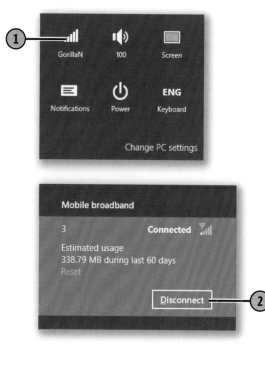

Set Connection Metering

① In the Settings panel, select the network icon. If you are currently connected to a wireless network, it will show the signal strength and name of the network.

② Tap and hold the mobile broadband connection for which you want to control metering.

③ In the pop-up menu that opens, tap Set As Non-Metered Connection to exclude the connection from all metering settings throughout Windows, or select Set As Metered Connection to include the connection in all metering settings throughout Windows.

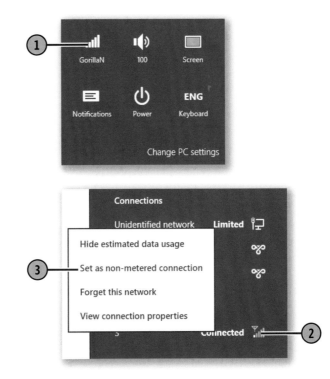

Caution

Be aware that setting a connection as non-metered means that extra usage of your mobile broadband connection will happen. For example, by default Windows Updates are set not to download over a metered connection, so if you set your mobile broadband connection as non-metered, those updates will download over that connection. Updates can be very large and can incur data costs against your cellular plan.

Control Activity on Metered Connections

① In the Settings panel, tap the Change PC Settings link, and scroll down to tap Devices.

② Toggle the switch for Download Over Metered Connections to On to allow Windows to download device drivers over a metered connection.

Drivers are small programs that assist Windows 8 in communicating with your hardware devices.

③ Scroll down further to the Sync Your Settings category.

④ Toggle the Metered Internet Connections switch to determine whether settings will be synced with your Microsoft Account and other devices across a mobile broadband connection or when roaming on that connection.

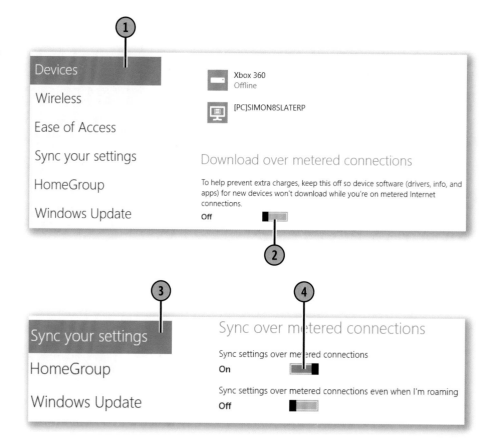

Caution

Enabling syncing of your settings or downloading drivers over a mobile broadband connection might cause excessive use of data and therefore incur extra cellular charges.

Configure Advanced Settings

(1) In the Settings panel, select the network icon. If you are currently connected to a wireless network, it will show the signal strength and name of the network. Tap and hold the mobile broadband connection.

(2) In the pop-up menu that opens, tap View Connection Properties.

(3) Tap the Subscription tab to view information about the connection, including phone numbers, IMEI numbers and IDs, and the service provider.

(4) Tap the Profile tab to access connection settings.

(5) Use The Access Point drop-down menu to select from a list of preconfigured profiles that Windows detects that match the issuing service provider of your SIM card.

(6) Enter the APN, APN User Name, and APN Password for your connection. These are not usually unique for you; you can find them on your service provider's website or by calling them.

(7) Select the Connect Automatically When This Network Is In Range check box to automatically connect when in range of the cellular network.

(8) Select the Allow Roaming On This Network check box to enable roaming automatically when traveling outside your cell provider's coverage.

(9) Tap OK to save any changes.

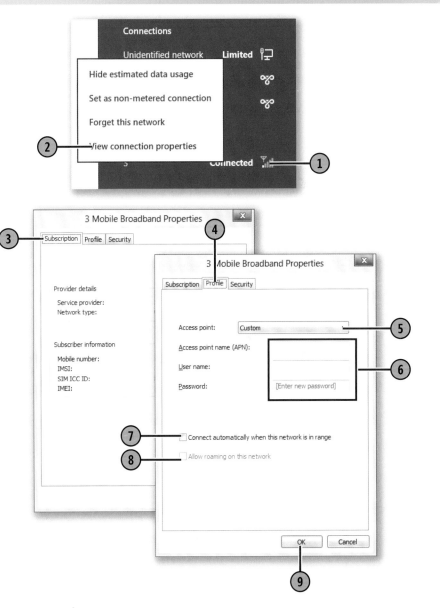

Connecting to Bluetooth Devices

There are many devices that you can connect to your tablet, and depending on what type they are, they might not require a physical connection. Many devices can be connected by using Bluetooth. This includes headsets, printers, mobile phones, wireless speakers, and many more.

Connect Bluetooth Devices

① In the Settings panel, tap the Change PC Settings link, and scroll down to select Devices.

② Tap Add A Device.

③ Wait for your Bluetooth device to be detected. Ensure that the Bluetooth device you want to connect is set to pairing mode. (You might need to consult the device's manual.) When detected, select the device.

④ Depending on the pairing type, you will be presented with either a code to match with that of your device or you will be asked to provide a code for your device. Follow the on-screen instructions to complete the pairing.

Allow Your Tablet to Be Discovered by Other Bluetooth Devices

1. In the Settings panel, type **blue** into the search box and select the Settings category.

2. In the results pane, tap the Change Bluetooth Settings item.

3. The Bluetooth Settings dialog box opens on the desktop. Select the Allow Bluetooth Devices To Find This Computer check box to make your tablet discoverable by other Bluetooth devices.

4. Tap OK to save the changes.

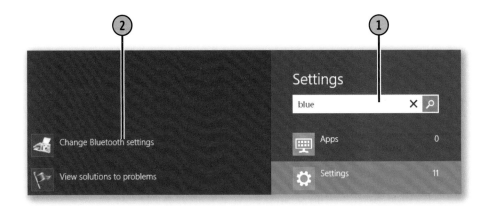

Using Advanced Network Settings

Sometimes, connecting to networks can be a little more complicated than simply looking for what Wi-Fi networks are out there and selecting the one you like. You might be slightly more security-minded than most, having added extra security to your home network by hiding the name of your network (SSID). Control might be your thing, so you might want to be able to better control your sharing settings.

Change Advanced Sharing Settings

1. In the Settings panel, type **network** into the search box, and then in the results pane, tap Network And Sharing Center

2. In the Control Panel, tap Change Advanced Sharing Settings.

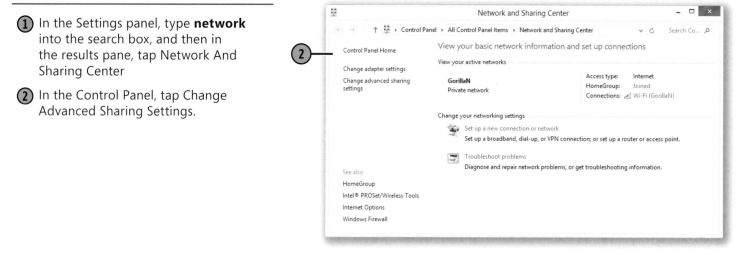

(3) Select either the Turn On Network Discovery option or the Turn Off Network Discovery option, as desired, to enable or disable discovery of other computers on the network and to make your tablet discoverable.

(4) Select the option as desired to either allow or not allow any printers shared on your tablet to be visible or to be able to view printers on other computers.

(5) Select the option as desired to either allow passwords to be managed by Windows, or to create user names and passwords that match on all computers in your homegroup.

(6) Tap Save Changes to save the changes you've made.

Change sharing options for different network profiles

Windows creates a separate network profile for each network you use. You can choose specific options for each profile.

Private (current profile)   ⌃

Network discovery

When network discovery is on, this computer can see other network computers and devices and is visible to other network computers.

● Turn on network discovery
  ☑ Turn on automatic setup of network connected devices.
○ Turn off network discovery

File and printer sharing

When file and printer sharing is on, files and printers that you have shared from this computer can be accessed by people on the network.

● Turn on file and printer sharing
○ Turn off file and printer sharing

HomeGroup connections

Typically, Windows manages the connections to other homegroup computers. But if you have the same user accounts and passwords on all of your computers, you can have HomeGroup use your account instead.

● Allow Windows to manage homegroup connections (recommended)
○ Use user accounts and passwords to connect to other computers

Guest or Public   ⌄

All Networks   ⌄

Save changes   Cancel

Manually Connect to a Wireless Network

(1) In the Control Panel, in the Network And Sharing Center, tap Set Up A New Connection Or Network.

(2) Tap Manually Connect To A Wireless Network.

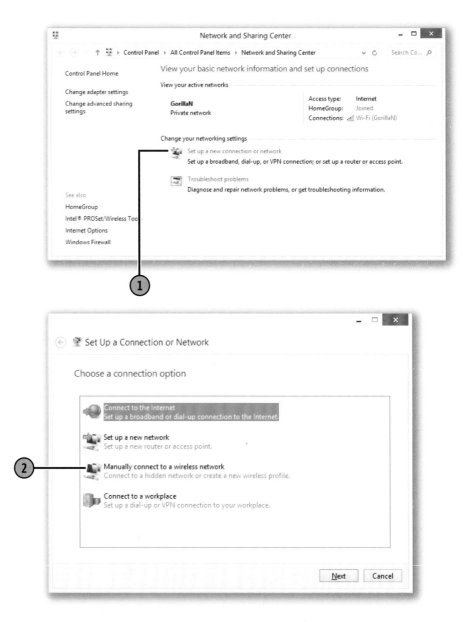

Caution

If you select the Connect Even If The Network Is Not Broadcasting check box, you might find that it's possible for someone running special software to lure you into a fake network to steal your data. Be careful with this setting.

③ Enter the network name and the type of security and encryption used by the network, along with the security key for the network.

④ Select this check box to have your tablet automatically connect to the network when it's available.

⑤ Tap Next to save the settings and attempt to connect.

_ □ ×

(←) 🖳 Manually connect to a wireless network

Enter information for the wireless network you want to add

Network name: [   ]

Security type: [Choose an option] ▾

Encryption type: ▾

Security Key: ☐ Hide characters

☐ Start this connection automatically

☐ Connect even if the network is not broadcasting

Warning: If you select this option, your computer's privacy might be at risk.

[Next]   [Cancel]

Sharing Files and Media with HomeGroup

Connecting your tablet to a home network is not only useful for gaining access to the Internet, it's also useful for sharing files and media between other computers in your house. Windows includes a feature to make this much easier, called Home-Group. With HomeGroup, you can easily access files on other computers in your home, share files from your tablet with other computers, use printers attached to other computers, and stream media such as music, videos and pictures. HomeGroup is supported by Windows 7–based and Windows 8–based computers, and after a homegroup has been set up, any computers that use Windows 7 or Windows 8 can be added to the existing homegroup.

Start a Homegroup

① In PC Settings, scroll down to tap HomeGroup.

② Tap the Create button to set up a homegroup; note that this button will be unavailable if a homegroup already exists on the network.

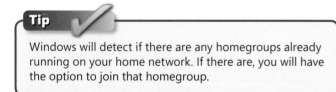

PC settings

Wireless

Ease of Access

Sync your settings

HomeGroup

Devices

HomeGroup

Create a homegroup

With a homegroup you can share libraries and devices with other people on this network. You can also stream media to devices.

Your homegroup is protected with a password, and you'll always be able to choose what you share.

Create

Tip ✓

Windows will detect if there are any homegroups already running on your home network. If there are, you will have the option to join that homegroup.

③ Note the homegroup password; you will need this to add other computers to it.

Tip

HomeGroup isn't the only way to share files around your home network, but it is the easiest to set up. You don't need any special equipment or software, other than the Windows 8 or Windows 7 computers you already own.

Try This!

Once you've set up your HomeGroup, go to another computer in your home and try to stream some music, videos, or pictures from your tablet. Just launch Windows Media Player and you should see your tablet under "Other Libraries" on the left side.

⊙ Libraries and devices

When you share content, other homegroup members can see it, but only you can change it.

Documents
Not shared

Music
Not shared

Pictures
Not shared

Videos
Not shared

Printers and devices
Not shared

Media devices

Allow devices such as TVs and game consoles to play my shared content.
On

Membership

If someone else wants to join your homegroup, give them this password:

A8JU1Qv2kM

If you leave the homegroup, you won't be able to get to shared libraries or devices.

Leave

③

Join an Existing Homegroup

1. In PC Settings, scroll down to tap HomeGroup.

2. When a homegroup is detected on the network, the option to join it is available. You will need to obtain the password from another member of the homegroup.

3. Tap the Join button to join the homegroup.

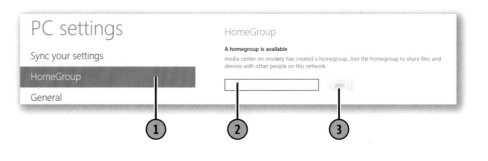

Leave a Homegroup

1. In PC Settings, scroll down to tap HomeGroup.

2. Tap the Leave button to immediately remove your tablet from the homegroup, stopping sharing of any files, printers, or media.

Decide What Your Device Shares

① In PC Settings, scroll down to tap HomeGroup.

② Toggle the switch to enable or disable sharing of the documents in your personal Documents folder.

③ Toggle the switch to enable or disable sharing of the music in your personal Music folder.

④ Toggle the switch to enable or disable sharing of the pictures in your Pictures folder.

⑤ Toggle the switch to enable or disable sharing of the videos in your personal Videos folder.

⑥ Toggle the switch to enable or disable sharing of printers and other sharable devices attached to your tablet.

⑦ Toggle to allow or block media devices such as smart TVs or games consoles like Xbox 360 to stream media from your tablet.

See Also

See page 337 for more information about changing sharing settings by using File Explorer.

PC settings

Wireless

Ease of Access

Sync your settings

HomeGroup

Windows Update

Libraries and devices

When you share content, other homegroup members can see it, but only you can change it.

Documents
Not shared

Music
Not shared

Pictures
Not shared

Videos
Not shared

Printers and devices
Not shared

Media devices

Allow devices such as TVs and game consoles to play my shared content.

On

Access Shared Files

① On the Start screen, tap the Search charm to find File Explorer.

② Scroll down the location pane to find HomeGroup.

③ Select the homegroup member whose files you want to explore. Both Windows 7 and Windows 8–based computers will be listed.

④ Navigate to the libraries, folders, and files you want to view.

Access Shared Media from Older Computers

① On the Start screen, tap Windows Media Player.

② Select the computer or user from which you want to stream.

③ Select the type of media to stream.

④ Browse the media you want to stream.

⑤ Tap the Play button to begin streaming.

Syncing Your Tablet and Other Computers

Your Windows 8–based tablet might not be the only computer you use, but you might spend quite a lot of time making sure you get the look and feel just right. Windows 8 allows you to sync your settings and passwords with many computers over a network or over the Internet by using a Microsoft Account. The first thing you will need is a Microsoft Account, such as one you use for Hotmail or for Xbox 360, which must then be connected to the account on your tablet.

Connect a Microsoft Account

① In the Settings panel, tap the Change PC Settings link, and then in PC Settings, tap Users

② Tap Switch To A Microsoft Account.

③ Enter the password for the account with which you are currently signed in.

④ Tap Next.

(5) Enter the email address of your Microsoft Account.

(6) If you don't have a Microsoft Account, tap the link to sign up.

(7) Tap Next to complete the process; you are asked to confirm your Microsoft Account password and security information.

(5)

(←) Sign in with a Microsoft account

Use your favorite email address to sign in to Windows. If you already use an email address to sign in to PCs running Windows 8 Consumer Preview, enter it here.

Email address

Users who sign in to PCs with a Microsoft account can:

- Download apps from Windows Store.
- Access files and photos anywhere.
- Sync settings online to make PCs look and feel the same–this includes settings like browser favorites and history.

Sign up for a new email address

Next   Cancel

(6)

(7)

Tip

Signing in with a Microsoft Account will allow your settings to follow you to any Windows 8 device you use. This is especially useful if your kids use multiple accounts because Parental Controls will be applied wherever they log on.

Customize Sync Settings

① In PC Settings, select Sync Your Settings.

② If you want settings synced, ensure that this toggle is turned on; otherwise, no settings will sync.

③ Determine precisely which settings are synchronized to your other computers.

④ Syncing over metered connections can cause costs to increase quickly. By default, this is enabled, but if you don't have an unlimited data plan for mobile data, you might want to disable the setting.

PC settings

Devices

Wireless

Ease of Access

Sync your settings

Sync your settings

Sync settings on this PC
On

Settings to sync

Personalize
Colors, background, lock screen, and your account picture
On

Desktop personalization
Themes, taskbar, high contrast, and more
On

Passwords
Sign-in info for some apps, websites, networks, and HomeGroup
On

Ease of Access
Narrator, Magnifier, and more
On

Language preferences
Keyboards, other input methods, display language, and more
On

App settings
Certain app settings and purchases made in an app
On

Browser
Settings and info like history and favorites
On

Other Windows settings
Windows Explorer, mouse, and more
On

Sync over metered connections

Sync settings over metered connections
On

Sync settings over metered connections even when I'm roaming
Off

See Also

ahe message "Your passwords won't sync until you trust this PC." When this happens, everything but passwords will sync with your Microsoft Account. See page 92 for details about how to resolve this.

Taking Your Tablet on a Plane

Tablets are such mobile and convenient devices that we find ourselves using them all the time, and they make especially good companions on long journeys. When flying, aviation authorities and airlines prefer that we turn our devices off so as not to interfere with the systems on the airplane. However, you probably have heard the notifications on most flights that it's safe to turn devices back on in a flight-safe mode when airborne. Windows 8 includes just that and also includes the ability to turn on a flight-safe mode but still utilize the inflight Wi-Fi now appearing on some routes.

Toggle Flight Mode

① Tap Wireless.

② To enable airplane mode, toggle the Airplane Mode setting to On; this will automatically disable all wireless radios, such as Wi-Fi. Bluetooth, and any cellular mobile broadband radios.

③ When in airplane mode, Wi-Fi can be turned on independently to enable access to inflight Wi-Fi services if your carrier and route have the service available.

PC settings

Search

Share

General

Privacy

Devices

Wireless

Airplane mode

Turn this on to stop wireless communication

Off

Wireless devices

Wi-Fi

On

Tip

Don't forget to turn airplane mode off again when you get off your flight (after the seatbelt sign has been turned off, of course!).

6

Staying Safe

Today our lives are constantly connected to the Internet through devices such as your tablet, and as a result, the information on them and the devices themselves need protection. The types of threats that we encounter on the Internet vary depending on what we do, our age and maturity, and on the latest methods of attack. Windows 8 uses multiple technologies to help defend your interests.

Malware is the term associated with software that intends to do something malicious to us or our computers. It's a nuisance that you can commonly encounter when opening webpages or downloading files. To help protect you from these attacks, Windows includes Windows Defender.

The second line of defense on your tablet is your firewall which actively watches and restricts what's talking to your computer and what your computer is talking to, to keep you safe. A third is Windows Update which keeps Windows 8 running with the latest Microsoft security fixes. Finally, Family Safety helps you monitor and control how your kids use your tablet device.

Using Windows Defender

Malicious software (malware) is a common threat online, with many different methods available to a would-be attacker. You can encounter malware in many places, such as email attachments, links on webpages, programs downloaded from the Internet, USB drives, and CDs and DVDs inserted into your computer. The list is endless, but one of the first points of protection is antimalware software that can detect, stop, and remove malware. Windows 8 comes with a number of measures to protect you from malware. Windows Defender provides protection against many forms of attack, but it's also possible that, if you're using a business tablet, your administrator has replaced this with corporate standard software. To protect against the latest attacks, you need to do a few things regularly, such as perform updates, scan often to see whether anything got through, and scan in real time as you're using your tablet.

Find Windows Defender

①On the Start screen, begin typing the word **defender**. Search kicks in and searches for the defender app.

②In the Results pane, tap the Windows Defender icon.

> **Tip**
>
> Windows includes protection from malware that attempts to affect the way that it starts, called Secure Boot. You don't need to do anything with Secure Boot, but it's good to know that Windows is protecting you from another common form of attack.

Run a Manual Scan for Malware

1. Tap Quick to perform a scan of areas and programs that are most likely to be targeted by malware, or select Full to do an exhaustive search of your tablet. (The latter option can take a long while to complete.)

2. Tap the Scan Now button to start the scan.

3. If you selected Custom, you'll be prompted to select the location to scan; this can be on a removable drive if needed.

4. Once the location has been selected, tap OK to initiate the scan.

When you see green, this means your PC is being protected, scans are in place and malware definitions are up to date.

View Malware Detection History

(1) Tap the History tab.

(2) Tap the type of detected items for which you want to view the history.

(3) If you don't have the advanced setting option selected to allow all users to view full history results, tap the View Details button.

④ Select one or more items identified as malware.

You can view details about the malware in the box below the Detected Items list.

⑤ Tap Remove All to remove all detected items from the list.

⑥ Use the Remove button to remove one or more selected items from the history list.

⑦ Tap Restore to recover an item that was incorrectly identified as malware.

Windows Defender

PC status: Protected

| Home | Update | History | Settings | ❷ Help ▾ |

View the items Windows Defender detected as potentially harmful and the actions that you took on them:

⦿ **Quarantined items**
    Items that were prevented from running but not removed from your PC.
◯ Allowed items
    Items that you've allowed to run on your PC.
◯ All detected items
    Items that were detected on your PC.

Detected item	Alert level	Date	Action taken
☐ ⊗ Virus:DOS/EICAR_Test_File	Severe	04/08/2012 12:59	Quarantined

Category: Virus

Description: This program is dangerous and replicates by infecting other files.

Recommended action: Remove this software immediately.

Remove all   Remove   Restore

Updating Malware Definitions

It's critically important to keep Windows Defender up to date so that it knows how to detect new malware threats. Updates can be performed manually or through Windows Update.

Tip

If you have a Windows RT-based tablet, Microsoft will keep your anti-malware definitions up to date for you.

Update Malware Definitions Manually

① If your malware definitions are out of date, the Windows Defender window will display a large Update button on the Home tab.

② If the Update button is not available on the Home tab, tap the Update tab.

③ Tap the Update button to start an update.

Windows Defender

PC status: Protected

Home | Update | History | Settings

? Help ▼

Virus and spyware definitions: Up to date

Windows Defender updates your virus and spyware definitions automatically to help protect your PC.

Definitions created on: 04/08/2012 at 03:00
Definitions last updated: 04/08/2012 at 13:02
Virus definition version: 1.131.1398.0
Spyware definition version: 1.131.1398.0

Update

...re definitions are files that Windows Defender uses to identify malicious or potentially

...tomatically, but you can also click Update to get the latest versions whenever you want.

Windows Defender

PC status: Potentially unprotected

Home | Update | History | Settings

? Help ▼

Virus and spyware definitions are out of date.

Scan options:

◉ Quick

○ Full

○ Custom

Scan now

⊘ Real-time protection: On
ⓘ Virus and spyware definitions: Out of date

Update

🔍 Scan details
Last scan: 12/05/2012 at 13:02 (Quick scan)

Tip ✓

If the definitions are considered up to date, you can still force an update by selecting the Update tab.

Configure Automatic Malware Definition Updates

1 On the Start screen, type **updates**, tap Settings, and then tap Turn Automatic Updating On Or Off.

2 Select a behavior for updates: Install Updates Automatically (Recommended) will download and install all types of updates unaided; Download Updates But Let Me Choose Whether To Install Them causes all updates to be downloaded but not installed—you will have to select the ones to install; Check For Updates But Let Me Choose Whether To Download And Install Them still enables Windows to notify you of new updates but downloads them only when you choose. Finally, Never Check For Updates leaves your tablet un-updated, causing potential security issues. This final option is safe only for non–Internet-connected devices.

3 Select OK to save the changes. Note that you need to be an administrator.

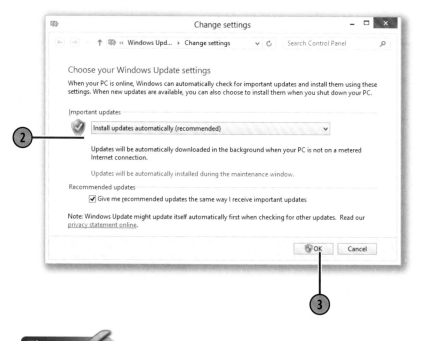

Tip

There are different types of updates available from Microsoft. Important updates are mainly fixes for vulnerabilities discovered in Windows security or to fix something that causes Windows to behave erratically. Recommended updates generally add functionality and include driver updates to get more from your hardware.

Configuring Windows Defender

If you don't have a Windows RT-based tablet and you don't want to use Windows Defender, it is possible to turn it off completely, or if you feel that real-time protection is impacting performance, you can turn off just that component.

If performance is being impacted by scans of particular files, file types, or processes, this too can be controlled.

Turn Windows Defender Off or On

1. In Windows Defender, tap the Settings tab.

2. Tap the Administrator category.

3. Select the Turn On Windows Defender check box to enable Windows Defender; clear the check box to disable it.

4. Tap Save Changes to save the changes. Note that administrator access is required.

Caution

Turning off Windows Defender will make your tablet more vulnerable to malware threats if you don't have other anti-malware software installed.

Turn Real-Time Protection Off or On

① In Windows Defender, tap the Settings tab.

② Tap the Real-Time Protection category.

③ Select the Turn On Real-Time Protection (Recommended) check box to enable scanning every time an app is opened, a link is clicked, a webpage is opened, and more.

④ Tap Save Changes to save the changes. Note that administrator access is required.

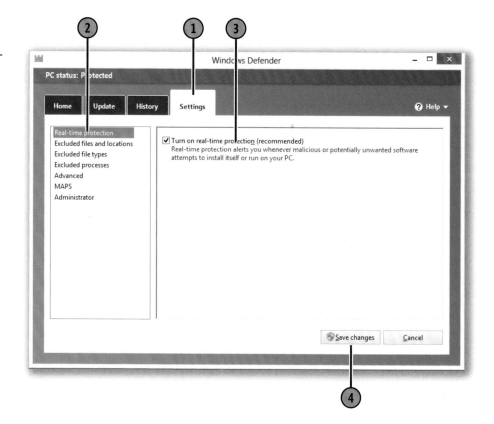

Caution

Turning off Real-Time Protection makes your tablet more vulnerable to malware threats if you don't have other anti-malware software installed. However, scheduled scans will still run.

Exclude Files, Locations, and Processes from Malware Scans

(1) In Windows Defender, tap the Settings tab.

(2) Tap the type of exclusion you want to use (files and locations, file types, or processes). All are configured similarly.

(3) Type the paths, file, file extensions, or process names to be included in the exclusion rule.

(4) With the exception of file extensions, the Browse button can be used to locate the file or processes to exclude.

(5) Tap the Add button to add the item to the exclusion list.

(6) Tap the Remove button, to remove any highlighted item from the exclusion list.

(7) Tap Save Changes to save the exclusions.

Caution

Be careful not to exclude drives such as C:, because this will prevent Windows Defender from scanning some critical locations.

Windows Defender

PC status: Protected

Home | Update | History | **Settings** | Help ▼

Real-time protection
Excluded files and locations
Excluded file types
Excluded processes
Advanced
MAPS
Administrator

Excluding certain files and locations can help speed up a scan, but may leave your computer less protected.
To add multiple files or locations, use a semicolon to separate the entries in the text box.

File locations:

c:\more locations

Browse
Add

Name
c:\book

Remove

Save changes | Cancel

Apply Advanced Settings

1 On the Settings tab, in the Advanced section, select the check box Scan Archive Files, to have Windows Defender scan zip, cab, and other archive files.

2 Select to have Windows scan USB drives or removable hard disks.

3 Select to have Windows create a restore point (a type of backup) before removing malicious hardware. The advantage is that nothing is lost, but the risk is that you potentially have an infected restore point.

4 Select to allow all users to see other user's history of detected malware. This can be a privacy concern for some people because users will be able to see what files or web-sites another user of the tablet was viewing when the malware was encountered.

5 Select to instruct Windows Defender for how long to keep quarantined files, using the drop-down to specify duration.

6 Click Save Changes to save your advanced settings.

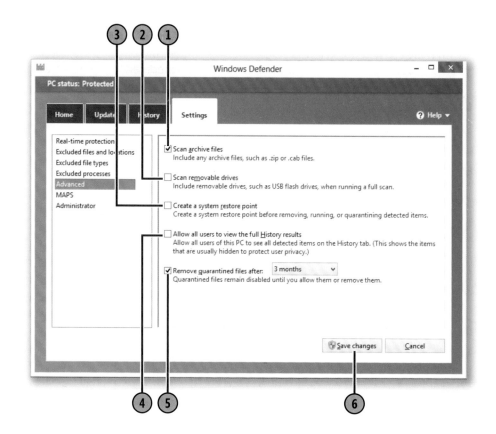

What to Do If Windows Defender Finds Malware

Windows Defender will find malware if it has definitions that match malware on your tablet when it is running a scheduled scan, a scan that you have started, or if you inadvertently interact with malware and the Windows Defender real-time scanner detects this activity. When the real-time scanner or a scheduled scan detects malware, it attempts to fix the problem for you. When a user-initiated scan detects malware, you are notified and asked what action Windows Defender should take. In either case, the malware is deleted, quarantined, or, in rare cases, it is unresolvable, in which case you should seek expert help.

When malware is detected, a popup like this will appear in the top right of the screen.

Malware Detected
Windows Defender is taking action to clean detected malware

When malware is detected by a scan, Windows Defender makes it obvious by changing the color of the window to red to indicate a problem.

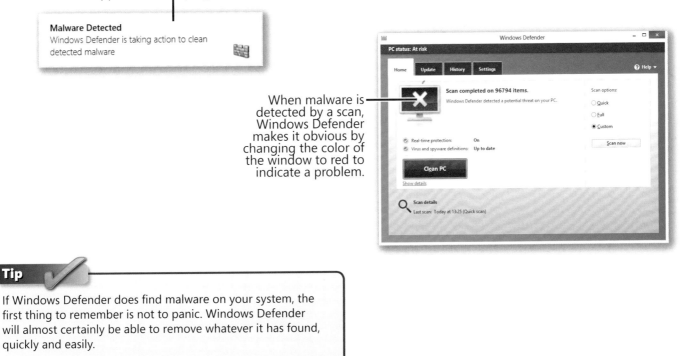

Tip

If Windows Defender does find malware on your system, the first thing to remember is not to panic. Windows Defender will almost certainly be able to remove whatever it has found, quickly and easily.

Remove Malware

① If a scan identifies malware, it will first display a warning alert while the scan completes.

② When the scan is complete, tap the Clean PC button to resolve the problem.

③ If you'd like to know more about what was found, select Show Details.

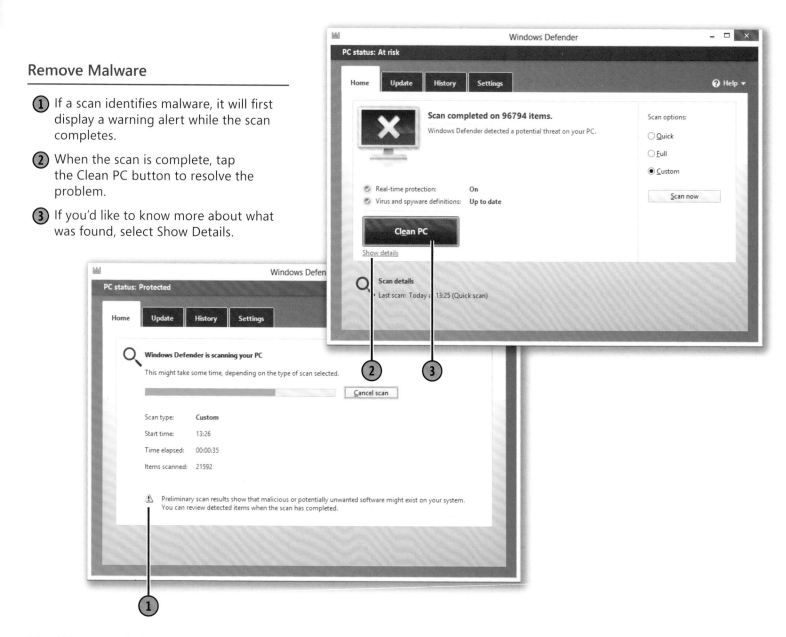

④ The Windows Defender Alert dialog box shows all instances of malware that it identified. To learn more about each detected item, select it and tap Show Details.

⑤ Select an action: Remove eradicates the virus; Quarantine holds it in an area for close examination by experts; Allow ignores it.

⑥ Tap Apply Actions to apply the changes you've selected. The red bar in this window will turn green again once the malware is removed.

Windows Defender Alert

Potential threat details

Windows Defender detected a potential threat that might compromise your privacy or damage your PC. Your access to this item might be suspended until you take action.
Click Show details to learn more. What are alert levels, and what should I do?

Detected items	Alert level	Status	Recommended action
Virus:DOS/EICAR_Test_File	Severe	Active	Remove

Show details >>   Apply actions   Close

Understanding Windows Firewall

Windows Firewall is built-in protection that prevents attackers from connecting to networking ports on your computer that are used for normal communication. The firewall looks at the source of a request coming to your computer and determines whether it is something you want to allow into your computer. If it is not, it is dropped; otherwise, the firewall allows the communication through.

View Windows Firewall Status

① In the Control Panel, tap Windows Firewall to view the status of the firewall and access its settings.

② Different types of networks have different firewall restrictions. For example, sharing is turned off on public networks where it might be a risk. Tap the drop-down arrow to view the settings for a particular zone.

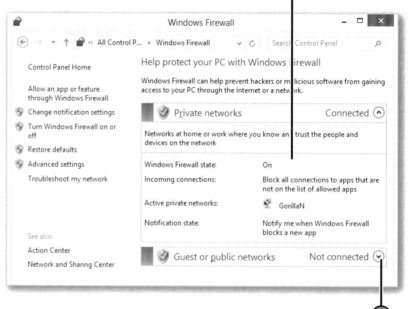

Windows Firewall tells you what it will do by default when something tries to contact an app on your computer if it's not on the allowed list.

Change Windows Firewall Notifications

(1) In the Windows Firewall dialog box, tap Change Notification Settings.

(2) Select the check box to enable notifications when Windows Firewall detects and blocks a new app attempting to use the network.

When this option is selected, you get a notification that gives you the option to say yes or no to access the app in the future.

(3) Select the check box to enable notifications for detecting and blocking new apps from accessing public networks.

(4) Tap OK to apply the changes.

Control Panel Home

Allow an app or feature through Windows Firewall

(1) Change notification settings

Turn Windows Firewall on or off

Restore defaults

Advanced settings

Troubleshoot my network

Customize Settings

Win... ▸ Custom...   Search Control Panel

Customize settings for each type of network

You can modify the firewall settings for each type of network that you use.

Private network settings

● Turn on Windows Firewall

☐ Block all incoming connections, including those in the list of allowed apps

(2) ☑ Notify me when Windows Firewall blocks a new app

○ Turn off Windows Firewall (not recommended)

Public network settings

● Turn on Windows Firewall

☐ Block all incoming connections, including those in the list of allowed apps

(3) ☑ Notify me when Windows Firewall blocks a new app

○ Turn off Windows Firewall (not recommended)

OK   Cancel

(4)

Restore Defaults

① In the Windows Firewall dialog box, in the Action pane, tap Restore Defaults.

② Tap the Restore Defaults button. A warning appears asking if you really do want to delete all settings regarding apps that are allowed through the firewall.

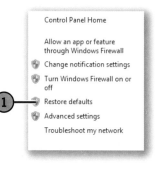

Control Panel Home

Allow an app or feature through Windows Firewall

Change notification settings

Turn Windows Firewall on or off

① — Restore defaults

Advanced settings

Troubleshoot my network

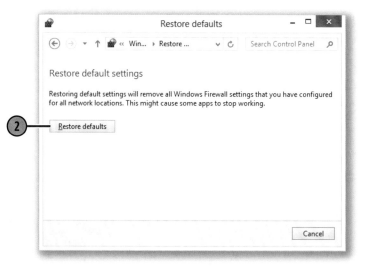

Restore defaults – ☐ ✕

← → ▾ ↑ 📷 « Win... ▸ Restore ...   ✔ ↻   Search Control Panel 🔎

Restore default settings

Restoring default settings will remove all Windows Firewall settings that you have configured for all network locations. This might cause some apps to stop working.

② — Restore defaults

Cancel

Tip ✓

Use Restore Defaults if you've made changes to your firewall that are causing you problems or that you made by mistake.

Allow Apps Through Windows Firewall

1 In the Windows Firewall dialog box, tap Allow An App Or Feature Through Windows Firewall link.

2 Tap Change Settings (if the button is available) to make changes to the allowed applications list.

3 Select the check box for an app or feature that you want to make available on Public and Private networks.

4 Tap Allow Another App to permit a non-listed app through the firewall.

5 If the app is listed in the app list, tap to select it.

6 If the app is not listed, use Browse to locate the app's files.

7 Tap the Network Types button to configure the network types on which to allow the app.

8 Tap Add to add a new rule for the app, or tap Cancel to abandon changes.

9 Tap OK when you're done making changes, or tap Cancel to abandon them.

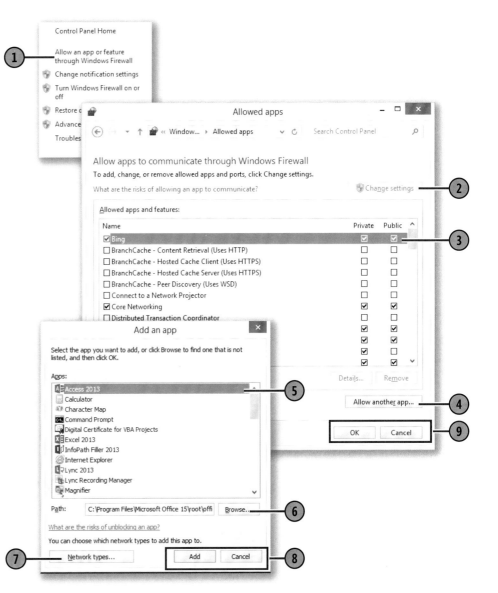

Turn Windows Firewall On or Off

1 In the Windows Firewall dialog box, in the Actions pane, select Turn Windows Firewall On Or Off.

2 For private networks, select whether Windows Firewall is on or off by selecting the appropriate radio button.

3 For public networks, select whether Windows Firewall is on or off by selecting the appropriate radio button.

4 Tap OK to apply the changes.

Control Panel Home

Allow an app or feature through Windows Firewall

Change notification settings

1 — Turn Windows Firewall on or off

Restore defaults

Advanced settings

Troubleshoot my network

Customize Settings — □ ×

Win... ▸ Customize...   ∨ C   Search Control Panel

Customize settings for each type of network

You can modify the firewall settings for each type of network that you use.

Private network settings

2 — ● Turn on Windows Firewall

☐ Block all incoming connections, including those in the list of allowed apps

☑ Notify me when Windows Firewall blocks a new app

○ Turn off Windows Firewall (not recommended)

Public network settings

● Turn on Windows Firewall

☐ Block all incoming connections, including those in the list of allowed apps

☑ Notify me when Windows Firewall blocks a new app

3 — ○ Turn off Windows Firewall (not recommended)

OK   Cancel

4

Caution

Disabling Windows Firewall without having other firewall software installed on your tablet could place it and the information on it at risk.

Keeping Windows Updated with Windows Update

Microsoft regularly releases updates to fix discovered security issues, usability issues, or even to release new drivers and software. Windows Update is a process that runs in the background on your Windows 8-based tablet (if, as recommended, you've enabled it), identifies any required updates, and applies those updates to your tablet at a convenient time.

Check Windows Update Status

1 Display the Control Panel and tap System And Security.

2 In the System And Security task view, tap the Windows Update item.

3 If Windows update shows anything other than green, it is worth checking to see whether all is well; Windows Update might be disabled or might not have been able to contact the Windows Update service for some reason.

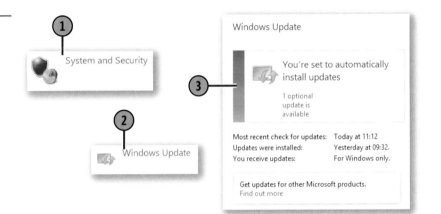

Manually Check for Updates

1 In the Settings panel, tap the Change PC Settings link and then tap Windows Update.

2 Tap the Check For Updates Now button to have Windows attempt to find new updates.

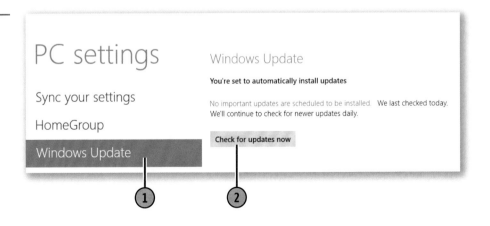

Knowing When Updates Are Available

Windows Update runs constantly and checks regularly for updates for your tablet. Periodically, when updates are available or after updates have been installed, you'll need to take some action. Windows notifies you with messages on your lock screen, sends notifications from Action Center, and more actively notifies you when you need to do something very soon, such as reboot.

Install Updates

1. On the Start screen, type **update**, and then tap Windows Update in the search results.

2. When updates have been downloaded and installed, you might be asked to restart. One way to do that is from the Windows Update dialog box; if they have not yet been installed, you will be asked to install updates.

Windows Update messages start to appear on your lock screen.

Changing Windows Update Settings

Occasionally, you might want to disable Windows Update—For example, if your tablet isn't connected to the Internet. However, generally, you should leave its default settings as is. If you find that updates occur at the wrong times, are too frequent, or take too long, you can configure these settings to make them more convenient for you.

Change Update Settings

1 Display the Control Panel, tap System And Security, and then in the left pane of the Windows Update screen, tap Change Settings.

2 Select the update style you would like.

3 In the Recommended Updates section, select the check box to have Windows treat recommended updates (which are lower priority than important updates and are generally not security related) the same as important updates.

4 Tap OK to save any changes.

Filtering Dangerous Downloads by using SmartScreen

Windows SmartScreen prevents you from accidentally down-loading files from the Internet that aren't recognized by Windows as being trustworthy. The trustworthiness of downloads is derived from how popular they are and any security infor- mation that the creator embeds into the download. Windows SmartSreen notifies you with a pop-up dialog box within Internet Explorer or when you try to open an untrusted file.

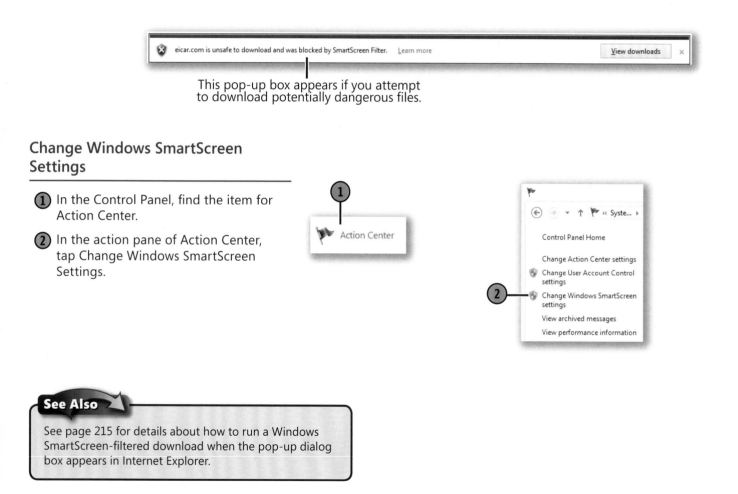

This pop-up box appears if you attempt to download potentially dangerous files.

Change Windows SmartScreen Settings

① In the Control Panel, find the item for Action Center.

② In the action pane of Action Center, tap Change Windows SmartScreen Settings.

See Also

See page 215 for details about how to run a Windows SmartScreen-filtered download when the pop-up dialog box appears in Internet Explorer.

(3) Select this option to have an administrator accept any download before an
unrecognized app can be run.

(4) Select this option if you want Smart-
Screen to warn only about running
unrecognized apps.

(5) Select this option to turn off Windows SmartScreen.

(6) Tap OK to apply the changes.

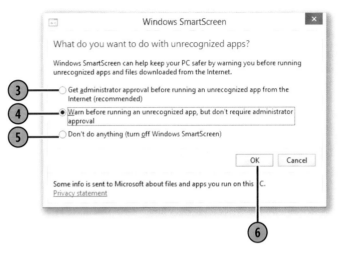

Caution

Turning off SmartScreen filter reduces
your tablet's anti-malware protection.

Securing Data with BitLocker Drive Encryption

Using BitLocker to encrypt hard disks can help with securing data, essentially by scrambling it and making it unreadable in other computers. It's possible to encrypt hard disks built into your device as well as USB-attached hard disks. When enabled,

BitLocker requires a password before you can access the data on your hard disk. BitLocker also needs your tablet to have a special piece of hardware called a *Trusted Platform Module (TPM)*.

Encrypt a Drive

① In Windows Explorer, right-click the drive to encrypt and select Turn On BitLocker.

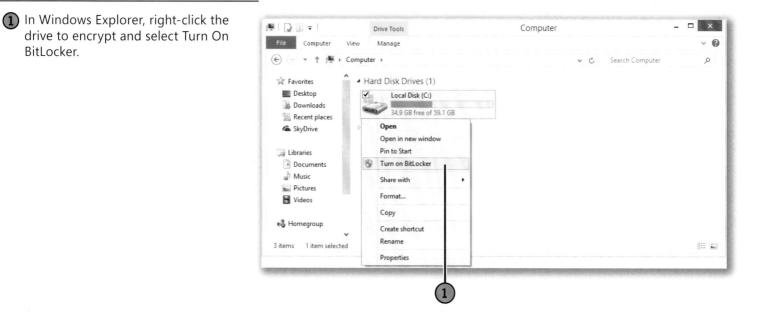

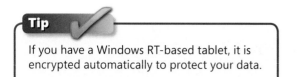
If you have a Windows RT-based tablet, it is encrypted automatically to protect your data.

② Select the Use A Password To Unlock The Drive check box.

③ Enter a password.

④ Confirm the password.

⑤ Tap Next to continue.

⑥ Select a location to which to save the recovery key to, which is needed to access the drive if you forget the password.

⑦ Tap Next to complete the process; you will need to specify whether to encrypt the empty space on the drive or just the existing drive and new data.

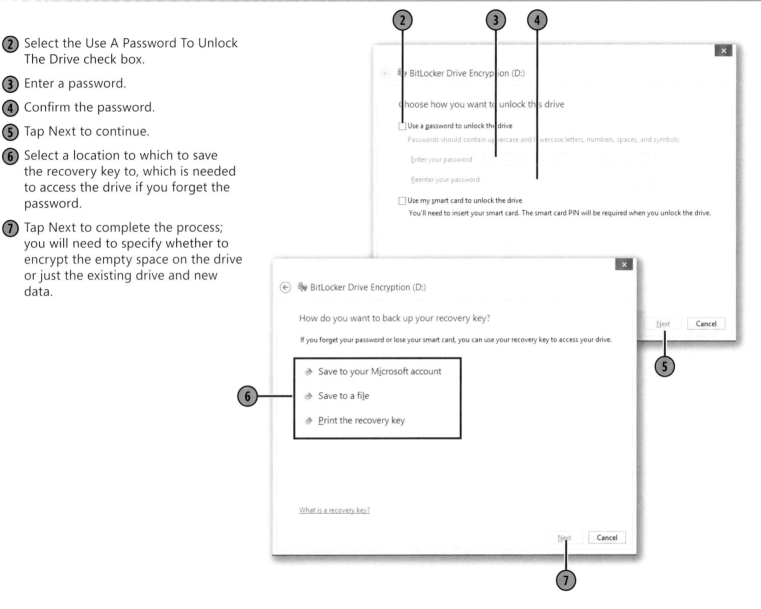

Enabling Family Safety to Keep Kids Safe

Your kids will want to use that lovely tablet of yours. When they're small, it will make an excellent travel companion for them on long journeys. When they're a little older and capable of using more of the tablet's features, you might want to put some protections in place to keep them away from content they aren't ready for. Family Safety can keep them safe from adult web content, from games that are too adult for them, and from apps they shouldn't use. You can also set time limits so that they don't play too long. However, if you don't want to prevent your children from accessing sites but you do want to know what they've been doing and how long they've been doing it, you can enable monitoring.

Set Family Safety Settings on an Existing Account

(1) In the Control Panel, tap Set Up Family Safety For Any User.

(2) Select the account to which to apply Family Safety.

Tip

When creating a new user account, you are asked if you'd like to enable Family Safety for the account.

③ Select the desired option to either enable or disable the current Family Safety settings.

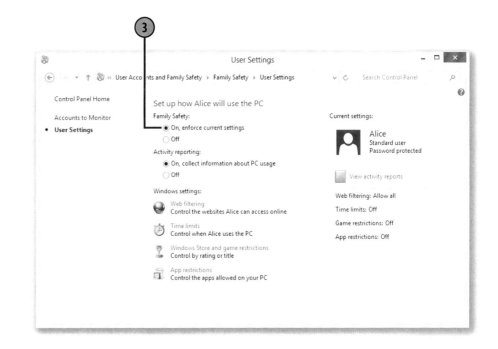

Tip

You can choose to manage your Family Safety settings from the Family Safety website. This gives you the opportunity to remotely add and subtract rules for your kids, which is useful if their tablet never leaves their side.

Monitoring What Your Children Do on Your Tablet

Monitoring what your children are doing with your tablet might be a better way for you to help educate them, depending on your parenting style. Windows 8 includes monitoring that, when tied to a cloud service, will watch what your kids do across multiple devices when they sign in with their Microsoft Account. This same service will send you a weekly digest of their activities, giving you an opportunity to intervene and discuss those activities with you child, if necessary. Activity monitoring is turned on by default.

View a Child's Activity

(1) In Family Safety, tap the child for whom you want to view activity.

(2) Tap View Activity Reports to view the last week's activity on this device.

(3) Tap Family Safety Website to view a more detailed activity history.

Note that to view this report, you need to sign in with your Microsoft Account to the Family Safety website.

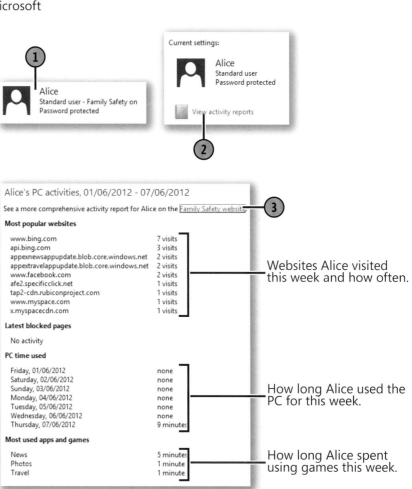

Websites Alice visited this week and how often.

How long Alice used the PC for this week.

How long Alice spent using games this week.

> **Tip**
>
> If you don't like the idea of your kid's activity being sent to Microsoft, don't worry. You can disable this by selecting the Remove It From The Family Safety Website link at the bottom of the Family Safety window—but you will lose access to more detailed reports.

Shows the websites
Alice visited and allows
easy access to block
unsuitable ones.

Shows how long Alice used the
PC, what apps she used, what
files she downloaded, games she
played, and apps she downloaded
from Windows Store.

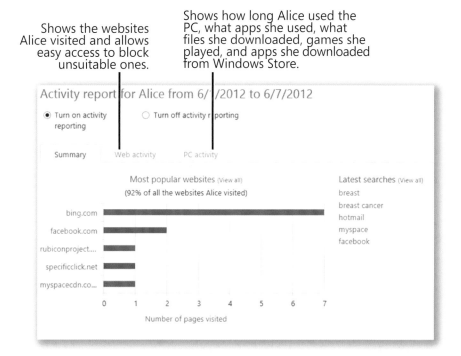

Tip

Through the Family Safety website, you'll receive a weekly
email activity report for all the protected members of your
family. The report details much more than those you can view
on your tablet alone and will aggregate what your kids have
been doing across any devices that they log on to with their
Microsoft Account.

Filter Websites

① In Family Safety, tap the Web Filtering link.

② Select the option to only allow specific websites.

③ Tap Set Web Filtering Level to filter a managed list of websites based on their content.

④ Select the level to which you want to allow access. The levels become less restrictive down the screen.

⑤ Select the Block File Downloads check box to prevent your kids from downloading anything from the Internet.

⑥ Tap Allow Or Block Specific Websites to create an allowed or blocked website list.

⑦ Enter a website address.

⑧ Tap Allow or Block to add the site to the respective list.

Set up how Alice will use the PC

Family Safety:
- ● On, enforce current settings
- ○ Off

Activity reporting:
- ● On, collect information about PC usage
- ○ Off

Windows settings:

🌐 Web filtering
Control the websites Alice can access online

Which websites can Alice view?
- ○ Alice can use all websites
- ● Alice can only use the websites I allow

Allow or block websites by rating and content types

Set web filtering level

Allow or block all websites

Allow or block specific websites

Which websites can Alice visit?

Choose a web restriction level:

- ○ Allow list only
  The child can view websites on the Allow List. Adult sites are blocked.
  Click here to change Allow List.

- ○ Child-friendly
  The child can view websites on the Allow list and in the child-friendly category. Adult sites are blocked.

- ○ General interest
  The child can view websites on the Allow list and those in the child-friendly and general interest categories. Adult sites are blocked.

- ● Online communication
  The child can view websites on the Allow list and those in the child-friendly, general interest, social networking, web chat, and web mail categories. Adult sites are blocked.

- ○ Warn on adult
  The child can view all websites, but receives a warning when a site contains suspected adult content.

☐ Block file downloads

Turning on web restrictions also turns on SafeSearch settings for Bing, Google, Yahoo! and other popular search engines. Ad

Allow or block specific websites for Alice

Enter a website to allow or block.

[   ]   [Allow] [Block]

Allowed websites: Blocked websites:

[Remove]

Tip ✓

It's very difficult to decide what's safe and what isn't on the Internet. New sites appear every second, so using the automatic filters might be a good idea, especially because it could mean the difference between incorrectly blocking access to a site critical for Johnny's term paper versus giving him access to the site and getting an A!

Control What Games Your Kids Play

(1) In Family Safety, tap the Windows Store And Game Restrictions link.

(2) Select this option to allow your child to play only those games and download only those apps you allow from the Windows Store.

(3) Tap to set ratings for games and Windows Store apps. This feature uses your local rating system, in this case PEGI and BBFC in the United Kingdom.

(4) Tap to allow games and apps with no rating. (All Windows Store apps are rated.)

(5) Tap to select the level to allow. The most restrictive (youngest age) is at the top, and the least restrictive (oldest age) is at the bottom.

(6) Tap to create a list of specific games that are installed that this child cannot play. There is no OK button to make these changes; when you change any setting, the change is made for all Family Safety restricted accounts.

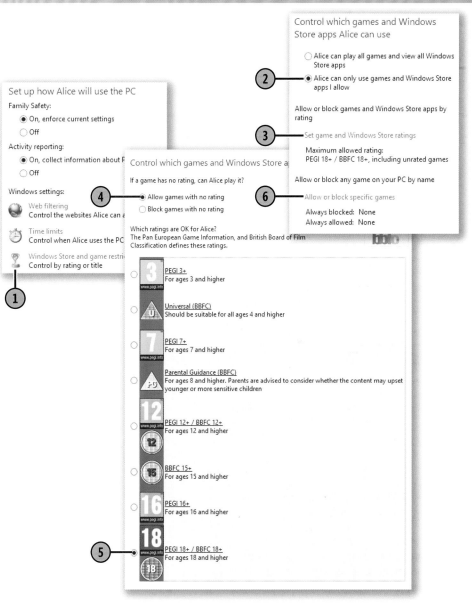

Set Time Limits for Computer Use

1 In Family Safety, tap Time Limits.

2 Tap Set Time Allowance to set an amount of time that your child can use the tablet per day. Times can vary from day to day and on weekends.

3 Tap Set Curfew to set times when the tablet cannot be used.

4 Highlight the times when the child will be unable to use the tablet.

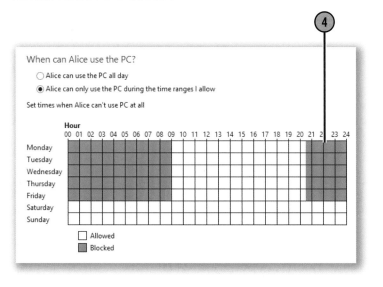

Set up how Alice will use the PC

Family Safety:
- ⦿ On, enforce current settings
- ○ Off

Activity reporting:
- ⦿ On, collect information about PC usage
- ○ Off

Windows settings:

Web filtering
Control the websites Alice can access online

Time limits
Control when Alice uses the PC

Control when Alice can use the PC

Set the number of hours Alice can use the PC per day

Set time allowance

Set the time of day Alice can use the PC

Set curfew

When can Alice use the PC?
- ○ Alice can use the PC all day
- ⦿ Alice can only use the PC during the time ranges I allow

Set times when Alice can't use PC at all

| | Allowed |
| | Blocked |

Tip

Setting a time allowance determines how many hours per day your child can use her computer; setting a curfew determines specific times when she can use it. Curfew and time limits can work together.

Restrict Specific Apps

①　In Family Safety, tap App Restrictions.

②　Select this option to allow only specific apps.

③　Select the check boxes for the apps you want to allow.

④　Tap Browse to browse for apps that you want to allow if they aren't on the list already.

App restrictions
Control the apps allowed on your PC

Which apps can Alice use?
○ Alice can use all apps
◉ Alice can only use the apps I allow

Check the apps that can be used:

File	Descriptio ^
Windows Store apps	
☑ Camera	Microsoft
☐ Finance	Microsoft
☐ Mail, Calendar, People and Messaging	Microsoft
☐ Maps	Microsoft
☐ Music	Microsoft
☐ News	Microsoft
☐ Photos	Microsoft
☐ Reader	Microsoft
☐ SkyDrive	Microsoft
☐ Sport	Microsoft
☐ Travel	Microsoft
☐ Video	Microsoft ∨

Add an app to this list:
Browse...

Check all
Uncheck all

Caution

Be careful when restricting some specific apps; for example, if you browse and restrict File Explorer, Windows might not function properly.

7

Browsing the Internet

We've become a world made up of information and sharing junkies, always connected to our friends on social networks with almost any information available at the click of a mouse or a tap of our finger.

Windows 8 helps to literally put that information at your fingertips by making the browsing experience on your Windows 8 tablet fantastic to use with touch. Most of the time, you will use your tablet with touch and will therefore navigate websites with using your fingers, swiping to go back and forward and pinching to zoom in and out. However, much of the experience you have on the web relies on the developers of your favorite websites, and they don't all (yet) make sites that are touch friendly.

Some websites have been designed solely with the use of keyboard and mouse in mind and don't respond too well when you want to use touch. Luckily, Windows 8 also includes a desktop-based mouse and keyboard-friendly web browser. You don't need to put down your tablet and go find a computer to use the non-touch website; you can still do it with your tablet.

Getting to Know Internet Explorer 10

Your Windows tablet comes with an advanced, built-in web browser in the form of Internet Explorer 10. Internet Explorer is available by tapping the Internet Explorer tile on the Start screen; it also appears when you tap a link in an email or in another app.

Top and bottom navigation bars retract when not in use so the web page is your focus

Open web pages appear as tabs

Tab tools, InPrivate Browsing

Open new tab

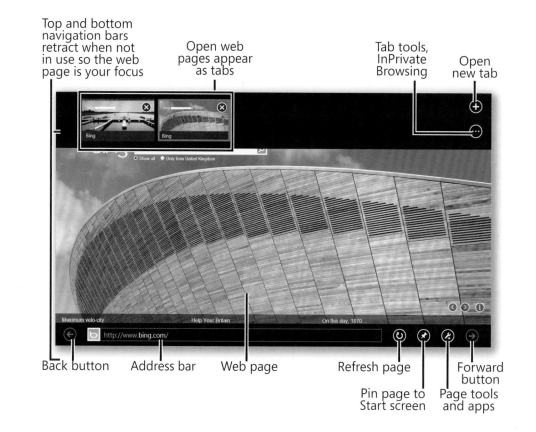

Back button

Address bar

Web page

Refresh page

Pin page to Start screen

Page tools and apps

Forward button

Opening Webpages with Internet Explorer 10

Internet Explorer is only as fun, interesting, or useful as the pages you visit. Internet Explorer will keep a history of frequently visited websites and makes it easy to go back to them in a single tap.

Enter a Web Address

1 Swipe upward from the bottom of the screen to show the address bar.

2 Tap the current web address and start typing the address of the page you want to go to. You can also type related words to have your selected search engine search the web for results.

3 When you start typing, Internet Explorer attempts to automatically complete the results for you by looking at the history of pages you've been to, your pinned pages, and by searching the web.

4 If Internet Explorer suggests a page you want to view, simply tap that suggestion to open the page.

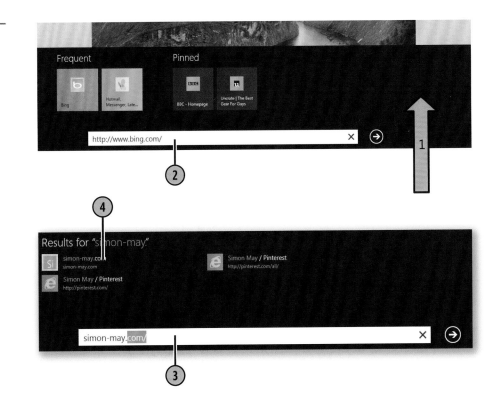

Tip

Opening the address bar also delivers a list of frequently used pages; just tap a page to go there quickly.

Navigate Backward and Forward

(1) Swipe up from the bottom of the screen to show the address bar.

(2) To go forward to the next webpage, tap the right-facing arrow. (You will have had to have already tapped back at least once for this to be available.)

(3) To go back to the page previous page you were on, tap the left-facing arrow. You can go back through several pages of your history this way.

Navigate Backward and Forward with Swipes

(1) Swipe from right to left to go forward.

(2) Swipe from left to right to go back.

Tip

The first time you swipe forward, you'll be asked whether you want to enable the Flip Ahead feature, which makes browsing to the next page on a website easier by swiping right to left. Be aware that if you do this, you will be sharing your browsing history with Microsoft.

Refreshing Pages

1. Swipe upward from the bottom of the screen to show the address bar.

2. Tap the refresh icon to refresh the webpage.

   A new copy of the page is fetched from the site with the latest information.

Zooming In and Out

There might be times when it's difficult to view a webpage, perhaps because the content is too large or too small. Internet Explorer supports zooming in and out by using pinching so that you can adjust the size of the elements on your screen.

Zoom In

① To zoom in, place two fingers on the screen and move them apart.

Zoom Out

② To zoom out, place two fingers on the screen and pinch them together.

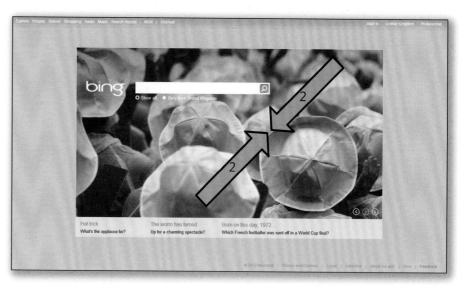

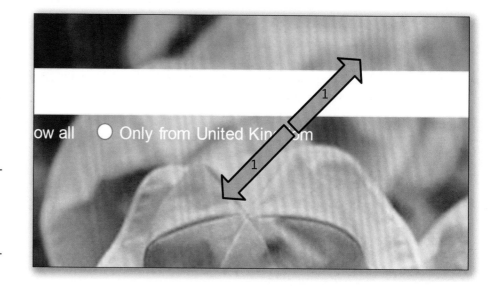

Downloading Files and Programs

When we browse the Internet, we often come across documents we want to download or programs we think will be useful. Internet Explorer can download those for you, and will assist you if you need to take any action after the file or program has downloaded. It also scans the file by using Smart-Screen to assess the reputation of the download and advises you which action is most appropriate.

Download and Run Programs or Open Files

① When you tap a link to download a program or file, pop-up dialog box appears, presenting you with options for what action to take. Tap Run or Open to run an app or open a file in the default app for that type of file.

② If you want to save the app or file rather than open it, tap Save. By default, the file will be saved to your Downloads folder. Once it has been saved (if the file you downloaded was an app), you'll be asked if you wish to run it.

③ When an app is downloaded, Smart-Screen will check that the file is reputable. If it finds that it's not, a message appears to let you know and the file will not be downloaded. Tap Close to dismiss the message.

 Tip

If you wish to download the file anyway, you'll need to open Internet Explorer on the desktop and download the file again. It will be blocked again, but you'll have the option to View Downloads; from here, you can override SmartScreen..

Pinning Webpages for Later

Webpages can be pinned in Internet Explorer 10 to make it easier for you to find them in the future. Pinning a page places a tile for that page on the Start screen.

Pin a Webpage

① Swipe upward from the bottom of the screen to bring up the address bar and then tap the Pin icon. The website name will be highlighted.

② Optionally, tap to change the name for the pin. You can use the X at the end of the address bar to clear the current text.

③ Tap the Pin To Start button to pin the page to the Start screen.

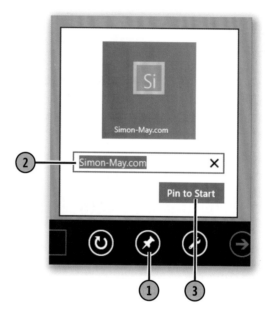

Tip

If you log on with a Microsoft Account and sync your settings, your pinned sites will follow you and appear on any Windows 8 device you log on to with your Microsoft Account.

Open a Pinned Webpage from Internet Explorer

① Swipe upward from the bottom of the screen to bring up the address bar and then tap the web address area.

② Above the address bar, tap an item in the Pinned section to open it in the browser.

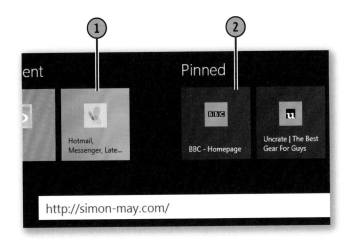

Open a Pinned Webpage from the Start screen

① On the Start screen, swipe left and right to locate the pinned site to open.

The tiles display the names of the their respective websites (unless you changed it when pinning the site).

② Tap the tile of the page you want to open.

Unpin a Webpage

① Tap and pull down a little on the pinned webpage you want to remove from the Start screen.

② In the lower-left corner of the screen, tap Unpin From Start.

See Also

For more information about how to rearrange items on the Start screen, see page 18.

Browsing with Tabs

When browsing the Internet, you might want to change sites frequently. You can do this easily in Internet Explorer 10 by using tabs. Each tab is like a browser in its own right, isolating what happens in other tabs, so if one tabs crashes you won't lose everything. Tabs can also be set to InPrivate browsing, which keeps your browsing private by not recording your browsing activity in the History folder. When you close the tab, your browsing activities are removed from your tablet.

Open a New Tab

① Swipe downward from the top of the screen to show the tab bar.

② Tap the plus sign to create a new tab and then enter the address to which to navigate via the address bar.

③ To switch back to an another tab, tap the tile for that tab.

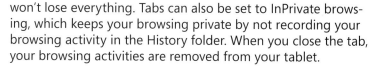

Open an InPrivate Tab

① On the tab bar, tap the three dots (ellipsis) icon.

② In the options panel that opens, tap New InPrivate Tab.

Everything you browse in this tab is hidden from your history, and cookies (used to track your activity and preferences by webpages) are deleted when you close the tab.

InPrivate tabs show the InPrivate logo to mark their privacy status

Close a Tab

1. Swipe downward from the top of the screen to show the tab bar.

2. Tap the close button (X) in the upper-right corner of each webpage tile to close the page.

Close All Tabs

① Swipe downward from the top of the screen to show the tab bar.

② Tap the Tab Tools button to open the tools menu.

③ Tap Close Tabs to close all tabs except the one you're currently viewing.

Finding Related Apps

The Internet has changed dramatically over recent years, and many people now prefer to consume their information from the Internet by using specialized apps. For example, you might find apps that show a news website in a style similar to a newspaper and decide that you'd prefer to use this app to consume the information on the site.

Windows 8 and Internet Explorer 10 make it easy to find apps for websites by introducing the ability to fetch them in a single tap.

Find Apps Related to a Page

1. Swipe upward from the bottom of the screen to show the address bar.
2. Tap the Page Tools icon to open the tools menu.
3. Tap Get App For This Site to go to the app associated with the webpage in the Windows Store.

Tip

When a webpage has an associated app, a small plus sign is added to the wrench icon on the address bar.

Viewing Webpages on the Desktop

Internet Explorer 10 operates a "plug-in–free" model, meaning that it does away with reliance on additional software (plug-ins) previously used to enable rich media software and other programs. The downside is that not all websites have enabled this capability. For this reason, you also have the option to open a webpage on the desktop (where plug-ins continue to be supported) in one tap.

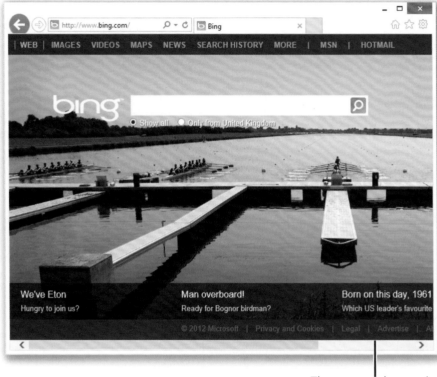

The same web page is opened in an Internet Explorer tab on the desktop.

Move a Webpage to Desktop Internet Explorer

① Swipe upward to show the address bar.

② Tap the Page Tools icon to open the tools menu.

③ Tap View On The Desktop to open the page in a new tab in Internet Explorer on the desktop.

Getting to Know Internet Explorer 10 on the Desktop

Internet Explorer 10 on the desktop is probably the most familiar web browser to experienced Windows users. The layout has been refreshed, but fundamentally, it's still very easy to use with a mouse and keyboard.

Internet Explorer on the desktop can use plug-ins, so you can still run videos by using a plug-in such as Silverlight or Java. Custom toolbars are also available on the desktop.

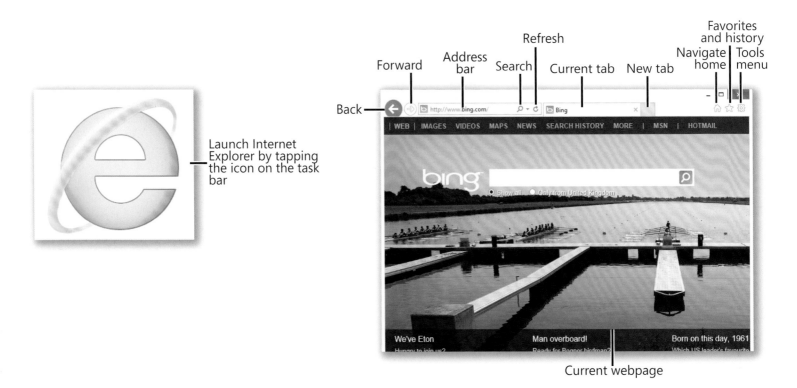

Launch Internet Explorer by tapping the icon on the task bar

Back

Forward

Address bar

Search

Refresh

Current tab

New tab

Navigate home

Favorites and history

Tools menu

Current webpage

Open a Webpage

① Type the address of the site you want to open or enter some words to search in the address bar.

② Press the Enter key on your keyboard or tap the Go arrow.

A drop-down menu opens, displaying addresses that you've typed recently.

③ Webpages you've visited previously that match part of the address or search you've entered start to appear.

④ Tap the desired address to go there without having to type the rest of the address.

⑤ Internet Explorer accesses your specified search engine immediately. Tap a result to go to the search results page that matches the terms.

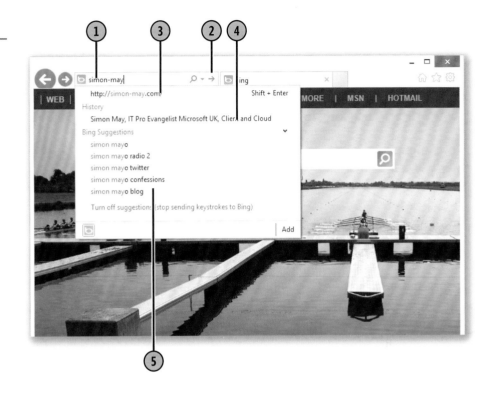

Using Favorites and History

Favorites are a way to keep a note of webpages you visit often so that you can avoid having to type in the address of the page every time you want to go there. They're just like pinned pages, but they don't appear on the Start screen. Internet Explorer also records a history of the sites you've been to so that it can provide you with relevant information as you browse the web and can suggest sites that you might want to visit when you start typing addresses. History is also incredibly helpful if you want to go to a site you were on yesterday, or even two weeks ago, but don't know the address.

Add a Webpage to Favorites

1. Enter the address of the webpage to which you want to navigate.

2. When the page has loaded, tap the Favorites icon (star).

3. Tap the Add To Favorites button.

4. Enter a name for the page that is meaningful to you; by default, this will be the page title.

5. Select a Favorites folder in which you want to place the favorite.

6. If the folder doesn't exist, tap New Folder to create one, enter a folder name, and then tap the Create button.

7. Tap Add to add the favorite.

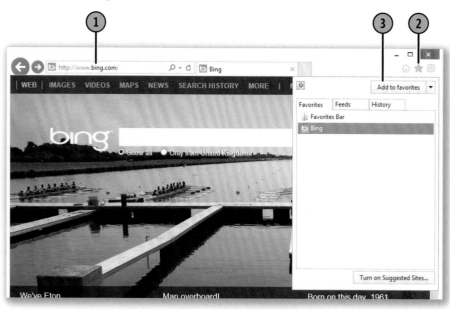

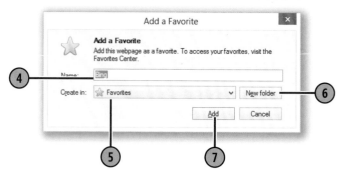

Open a Favorite Webpage

(1) Tap the Favorites icon at the top of Internet Explorer.

(2) Tap a Favorite to open that page.

(3) Alternatively, start typing part of the name you've given to a favorite.

(4) In the drop-down list that appears, tap the name of the favorite you want to open.

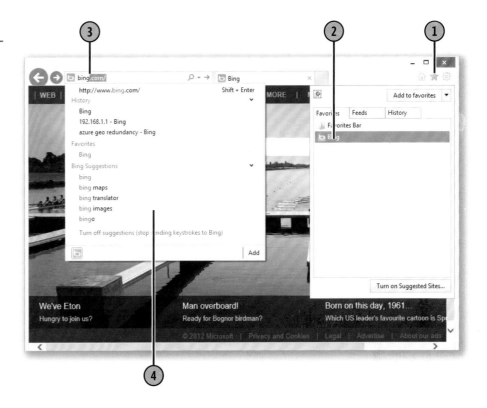

Open History

① Tap the Favorites icon.

② Select the time period for which you want to view the history. For the last week, each day is visible. Next, past Sunday weeks are grouped together. And then finally, months are grouped.

③ Tap the website you want to go to from your history.

Managing Downloads

When you're online, you will come across files that you want to download; it could be a document, a video, an application, or something entirely different. When you tap a link to a file that Internet Explorer can't display, a yellow pop-up dialog box appears at the bottom of the window, asking if you want to download the file. From here, you have a couple of options; you can open the download by using an app on your tablet, or you can save the download to your tablet.

Download and save the file

Download and then run a program (this button is instead labeled Open if you have an app that can open this type of file)

Cancel the download before it starts

Tap Learn to learn more about Smart-Screen downloads

Open a previously downloaded file

Completed download

Blocked download

Active download

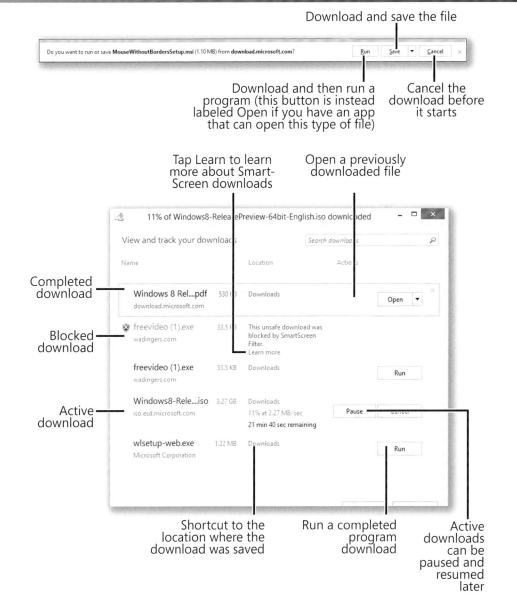

Shortcut to the location where the download was saved

Run a completed program download

Active downloads can be paused and resumed later

Tip

To override a blocked download, tap and hold the download, and then in the options panel that opens, tap Download Unsafe Program.

View Downloads

① In the toolbar of Internet Explorer 10 Desktop, tap the Tools (cog) icon.

② In the drop-down menu that opens, tap View Downloads.

Pause, Stop, and Restart Downloads

① During an active download, tap Pause to suspend the download at its current state of completion.

② When a download is paused, tap Resume to continue the download from the point at which it was stopped.

③ Tap Cancel to discontinue an active download.

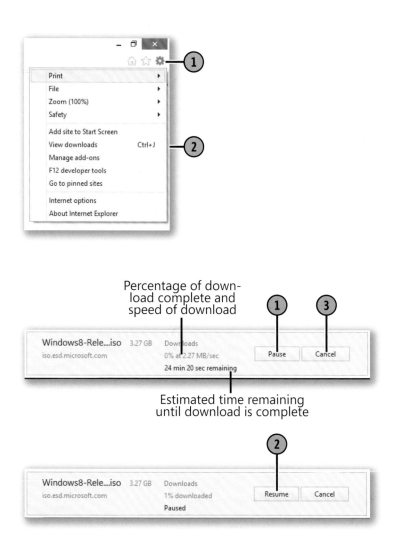

Percentage of download complete and speed of download

Estimated time remaining until download is complete

Open and Run Downloads

1 When you tap a file to download, Internet Explorer Desktop displays a pop-up dialog box that presents three options. If the file is an app, tap Run to run the file. If the file is not an app, this button instead is labeled Open and will open the file in a suitable app or request that you select an app if one is not already known to Windows.

2 If you don't select an action from the previous pop-up dialog box, you can still run and open a file from within the download manager. Tap Run for programs or Open for files.

3 When opening files, you can tap the optional arrow and select an alternative program with which to open the file.

Setting Common Internet Options

Internet Explorer 10 has many options with which you can customize the way the browser works and behaves. Many of these are advanced settings that you will probably never need to use. However, there are some things you might want to modify. For example, you might want to change the home page—this is the webpage (or webpages) you first see when you start Internet

Explorer. Your home page need no longer be just a single page; Internet Explorer can open multiple home pages, each in a different tab. Of course, you might find it easier to have Internet Explorer open with the page you were last looking at before you exited the program. You can also control this as well as other startup settings.

Set How Internet Explorer Desktop Starts

1 Tap the Tools icon.

2 In the drop-down menu that opens, tap Internet Options.

Print	▶
File	▶
Zoom (100%)	▶
Safety	▶
Add site to Start Screen	
View downloads	Ctrl+J
Manage add-ons	
F12 developer tools	
Go to pinned sites	
Internet options	
About Internet Explorer	

③ Enter the web addresses of each page you would like to open when Internet Explorer starts on the desktop. Enter each address on a new line.

④ Tap Use Current to set the current page you're viewing as a home page.

⑤ Select Start With Home Page to use the home page settings specified. Or, select Start With Tabs From The Last Session to open the pages you were looking at when you last exited Internet Explorer.

⑥ Tap OK to save the settings and close the dialog box. Tap Apply to save the settings but keep the dialog box open, or tap Cancel to abandon changes.

Change How Tabs Work

(1) In the Internet Options dialog box, on the General tab, tap the Tabs button.

(2) Select the Enable Tabbed Browsing check box.

Each page you view will open in a new Internet Explorer window without tabs.

(3) Select this check box to enable a warning when you are about to close more than one tab at the same time.

(4) Select this check box to automatically switch to new tabs as they are created. (This can be annoying if a page pops up information that isn't important to what you're doing.)

(5) Select this check box to display a preview of open tabs when you hover over the Internet Explorer icon on the taskbar.

(6) Select the Enable Quick Tabs check box to display a thumbnail preview of open tabs when two or more tabs are open.

(7) Select the Enable Tab Groups check box to gather tabs together so that, if a webpage creates a second tab, the tabs are color coded for related pages.

⑧ Select this check box to open only the first of your homepages when you start Internet Explorer; you can still open them all by tapping the Home button.

⑨ Specify what happens when you open a new tab, displaying a special page with frequent websites listed, a blank tab, or the first home page in your list.

⑩ Select one of these three options to specify what happens when a web-page asks to open a new window.

⑪ Select one of these three options to specify how links open when you tap them in other apps, such as email or messages.

⑫ Tap to restore the default settings.

⑬ Tap OK to save your settings or tap Cancel to abandon changes.

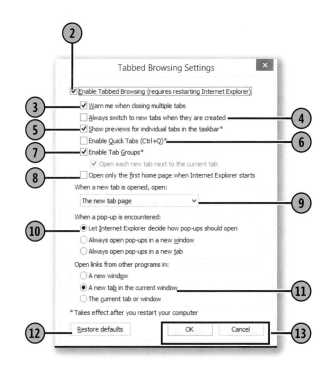

Staying Safe Online with Internet Explorer

Online Safety is an important aspect of any web browser, and Internet Explorer has some particularly useful features to keep you safe. SmartScreen technology is used to identify websites that you attempt to visit, either by typing the address or tapping a link, that could contain malicious content. Malicious content is a program that might attempt to steal your information, trick you into providing information, or download malware to your tablet. SmartScreen Filtering checks webpages before you get to them and alerts you if it detects something suspicious. SmartScreen does the same thing for downloads. You can override SmartScreen if you are sure that you want to view the site or proceed with a download.

Online privacy is a prime concern for many, so Internet Explorer also has protections to prevent your web activity from being tracked.

Use SmartScreen Filtering

1. Enter an address to open any webpage.

2. When a page is encountered that has been reported to SmartScreen as being unsafe, the webpage is blocked. A warning message with a red background appears, and the address bar is shaded red.

3. Tap More Information to learn more about the threat.

4. If you are certain that the page does not represent a threat, at the bottom of the More Information section, tap Disregard And Continue.

Caution

SmartScreen is designed to protect you from threats. Disregarding its warning could lead to information loss or malware infection.

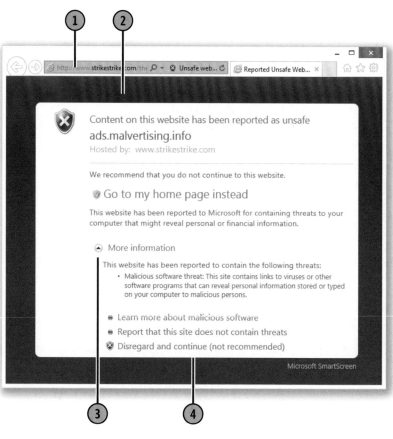

Use SmartScreen with Downloads

1 When you attempt to download a file that doesn't have a sufficiently high reputation in SmartScreen for it to be trustworthy, SmartScreen blocks the download. Tap View Downloads to open the Download Manager and view the download.

2 If you want to accept the warning, tap the Close button (X) to dismiss the message; your file still is not downloaded.

3 Tap Run or Open (for documents) to run or open the file despite Smart-Screen's protests.

4 If you still wish to download a file that is blocked because it has been reported as unsafe (not rec-ommended), first tap and hold the download.

5 Tap Download Unsafe Program.

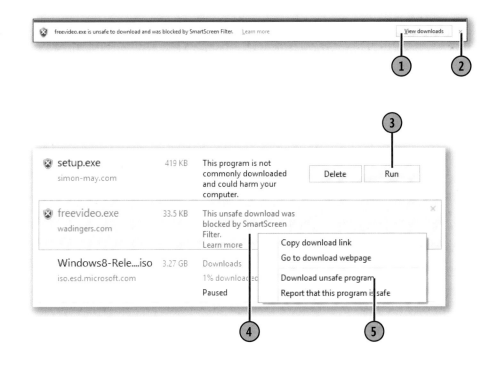

Caution

SmartScreen is designed to protect your interests. However, it can sometimes be overcautious. If you can trust the download, you can choose to run it anyway, but exercise extreme caution. It's always pos-sible that the file is not what it purports to be. Check that the site you are downloading from is reputable; when in doubt, heed the warning.

Using Do Not Track

Because of the way the web works, it's possible for websites to track your activity on the web; this is a completely normal practice for many websites, and it's how they understand what you've done on their website to help them create a better experience for you. It's also one way that advertising on the web is targeted to you. However, some people don't like being monitored and want to stop it to protect their privacy. To address these concerns, Internet Explorer 10 includes a new feature called "Do Not Track," which, when enabled, alerts website owners that you don't want them to track what you're doing on their site. Website owners can then choose to respect the setting, based on an honor system. Although we show these settings on the desktop here, the same settings apply in Internet Explorer on the desktop.

Enable or Disable Do Not Track

1 Tap the Tools icon.

2 Tap Internet Options.

3 Tap the Advanced tab.

4 Select the Always Send Do Not Track Header check box to enable the Do Not Track feature, or clear the check box to disable it.

5 Tap OK to apply your changes.

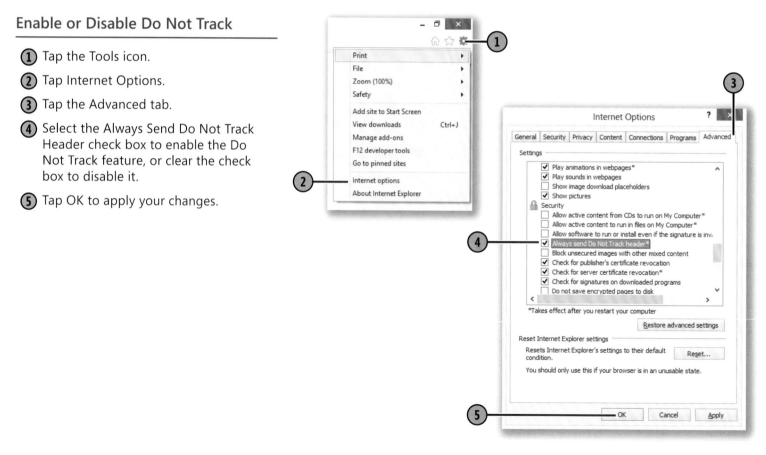

Keeping Your Tracks Private

When you use Internet Explorer 10, it keeps a history of all the pages you've visited. If someone wants to, she can use this information to see where you've been, which can be frustrating if you're buying your spouse a fantastic birthday present, only to have the surprise ruined. Internet Explorer also keeps note of everything you enter into web-based forms and uses this to make suggestions when you visit new forms. For example, it remembers your email address and shipping address to make activities like online shopping easier. Websites also like to store information on your tablet in small files called cookies to keep track of what you do on their sites. These are usually intended to make things easier for you when you visit their site or to have the site remember you. However, cookies can also be read by others, who can then target ads to you based on things you've been browsing for.

Internet Explorer can help in all these areas. First, by enabling InPrivate browsing, you can browse without any of this information being stored. When you close an InPrivate tab, all the cookies, history, and form data are lost. But even, if you don't use InPrivate, you can still quickly delete parts of this browsing history information at any time.

Enable InPrivate Browsing

① Tap the Tools icon.

② In the drop-down menu that opens, tap Safety.

③ Tap InPrivate Browsing to open an InPrivate tab.

InPrivate tabs display this logo in the address bar

InPrivate | about:InPrivate

Delete History

1 Tap the Tools icon.

2 In the drop-down menu that opens, tap Safety.

3 Tap Delete Browsing History, and then in the dialog box that opens, select or clear the check boxes adjacent to the individual items in your browsing history to delete or keep them, respectively.

Delete browsing history...	Ctrl+Shift+Del
InPrivate Browsing	Ctrl+Shift+P
Tracking Protection...	
ActiveX Filtering	
Webpage privacy policy...	
Check this website	
Turn off SmartScreen Filter...	
Report unsafe website	

Print	▶
File	▶
Zoom (100%)	▶
Safety	▶
Add site to Start Screen	
View downloads	Ctrl+J
Manage add-ons	
F12 developer tools	
Go to pinned sites	
Internet options	
About Internet Explorer	

Managing Add-Ons

Internet Explorer on the desktop provides the ability for other additional software to be included in your browsing experience. This might be a toolbar, such as the Bing bar, that makes finding Bing services easier. It could be software that makes particular types of video viewable, such as Microsoft Silverlight. You might want to use a different default search engine or use custom Accelerators that make tasks like sending emails from webpages more convenient.

Manage Toolbars and Extensions

1 Tap the Tools icon.

2 Tap Manage Add-Ons.

3 In the Manage Add-Ons dialog box, in the Add-On Types pane, tap Toolbars.

4 Select the add-on with which you want to work.

5 To learn more about the selected add-on, in the lower-left corner of the dialog box, tap the More Information link. This information includes when it was installed and where its files are on your tablet.

6 Tap Disable to prevent the add-on from being used. You might want to do this if Internet Explorer has alerted you to a performance concern or if you see an add-on that you don't trust.

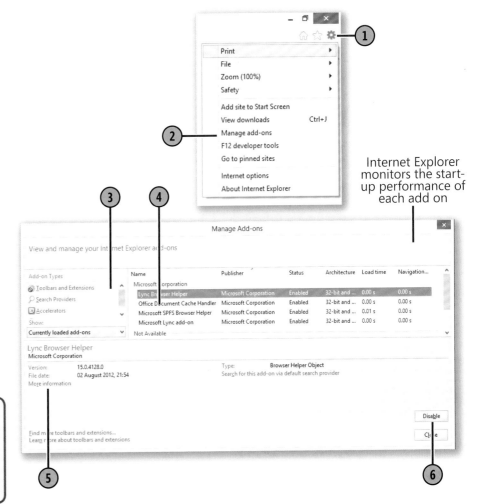

Internet Explorer monitors the start-up performance of each add on

Tip

Review the add-ons running on your tablet regularly to make sure that nothing unwanted has appeared. For example, if you start to find Internet Explorer is a little slow, check here first to see whether anything unexpected is running.

Manage Search Providers

(1) In the Manage Add-Ons dialog box, in the Add-On Types pane, tap Search Providers.

(2) Select the search provider to manage.

(3) Use the links to reorder the search providers; enabled search providers are searched in order when you enter search terms in the address bar.

(4) Enable or disable search suggestions and the display of top search results in the address bar. Search suggestions search as you type and attempt to complete what you're typing before you finish, making search faster.

(5) Select the Prevent Programs From Suggesting Changes To My Default Search Provider check box to stop some programs from promoting a different search engine.

(6) Select the Search In The Address Bar check box to enable search from the address bar. Clearing this check box means that the specified search provider will not be used in the address bar.

(7) Tap Set As Default to set the currently selected provider as your preferred search provider.

(8) Tap Remove to remove the search provider, making it unavailable.

8

Using Apps

Apps are among the jewels of Windows 8, providing unlimited options for extending what you can do with your tablet. Those apps are available for your tablet from the Windows Store, which provides a store front or catalog for you to choose your apps from. You can browse the store by flicking through all the available apps, which are organized into categories such as Entertainment, Books & Reference, Productivity, Photos, and more. If browsing isn't your thing, you can find apps by searching the store for specific titles or for apps produced by specific developers or with specific features or purposes.

When you find an app you like, you will need to install it, but before you do, you'll want to check the price. Some developers charge for their apps, others offer theirs free of charge. After you've decided on trying, buying, or using a free app, you then need to install it. It's a one-click process to do so, and Windows takes care of the installation for you. Windows also takes care of ensuring that you can install the same app on up to additional four Windows 8 devices.

What's What in an App?

Apps in Windows 8 are full screen and immersive; thus, many of the menus are hidden from view to focus on the content of the app. Knowing where to swipe to make options available is key.

Apps are full
screen and
immersive.

To access charms,
swipe inward from the
right edge.

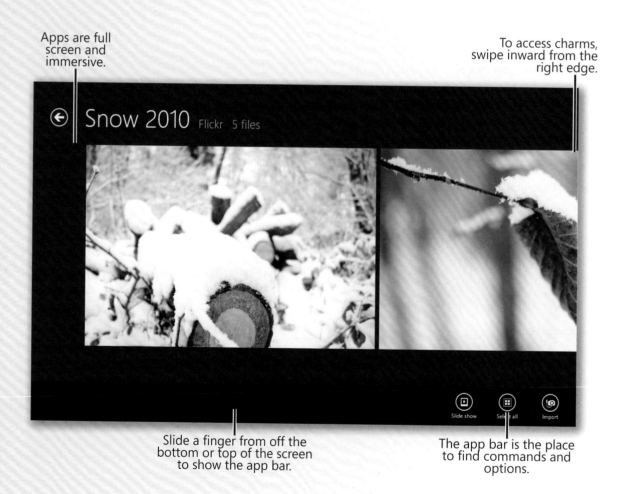

Snow 2010 Flickr 5 files

Slide show   Select all   Import

Slide a finger from off the
bottom or top of the screen
to show the app bar.

The app bar is the place
to find commands and
options.

Using the Store to Get Apps

The Store is where you go on your Windows 8 tablet to get apps. There are apps for every occasion, but the store categorizes them to help you find your way through, and you can also search within the store to find apps if you know the name or what you want the app to do. Some apps are free, and some you must buy. You'll need to have a payment method set up in your Microsoft Account if you intend to purchase apps.

Open the Store

① On the Start screen, select the Store tile.

② When the Store app opens, you can pan through the items in the store from left to right by placing a finger on the screen and moving or flicking left or right, just like the Start screen.

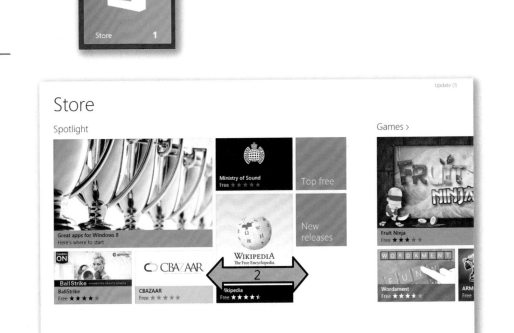

Paying for Apps

Not all apps are free. Many require that you purchase them to unlock all their functionality. Therefore, you will need to set up a payment method. Keep in mind that all purchases are final.

Set Up Billing

1. Within the Windows Store, select the Settings charm and tap Your Account.

2. In the Payment And Billing Info section, tap Add Payment Method.

③ Choose to pay by either a credit card or a PayPal account.

④ Enter the details of your credit card and your credit card billing address, or if using PayPal, enter your PayPal billing address.

⑤ Tap Next to complete the credit card setup process and validate your card, or if using PayPal, tap Next to enter your PayPal details at the PayPal site.

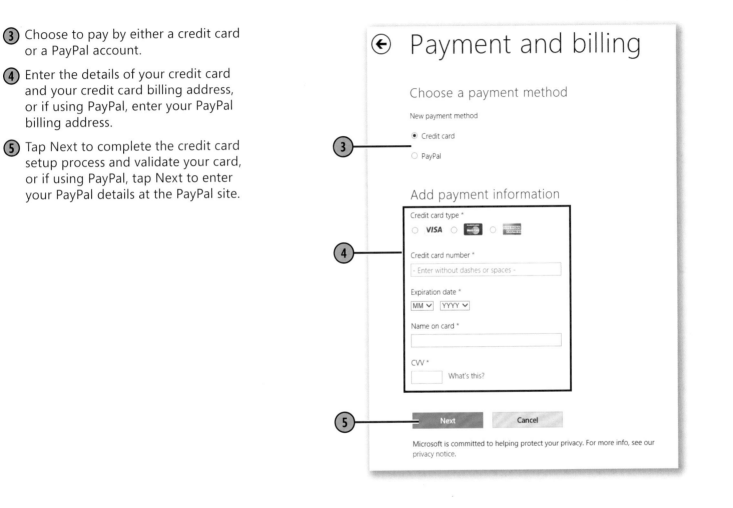

Installing Your First App

The store is a great place to select and install apps. The process is made as simple as possible by giving you a few options while presenting you with as much relevant information as possible to make choices about the app that you want to install. Apps are rated by others, using a star rating system (zero through five stars), and the apps are divided into categories, such as Games, Social, Entertainment, Photo, Shopping, Productivity, and many more. Microsoft also curates the store to highlight apps that win contests, are seasonal, or are likely to be relevant to you, based on the apps you've installed in the past.

Browse the Store

1. On the store's main page, pan to find a category of apps you want and then tap the title of the category.

2. If you want to view a curated list, tap the tile for that list.

Tip

Microsoft highlights some of the best apps for you to install, but you'll want to look at what an app does (and its reviews) to help determine if it's right for you.

(3) If you want to filter the available apps by price, tap the Sort By Prices drop-down list and select from Free or Free And Trial (to include apps that have a trial period), or tap Paid to show only paid apps.

(4) Choose to sort the list of apps by noteworthy, newest, highest rated, lowest price or highest price.

(5) Tap an App tile to view more details or to install it.

App Star Rating

App Price

Install an App

(1) Tap and hold to scroll up and down the overview of the app.

(2) Tap and hold the picture of the app, and move your finger left and right to scroll through images of the app at different stages.

(3) Tap Details to view information about the app, such as what languages it's available in and what information and features of your tablet the app can access.

(4) Tap Reviews to read reviews of the app from other users.

(5) Tap Install if the app is free, or tap Buy if the developer charges for the app. Sometimes a paid app has a Try button so that you can use it free of charge for a limited period.

(6) When the app has installed, a pop-up will briefly appear in the upper-right corner of the screen; tap it to launch the app. The app will also appear automatically on your Start screen.

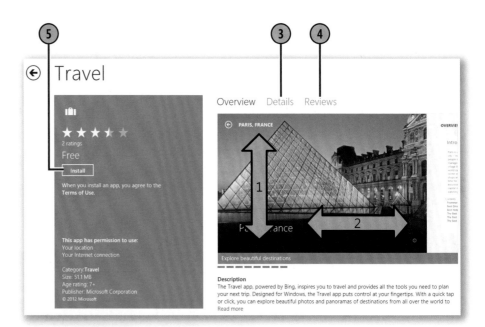

Caution

All app purchases are final. You cannot get your money back if you buy an app and you don't like it.

Searching the Store

You might have a very specific idea of the app you want from the store, in which case browsing to locate the app would be cumbersome. Instead, you can simply use the Search charm.

Search for Apps

① Swipe in from the right, and tap the Search charm.

② Enter a term to search for in the store; it could be the name of the app, the name of an app developer, or the purpose of an app.

③ Tap the search button if you're in the Store; otherwise, tap the Store icon.

④ Results will appear to the left.

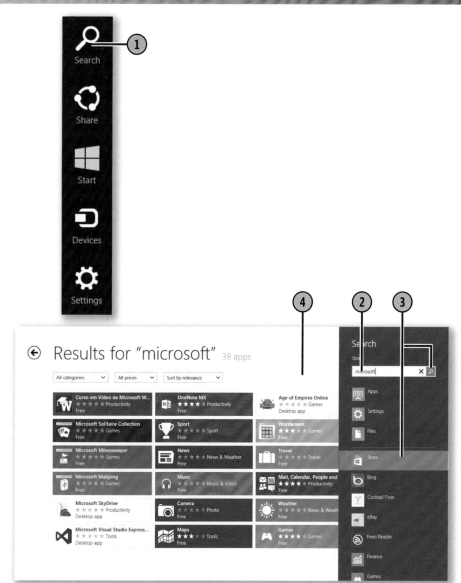

Managing App Licenses

To make your experience as consistent as possible across a number of different devices, Microsoft has made it possible to buy an app once and install it onto multiple devices. If you log on to lots of devices regularly, you might need to manage the devices that your account uses because there are limits to how many devices you can have.

Remove Unwanted Devices

1. While in the Store, swipe in from the right and tap the Settings Charm.

2. On the Settings menu, tap Your Account.

3. Scroll down to the Your PCs section.

4. Locate the PC you want to remove and tap the Remove button. A confirmation pop-up appears. PCs are added automatically when you sign in to them with your Microsoft Account.

Search

Share

Start

Devices

Settings

Settings

Store
By Microsoft Corporation

Your account

Preferences

App updates

Terms Of Use

⬅ Your account

Add payment method

Always ask for your password when buying an app
Yes

Your PCs

When you install an app on a PC from the Windows Store, the name of that PC will appear here. You can install the apps you get from the Store on 15 PCs.

SIMON8SLATERP

Remove

SIMMAYW8CP

Remove

zoostorm

Remove

Changing Settings in Apps

Most applications have settings or preferences for customizing the app to your needs. These could be user account names, email addresses, color schemes, or virtually anything else useful to the app. Windows 8 introduces a standard way to access those settings for apps, from the Settings charm.

Windows 8 helps you to keep control of the information and features to which apps on your tablet have access, so you can stop apps from using your webcam or decide not to use an app that requires network access. These settings are visible and, in some cases, controllable through Permissions. To change app settings, you need to be in the app.

Open Settings

1. Tap the Settings charm and then tap the Settings menu item just below the name of the app.

2. Change any settings for the app; they will be unique to each app.

3. To return to the Settings menu, tap the arrow.

4. To stop changing settings and return to using the app, tap the app.

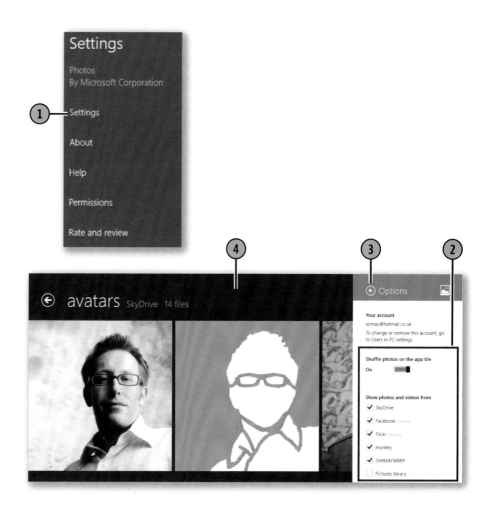

Set Permissions

1 Tap the Settings charm and then tap Permissions.

2 For devices such as webcams and GPS, you can choose to enable and disable the app's use of the device.

3 To go back to the Settings menu, tap the Back arrow.

Settings

Photos
By Microsoft Corporation

Settings

About

Help

1 —Permissions

Rate and review

3

⊙ Permissions

Camera
By Microsoft Corporation
Version 6.2.8376.0

Privacy
Allow this app to access your:

Webcam and microphone
On

2

This app has permission to use: —— Tap here to view a list of
Your pictures library   everything the app can
                                                   access, including devices,
                                                   information, networks,
                                                   social networks, cloud
                                                   connections, and more.

Tip ✓

You will also find that some apps include Options as well as settings. These will be accessible from the app menus within the app; they are normally focused on what you want the app to do, rather than how you want the app to behave.

Removing Apps

With all the apps that you can install on your tablet, sooner or later you'll want to remove one or two. Thankfully, the process is simple, and you can remove apps cleanly in moments.

Uninstall an App

(1) Open the Start screen and identify the item you want to remove. Tap and hold the tile and pull it down a little.

(2) From the pop-up menu that appears at the bottom of the screen, tap Uninstall.

(3) A confirmation box will appear. Tap Uninstall to remove the app, or tap outside the pop-up to cancel.

Tip

You can also Unpin apps on the Start screen. However, the app will still be available from All Apps on the app bar or through search.

This app and its related info will be removed from this PC.

Camera

Uninstall

(3)

Rating and Reviewing Apps

The Store strongly encourages peer review of apps, so when you're choosing an app, you should take a look to see what others think of it. Of course, it's also useful if you can express your opinion about an app, which you can. If you come across reviews that you think are helpful, you can highlight them to make it easier for others to find, or you might find a review that is unhelpful and vote it down. Finally, you might come across reviews that are offensive; you can report these to Microsoft for review.

Write a Review

1. From the Settings charm within the app you want to review, select Rate and review.

2. Provide a star rating by tapping the maximum number of stars you think the app deserves.

3. Enter a title for your review.

4. Enter the details of your review.

5. Tap Submit to have your review added to the app. (It might not appear right away.)

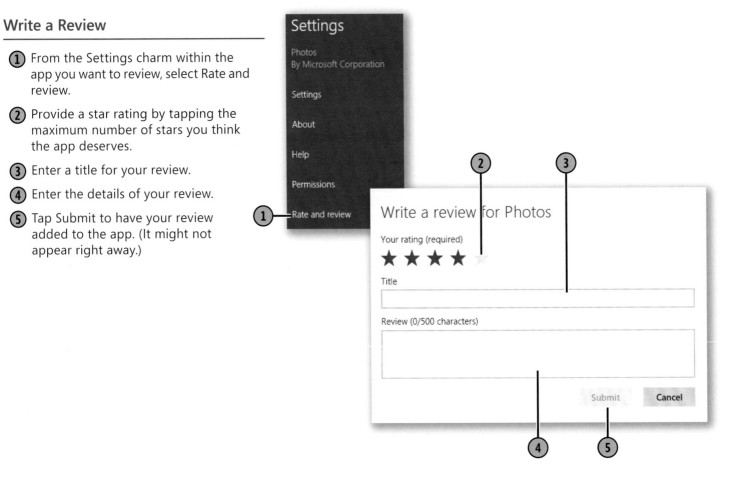

Report Someone Else's Review

① When viewing an app in the store, select the Reviews pivot.

② Tap the Report This Review link if you feel the review is unsavoury in some way. The review will be reported, and the link is replaced with a thank-you note.

Mark Other Reviews as Useful or Not

③ If you feel a review was especially useful toward your decision to try or buy an app, tap the Yes link next to Was This Review Helpful?

④ If you feel a review was completely irrelevant toward your decision to try or buy an app, tap the No link next to Was This Review Helpful?

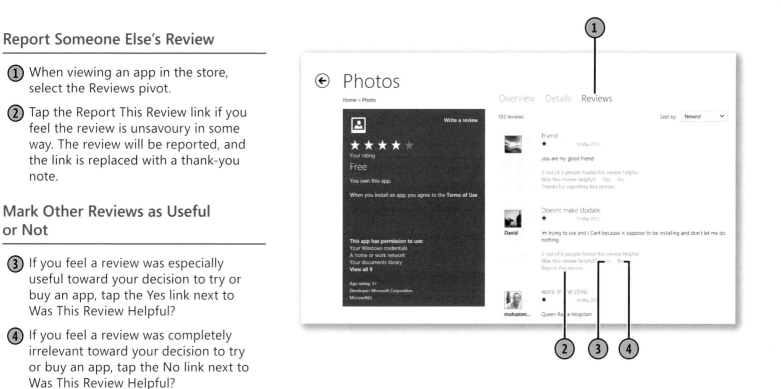

Having Two Apps On-Screen Simultaneously

Using a function called snapping, two or more apps can be on-screen at the same time. Using this feature, you can compare information between two apps. For example, you could look at the webpage of a restaurant and also look at its location on a map to see how to get there.

Use Snap to View Two Apps

① With an app open, drag a finger from the top of a screen. The app will pull away, and a dividing bar will appear one-third of the way down the screen. Drop the app into either section of the divided screen.

② Drag from the left side of the screen to bring up a previous app and drop this into the unused area.

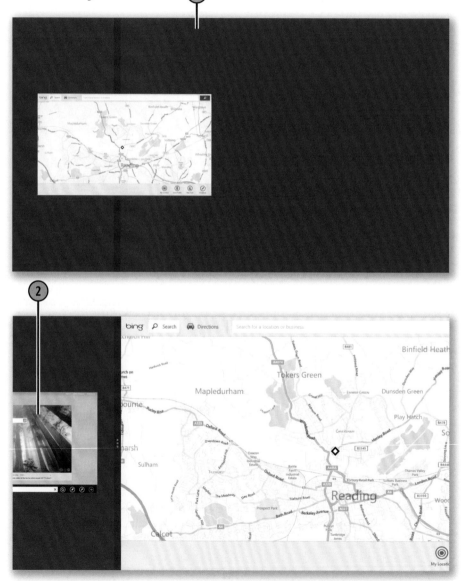

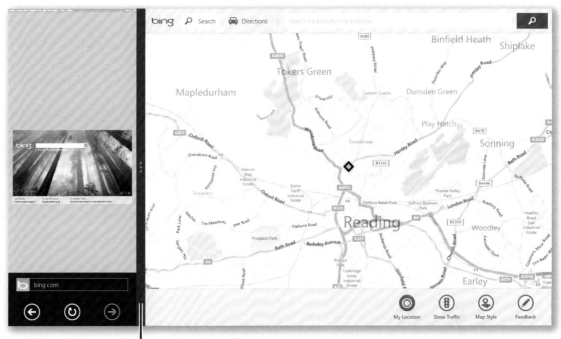

The divider can be moved to the other
side of the screen to make either snapped
app more prominent.

Tip

Many apps are designed to work brilliantly when snapped—for
example, the Mail app shows your email as it comes in, even
while you're working on something else.

Installing Desktop Apps

It is still possible to run apps designed to run on previous versions of Windows on your Windows 8 tablet. Apps designed for previous versions of Windows will run on the desktop, and nothing has changed in the way you acquire or install them. You can install any app on the desktop without the need to go through the Store, but you will need access to the installation files, which can be downloaded from the Internet or copied from a CD, DVD, USB device, or hard disk.

Install a Desktop App

1. On the desktop, use File Explorer to identify the installation file and then double-tap it to run the install.

2. You might be prompted by User Account Control to give the app permission to install. If you trust the source, tap Yes.

3. Most apps install with a wizard. Follow the wizard to complete the installation.

Tip ✓

Some desktop apps are available through the store. When you tap a desktop app in the store, it will direct you to the software developer's website, and you can download from there.

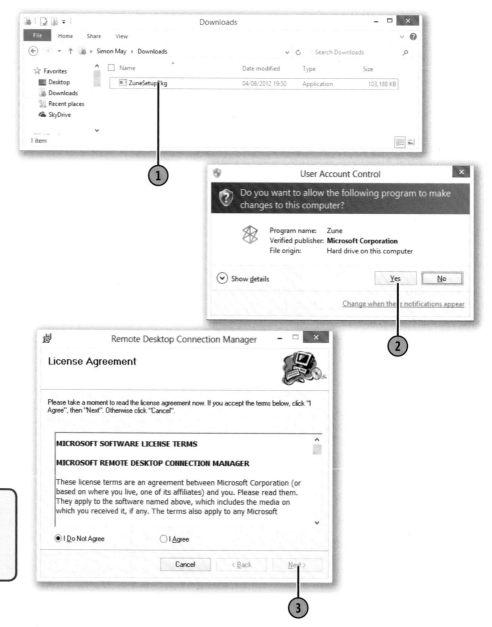

Uninstalling Desktop Apps

Unlike apps installed from the store, desktop apps cannot be uninstalled so easily. However, they can still be removed without too much effort. Control Panel is the place to control desktop apps.

Uninstall a Desktop App

It is still possible to run apps designed to run on previous versions of Windows on your Windows 8 tablet. Apps designed for previous versions of Windows will run on the desktop, and nothing has changed in the way you acquire or install them. You can install any app on the desktop without the need to go through the Store, but you will need access to the installation files, which can be downloaded from the Internet or copied from a CD, DVD, USB device, or hard disk.

① From the Control Panel, select Programs And Features.

② Identify the app to remove from the list and tap to select it.

③ Tap the Uninstall button to start the removal of the app by using the app's own installation program. Uninstallers vary from this point, but simply following the wizard instructions should be all that's required.

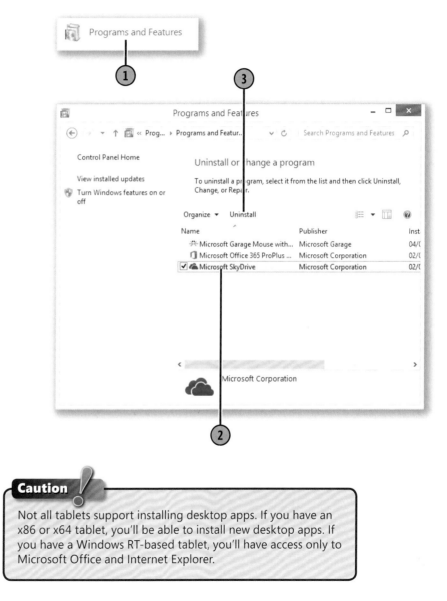

Caution

Not all tablets support installing desktop apps. If you have an x86 or x64 tablet, you'll be able to install new desktop apps. If you have a Windows RT-based tablet, you'll have access only to Microsoft Office and Internet Explorer.

9

Connecting with Email

Email has become almost a default communication method for people all over the world, in both their personal and social lives. Your Windows 8 tablet includes a Mail app that makes sending and reading email on your tablet very easy.

The Mail app includes additional apps for managing your calendar and your address book. The Calendar app and People apps are connected to your email account and to the Mail app so that you can easily create an appointment, select people from your address book, and email an invitation to a meeting or event. Setting up your email accounts in the Mail app automatically adds them to both the Calendar app and the People app, making your information available throughout your Windows 8 tablet.

It's also fine to have more than one email account on your tablet. In fact, it's encouraged; this way, you'll be able to easily switch between your work and personal email. When sending an email message, you can decide which account to send from, and when reading mail, you can view it in different accounts.

Identifying the Mail and Calendar Apps

The Mail and Calendar apps are both visible on the Start menu by default when you first start Windows 8. The tile for the Mail app displays a sealed envelope if it's not showing details of recently received emails. The live tile for Calendar always shows today's date, but it will also show your upcoming appointments. The lock screen displays your upcoming appointments, too, and it also tells you how many unread emails you have in your inbox.

Mail—The live tile can show the title and sender of a recently received email

Calendar—The live tile can show the next upcoming appointment

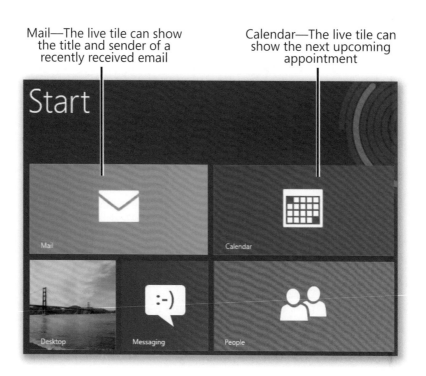

Setting Up Email

The first thing you'll need to do to get email on your tablet is to provide it with information about your email account. If you don't yet have email, you can sign up for Hotmail for free along with your Microsoft Account. You probably already have an email account somewhere though, and there is a good chance that your Windows 8 tablet can use that email account. The built-in Mail app in Windows 8 supports Hotmail, Google Mail, Microsoft Exchange (for corporate email), and Yahoo! Mail to name just a few.

Tip ✓

If you don't yet have an email account, you can sign up for a new account at *http://outlook.com*. Here you can create a new web-based email account that uses a web interface very similar to the Mail app in Windows 8—but with many more features. For example, Outlook.com has advanced rules and filters for fighting "grey mail" (also known as newsletters) that can fill up your inbox. Setting up this functionality is simple and requires just a few clicks. Outlook.com is fully compatible with Mail in Windows 8. When setting up your email, just select the option to add an Outlook account once you've signed up for the service.

Add a Hotmail, Exchange, or Google Mail Account

1. Tap the Mail tile on the Windows 8 Start screen to open the Mail app.

2. Swipe in from the right, and tap the Settings charm.

3. Tap the Accounts link in Mail.

4. Tap Add An Account.

5. Tap the type of account to add.

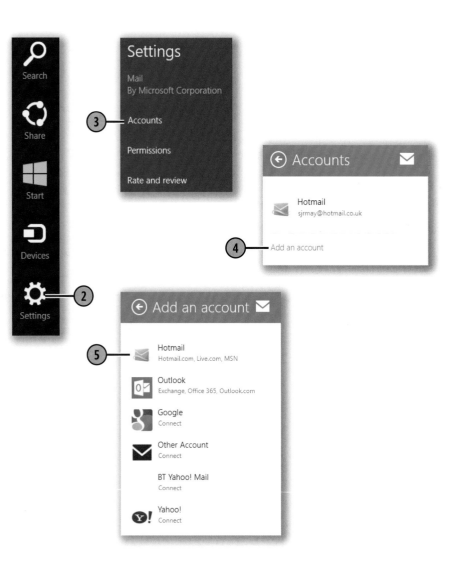

⑥ Enter your email address.

⑦ Enter your password.

⑧ Tap Connect.

Windows attempts to sort out the details.

⑨ The email account will be added into the Mail app and appears on the left side, along with a count of unread mail for the inbox you've just added.

Add your Hotmail account

Enter the information below to connect to your Hotmail account.

Email address

⑥ ─────────

Password

⑦ ─────────

Connect Cancel

⑧

Hotmail   2 ─⑨

Microsoft

Tip

Although the Mail app makes it easy to do most things from your tablet, you might also need to use a web browser to do more complex tasks. For example, the Mail app doesn't allow you to create new rules to automatically process your email. Hotmail will sweep your newsletters into a "newsletters" folder for you, but control of these rules are not available from the Mail app, only from the Hotmail website.

Reading Email

Reading email with the Mail app is as simple as opening the app. However, depending on how you have your Mail app and tablet configured, it might not always be instantly up to date. Although the default is to download mail when it's received, you might have set mail to update less frequently. In this case, you need to perform a *sync*. Also, sometimes you might have multiple email accounts set up (for example, one for work, one for home), so you might need the ability to switch between them.

Read Email

1. Open the Mail app and tap an email to read it.

2. Tap to reply to an email.

3. Tap to delete an email after reading it.

4. Tap to open a different account.

5. Tap to update your email (check for any new messages).

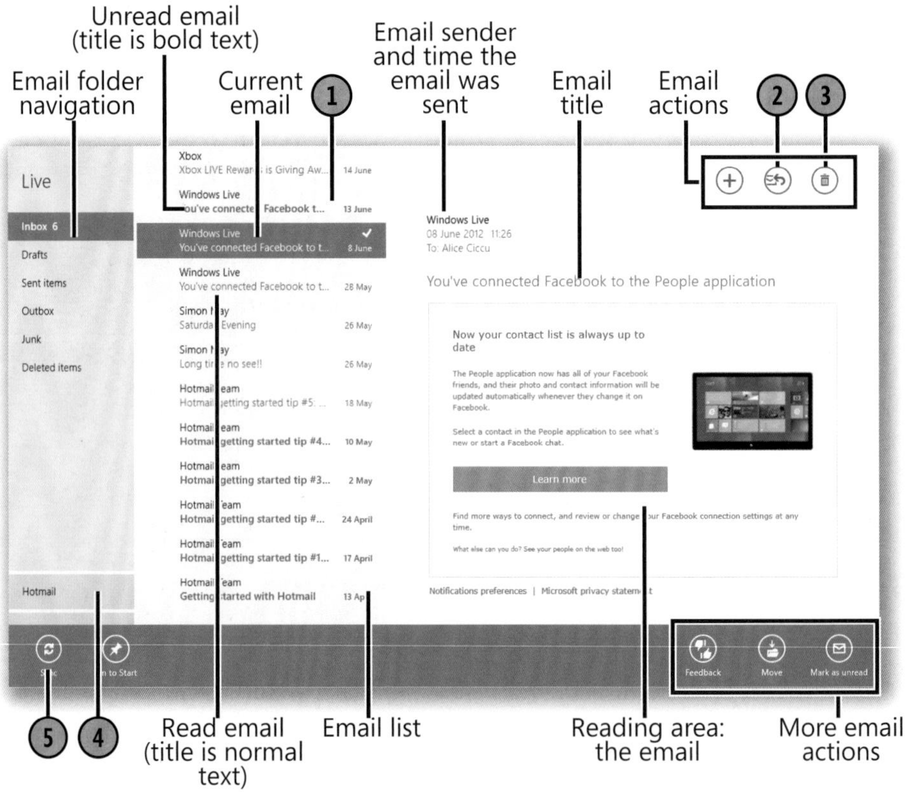

Unread email
(title is bold text)

Email folder navigation

Current email

Email sender and time the email was sent

Email title

Email actions

Live

Inbox 6

Drafts

Sent items

Outbox

Junk

Deleted items

Xbox
Xbox LIVE Reward is Giving Aw... 14 June

Windows Live
You've connected Facebook t... 13 June

Windows Live
You've connected Facebook to t... 8 June

Windows Live
You've connected Facebook to t... 28 May

Simon May
Saturday Evening 26 May

Simon May
Long time no see!! 26 May

Hotmail Team
Hotmail getting started tip #5... 18 May

Hotmail Team
Hotmail getting started tip #4... 10 May

Hotmail Team
Hotmail getting started tip #3... 2 May

Hotmail Team
Hotmail getting started tip #... 24 April

Hotmail Team
Hotmail getting started tip #1... 17 April

Hotmail Team
Getting started with Hotmail 13 Ap

Hotmail

Windows Live
08 June 2012 11:26
To: Alice Ciccu

You've connected Facebook to the People application

Now your contact list is always up to date

The People application now has all of your Facebook friends, and their photo and contact information will be updated automatically whenever they change it on Facebook.

Select a contact in the People application to see what's new or start a Facebook chat.

Learn more

Find more ways to connect, and review or change your Facebook connection settings at any time.

What else can you do? See your people on the web too!

Notifications preferences | Microsoft privacy statement

Feedback Move Mark as unread

Read email
(title is normal text)

Email list

Reading area: the email

More email actions

Making Accounts and Folders Accessible from the Start Screen

The Mail app tile on the Start screen shows an aggregated view of all of your mail. If you don't like that, you can pin accounts and folders to your Start screen for a more detailed view.

Pin to Start Screen

① Tap the account for which you want to create a tile.

② Tap the folder within the account to which you want the tile to take you.

③ Swipe upward from the bottom of the screen to show the App Bar.

④ Tap Pin To Start.

⑤ Confirm that the tile name is OK and then tap Pin To Start.

Tip ✓

This is a great way to make a folder easy to access or, if you receive your work email on your tablet, to separate your work and home email accounts.

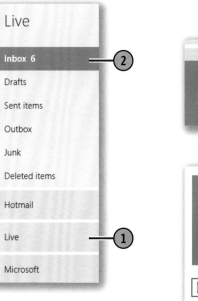

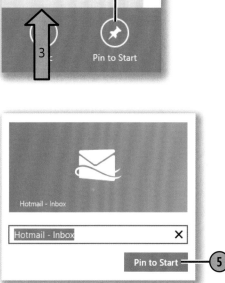

Writing Email

Writing emails to friends and family is a great way to keep in touch, and it's almost essential in any workplace today. The Mail app is designed with this in mind, making it easy to send a simple email.

Write Email

1. Tap the plus sign to create a new email.

2. Tap Add A Subject to replace the text with your own subject line for the email, making it descriptive of the content.

3. Tap the blank area to enter the body text of the email.

4. Tap in the To text box to enter an email address or a friend's name; Mail will checks names against your address book automatically.

5. Tap in the Cc text box to enter additional recipients.

6. Optionally, tap your account name to change to a different account if you've set up more than one account.

7. Tap the Send icon to send the mail, or if you've decided against it, tap the Close icon to save it as a draft or delete it altogether.

8. Tap Attachments to add files to send along with the email.

9. Tap More Details to blind copy the email to someone or to change its priority level.

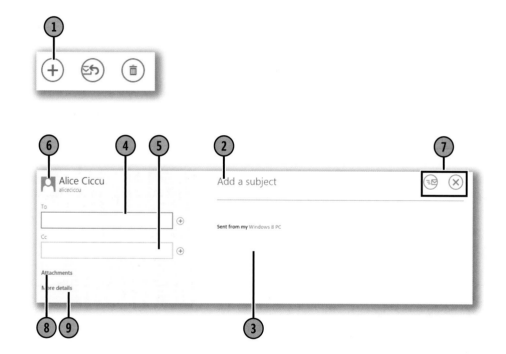

Format Email Text

① Highlight some text that you've typed in your email.

② Tap Font to change the font style of the lettering.

③ Tap Font Color to change the color of the text.

④ Tap Bold to make the text stand out.

⑤ Tap Italic to apply italic-style lettering.

⑥ Tap Underline to underline words.

⑦ Tap More to show additional options to format the text as a Bulleted or Numbered list.

⑧ Tap Copy/Paste to copy the text to the clipboard or paste text from the clipboard.

⑨ Tap Attachments to add an attachment to the email

⑩ Tap Save Draft to save the email for later without sending it

Organizing Email

With so much email coming and going, you will likely find that you need to keep some of it. Most email services, such as Hotmail, Google Mail, and Microsoft Exchange, provide a way for you to keep mail in folders, and the Mail apps lets you manage those folders. Sometimes you'll also read an email and want to mark it as unread so that you can remember to read it again later.

Move Mail into a Folder

1. Select the email you'd like to file to a folder.

2. Swipe upward from the bottom of the screen to show the App Bar.

3. Tap the Move icon.

4. In the highlighted Folders list, tap the folder into which to place the email.

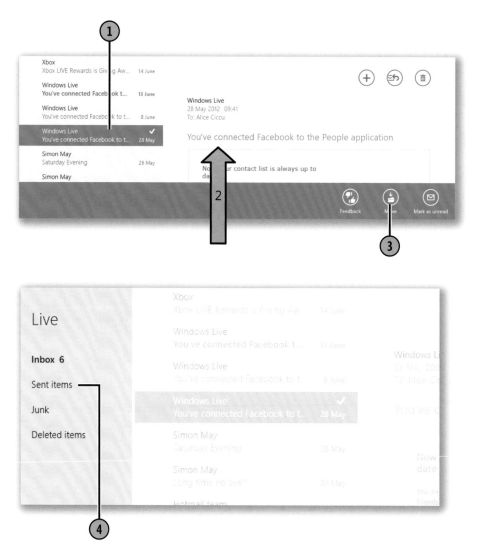

Mark Unread

① With an email selected, swipe upward from the bottom of the screen to show the App Bar.

② Tap Mark As Unread. (If the email is already unread, this displays as Mark Read and marks the email as read.)

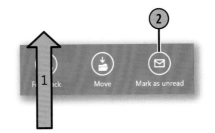

Showing Email Notifications

Windows 8 can check your email accounts regularly and let you know whether you've received any mail without you having to go into the Mail app. It does this by showing you notifications on the lock screen so that you will know that you've got mail as soon as you pick your tablet up, and by updating the live mail tile.

Check for Email in the Background

1 In the Mail app, tap the Settings charm and then tap Permissions.

2 Toggle the Lock Screen setting to On.

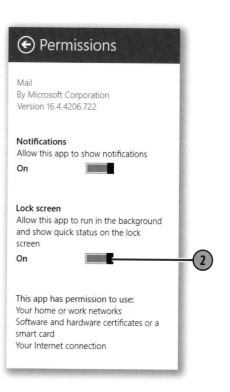

Allow Lock Screen Notifications

(1) In the Settings panel, tap Change PC Settings.

(2) Tap Personalize.

(3) Scroll down to Lock Screen Apps, and ensure that the Mail app icon is set to appear on the lock screen. If not, tap a plus sign (+) and select the Mail app or inbox from the choice that appears.

Changing Mail Settings

The Mail accounts that you set up on your tablet are preconfigured with some default settings, such as update frequency, how much history to download, and what name to use for the account. You can change these for each account; thus if your email is updating too often or if you don't like the name Windows gives your account, you can change the respective settings. You'll need to be in the Mail app to make any changes.

Access Account Settings

① In the Mail app, tap the Settings charm.

② Tap Accounts.

③ Tap the account for which you want to change the settings.

Change Account Name

1 Tap the current name of the account and enter a new name for it.

Change Sync Settings

2 Tap the Download New Content drop-down list and choose to download every 15, 30, or 60 minutes, or select Manual to require that you tap the Sync button on the App Bar to download new mails.

3 Tap the Download New Content drop-down list to select to have the last 3 or 7 days, 2 weeks, 1 month, or all of your mail history kept on your tablet.

4 Toggle the Automatically Download External Images control to On to have the mail app download images, even if they're just linked to an email. Setting this to No can provide higher security, but you won't get images in emails unless you specifically download them on a per-email basis.

Enable or Disable Notifications

5 Toggle Show Notifications For This Account to On to have a notification appear each time you receive a new email; this is off by default.

Tip

You can also remove an account from here by scrolling down and tapping the Remove button.

Tip

Other accounts have more settings. For example, a corporate Exchange email account might require a different user name for your email address, so there are extra user name boxes with that type of account.

Printing Emails

There might be times when you want to print out an email, perhaps for safekeeping, to show to someone, or maybe you need to print some concert tickets. Printing emails is the same as printing in any other app.

Print an Email

① Tap the email you want to print.

② Tap the Devices charm.

③ Tap the name of the printer you want to use.

④ Tap to select the page orientation.

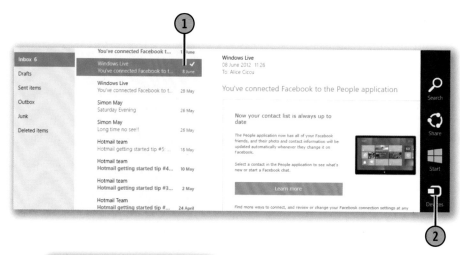

Tap to select the paper size.

 Tap Print to send the email to your printer.

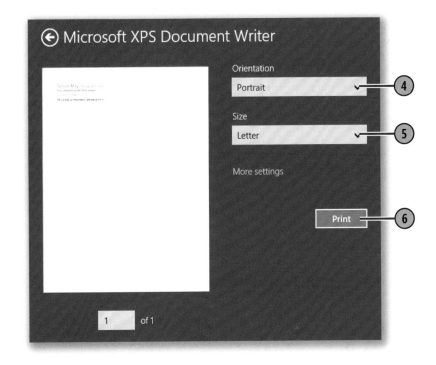

Using Calendar to View Your Schedule

The Calendar app connects to the calendar that is often associ- ated with your email account. Microsoft Exchange and Hotmail account, as well as Google Mail account, have this feature built in; your ISP, POP3, or IMAP4 email accounts might not.

View Your Schedule

1. On the Start screen, tap Calendar.
2. Swipe upward to show the App Bar.
3. Tap to show a single day.
4. Tap to show a week.
5. Tap to show a month.
6. Tap to go to today in the calendar.
7. Tap, hold, and drag your finger to the right to go to previous dates.
8. Tap, hold, and drag your finger to the left to go to future dates.

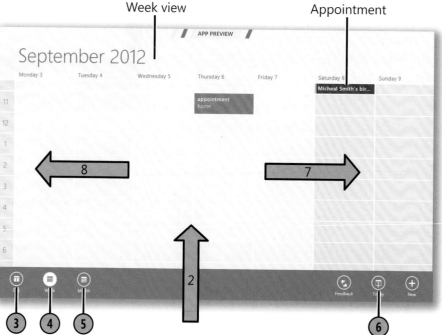

Add an Appointment

① Either tap an empty space in your calendar or show the App Bar and tap New.

② Enter a title for the calendar entry.

③ Enter any special details of the appointment.

④ Enter details about the appointment, such as the time and date of the appointment. There are many options; you can scroll down to reveal them all. You can set the following: where; when; start time; duration; recurrence details; reminder times; whether you'll be busy or free during the appointment; which calendar to use (if you have more than one); who to invite (each person you invite will receive an email invitation). You can also flag the event as Private so that only you can see it if you have shared calendars.

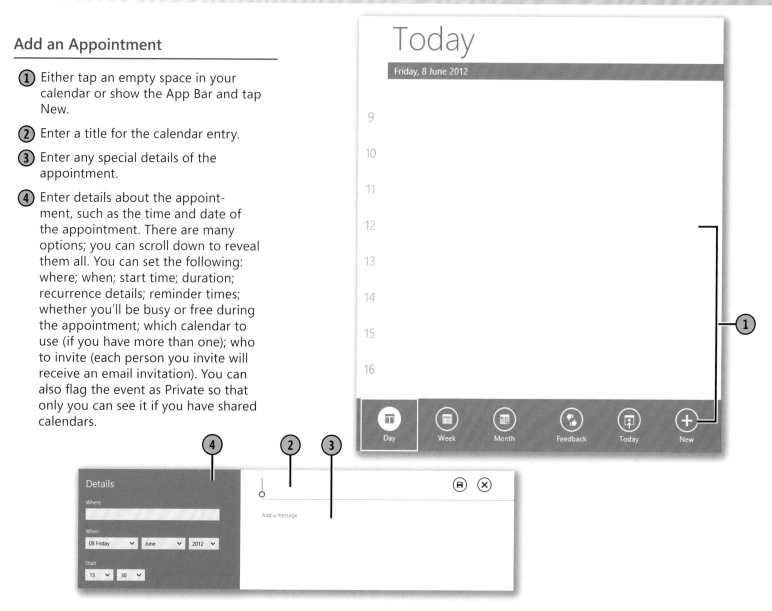

10

Connecting to Social Networks

Today, many of us are hyper-connected, using social networks and email to keep in touch. With email, we typically store the contact details of everyone we come across in our address books. Our social network connections typically link us to almost every individual we know, from our schooldays through our working adult lives, from friends through family through coworkers. It can be a challenge keeping all that information together, and this is where the People app can help make sense of it all.

The People app on your Windows 8 tablet connects all your email address books and social networks together so that your contacts are always easily accessible. Those contacts are available to you in other apps, such as Mail and Messaging, so you don't have to keep storing duplicate account details. Social networks are places where people share all types of information from status updates to conversations to photos of their kids or what they did on Friday night. The People app is again the hub for this information on your tablet. When you are connected to your Facebook account, photos will be available in the Photos app or in any app that can use photos, so you don't have to keep adding your Facebook details over and over.

Introducing People

The People app is the starting point for connecting your social networks to Windows. When networks are connected, you can access the information they store, such as pictures or names and addresses, in other apps such as Mail or Photos. The People app shows updates from your connected social networks as well as showing when those people are actually connected to and available on those social networks through chat.

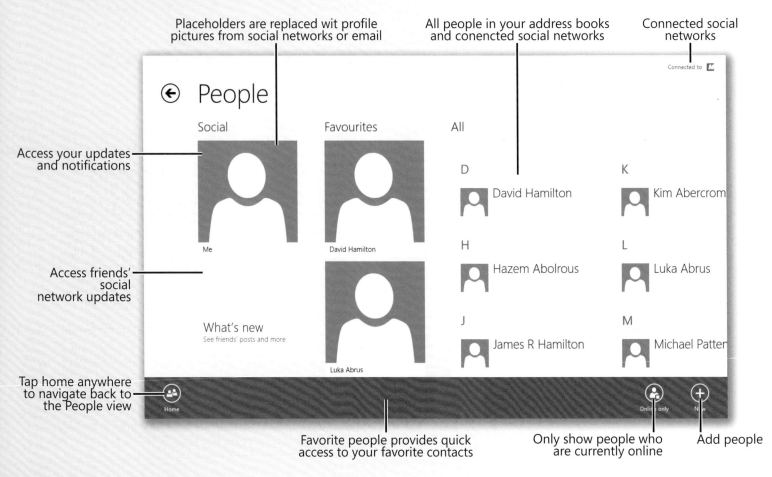

Placeholders are replaced wit profile pictures from social networks or email

All people in your address books and conencted social networks

Connected social networks

Access your updates and notifications

Access friends' social network updates

Tap home anywhere to navigate back to the People view

Favorite people provides quick access to your favorite contacts

Only show people who are currently online

Add people

Name of updater can be tapped for more updates from this person

Status update can be tapped for more detail

Photo shared on social network

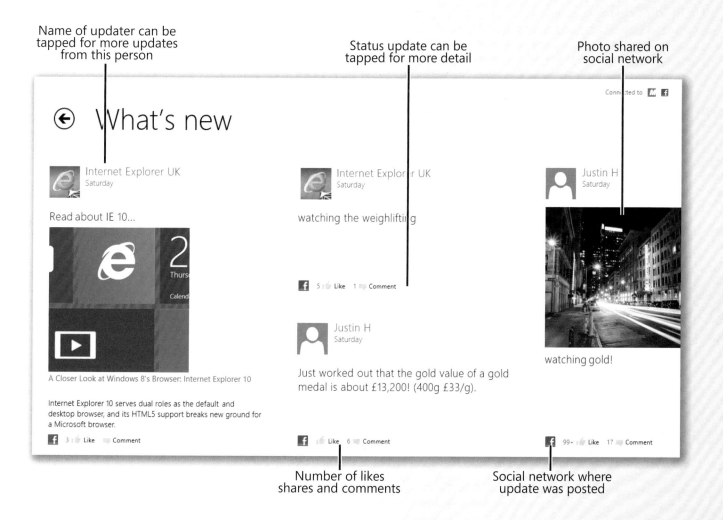

Number of likes shares and comments

Social network where update was posted

Linking Social Networks

The first step in using the Windows 8 social features on your tablet is connecting your social networks to the People app. Most social networks connect in the same way; the following steps show Facebook, but other networks work similarly. When connected, you can view status updates and chat with people with whom are friends on those networks.

Connect Facebook

1. Open the Start screen and tap the People tile.

2. Within the People app, tap the Settings charm.

3. Tap Accounts in the People settings list.

4. Tap Add An Account.

5. Tap the social network to add an account, in this example, it's Facebook.

People app tile on the Start screen-this tile will show photos of you and your friends once connected to your social networks.

Accounts already connected

6. Tap the Connect button to link to the social network.

7. If you aren't signed up to Facebook, tap the signup link.

8. Enter your Facebook user name.

9. Enter your Facebook password.

10. Tap Log In.

11. Tap Done to complete the process.

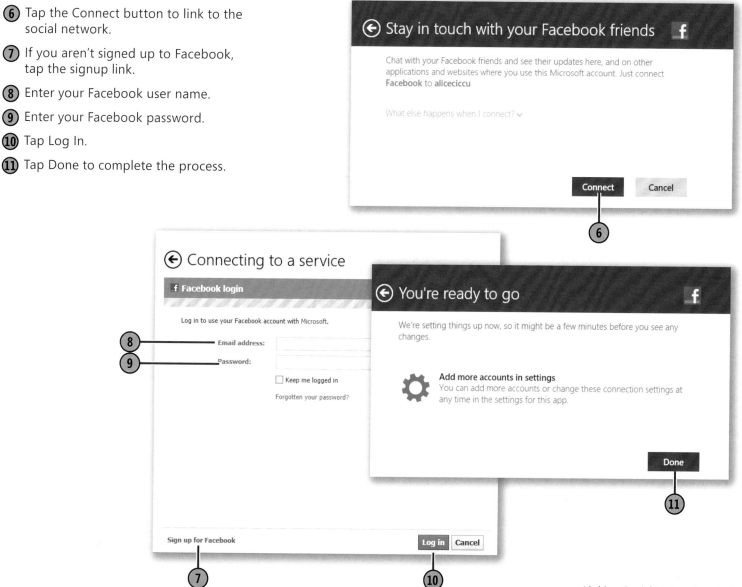

Linking Email Accounts

Connecting email accounts is a slightly different process from connecting social networks. When you've connected an email account, such as a Microsoft Hotmail, Google Mail, or Microsoft Exchange (for corporate email) account, any contact information you have stored in those email accounts will be brought into the People app.

Connect Hotmail

① Within the People app, tap the Settings charm.

② Tap Accounts in the People settings list.

③ Tap Add An Account.

④ Tap the email account you want to use, in this example, it's Hotmail.

⑤ Enter your Hotmail email address.

⑥ Enter your email password.

⑦ Tap Connect to connect to the account.

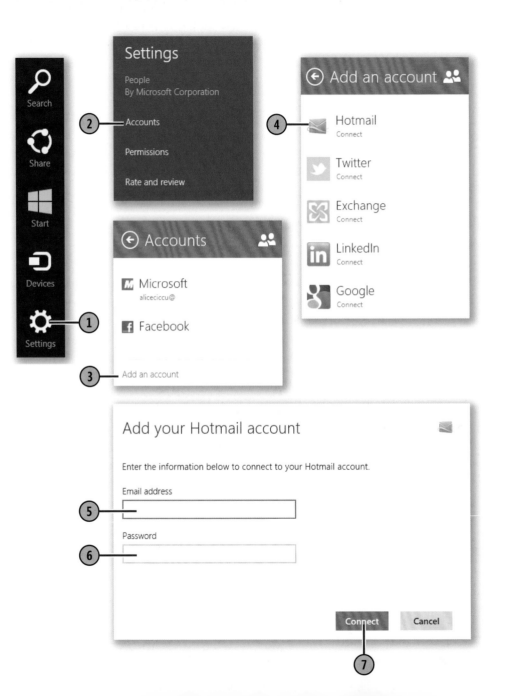

Removing Account Links

Sometimes you might want to stop the People app from conversing with your social network or email accounts. For example, you might decide to withdraw from a social network or to move your email to another provider. Account Links are managed through a web service, rather than just your tablet so that your services are connected, whatever device you use.

Remove Social Networks

1 Open Internet Explorer and navigate to *http://profile.live.com* and sign into the website if prompted.

2 Tap the Manage link.

3 Tap Edit Connection under the connection you want to remove.

4 Tap Remove This Connection Completely.

Changing Social Network Permissions

Social networks make it easy to share information with our friends, family, and coworkers, but sometimes we can have a tendency to overshare. Windows helps you manage this by deciding what your devices can share with the world. Again, this is managed from the web so that it works automatically with all your devices.

Manage Social Network Permissions

1. Open Internet Explorer and navigate to *http://profile.live.com* and sign into the website if prompted.

2. Tap the Manage link.

(3) Tap the Edit Connection link under the connection you want to manage.

(4) Select or clear the options as you prefer. These are different for each social network, but take note of any description in which the word *share* is used because this indicates that you will push information to this social network. Usually, *publish* implies you'll need to take additional action, such as tapping a Share With Facebook button.

(5) Tap Save to confirm the changes.

Finding People

With all this information about your friends in the People app, you might actually want to do something with that information.

View a Person's Details

(1) Tap a contact in the People view.

(2) Tap Map Address to open a Bing map of the contact's address in Internet Explorer.

(3) Tap Send Message to send the person an instant message using the service noted. Optionally, tap the down arrow to the right to change to a different service.

(4) Tap Send Email to send the person an email.

(5) Tap the View Profile item to view the person's profile on the selected social network. Optionally, tap the down arrow to the right to change to a profile on a different network where you know that person.

(6) Tap the back arrow to return to the All People view.

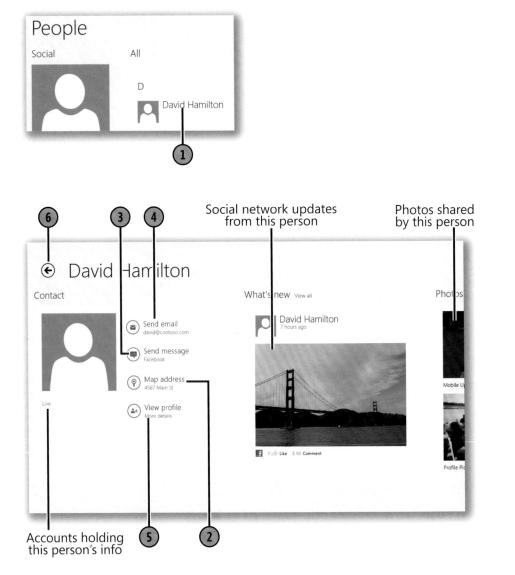

Search for People

① Within the People app, tap the Search charm.

② Type the beginning of a name into the People search box.

③ Results will be shown as they're found. Tap an individual to view more details.

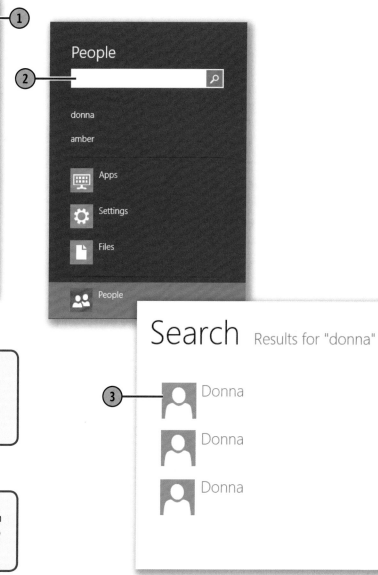

Tip

You don't need to be in the People app to search for people. Just as with any app, you can search within it from outside the app. Just tap the Search charm, and select People from the list of apps to search.

Tip

To quickly find people, use the pinch gesture to zoom out from the People view to see an alphabetical list in which you can tap a letter to go to friends whose names start with that letter.

Viewing Friends' Updates

We all like to know what our friends are up to, to share news with each other, and to plan events. The People app makes these things simple with the What's New view, which aggregates status updates from your friends' social networks. The actions you can take on an update depend on which social network generated the update.

View Updates

① Tap What's New to view your friends' updates.

② Scroll left and right to read more updates by tapping, holding, and dragging.

③ Tap an update to view more information about it.

④ Scroll comments up and down by tapping, holding, and dragging.

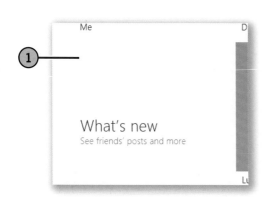

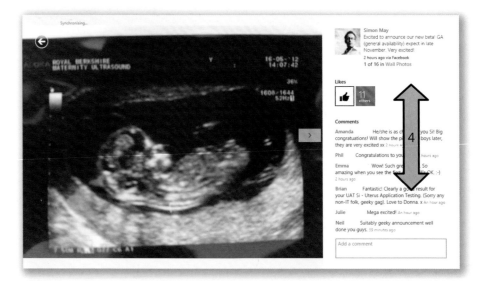

Comment on Updates

① When viewing an update, you can comment on it by tapping into the Add A Comment box and typing your comment. A Comment button appears; tap this to add your comment. If you're replying on Twitter, the button will say "Reply".

② Often on social networks, people "like" or "favorite" a post. Tap the thumbs-up icon or star icon to "like" or "favorite" an update.

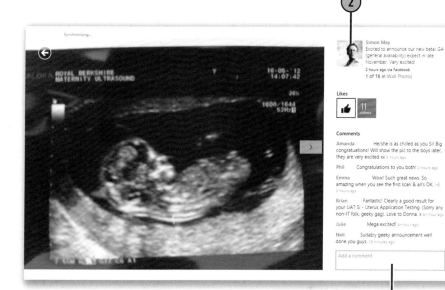

Caution

Be careful about the comments you make. Be as respectful online about a person, their thoughts, and opinions as you would be in person. Remember, all their friends and all your friends will see the comment. If you wouldn't make a comment to someone, face to face, in a room full of people, think twice about saying it online!

11

Enjoying Videos and Music

Your tablet is an entertainment hub that's just waiting for you to put some life into it with your music and videos. The music and video apps can play music stored on your tablet, on another computer in your homegroup, or downloaded from the Xbox Music and Video stores.

You can watch any movies or listen to any music that you already own, and the Music and Video apps make it very easy to acquire more. The first thing required is an Xbox LIVE account linked to your Microsoft Account to control how you'll pay for your purchases. When this is set up, getting new music or watching the latest movie releases is just a matter of tapping the Buy button and then tapping Play.

You don't have to own an Xbox to use the Xbox services. However, if you do own an Xbox, your music and video is available on more than just your tablet; you can tap the Play button on Xbox button wherever you see it to send the video or music to your TV via your Xbox.

The music and video apps play back in full screen, with cover art animation taking the place of a video for music playback. Controls are big and easy to see and use, and the App Bar helps by providing more careful controls and more options if you need them.

Setting Up Music and Video Accounts

You are able to pay for the movies and music that you download through your Microsoft Account. The first time you start the Video or Music apps, you're asked to confirm some Xbox settings or to set them up if you're new to Xbox.

Start Video or Music for the First Time

1. If you already have an Xbox Live account, tap the link to use that account. Provide the user name and password, and you're done.

2. Enter your first name.

3. Clear the Xbox Partner Marketing check box or leave it selected to allow Microsoft to send you useful info.

4. Select the Partner Marketing check box to allow Microsoft's partners (such as games makers) to send you information.

5. Read the usage terms.

6. Tap the I Accept button to create your account. You're presented with a Welcome screen.

See Also

See page 287 for details about how to change your account settings.

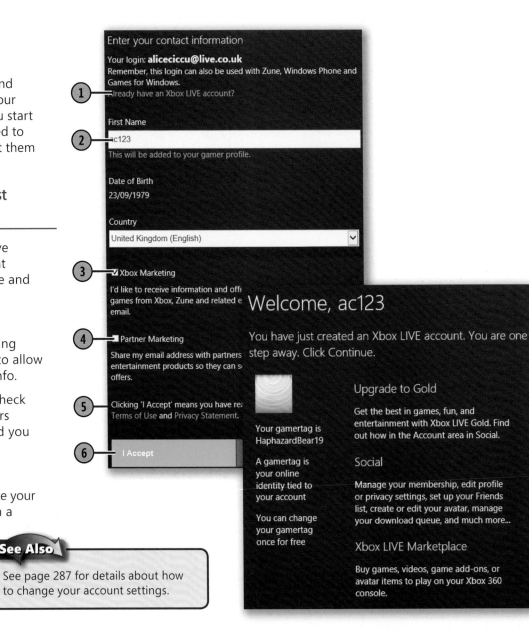

Enter your contact information

Your login: **aliceciccu@live.co.uk**
Remember, this login can also be used with Zune, Windows Phone and Games for Windows.
Already have an Xbox LIVE account?

First Name
ac123
This will be added to your gamer profile.

Date of Birth
23/09/1979

Country
United Kingdom (English)

☑ Xbox Marketing
I'd like to receive information and off games from Xbox, Zune and related e email.

☐ Partner Marketing
Share my email address with partners entertainment products so they can s offers.

Clicking 'I Accept' means you have re Terms of Use and Privacy Statement.

I Accept

Welcome, ac123

You have just created an Xbox LIVE account. You are one step away. Click Continue.

Your gamertag is HaphazardBear19

A gamertag is your online identity tied to your account

You can change your gamertag once for free

Upgrade to Gold

Get the best in games, fun, and entertainment with Xbox LIVE Gold. Find out how in the Account area in Social.

Social

Manage your membership, edit profile or privacy settings, set up your Friends list, create or edit your avatar, manage your download queue, and much more...

Xbox LIVE Marketplace

Buy games, videos, game add-ons, or avatar items to play on your Xbox 360 console.

Introducing Music with Xbox Music

One of the joys of listening to music is discovering songs that you've not yet heard. Xbox music makes this easy by integrating a music store into the app, placing new music front and center. To start the Music app, on the Start screen, tap the Music tile.

Browse Music Categories

(1) Tap and hold to pan left and right to view music categories.

(2) Optionally, tap a tile in a category to view details about that artist or album.

(3) Tap the category title to browse deeper.

(4) Tap Show Featured or Show Albums to change the filter.

(5) Tap a genre to view albums and artists in that genre.

(6) Tap an album, track, or artist to view information.

Currently playing track

Music recommendation

Music categories

Progress through current track

Tap current track to view more info

Getting New Music

After you've found some music that you'd like to acquire, it's time to start adding that music to your collection. There are two options for this. The first is to purchase the music, which makes it yours to own forever. The second option allows you to keep and play the music as long as you have a Music Pass, which, for a monthly subscription fee, allows you to download unlimited music. You can sign up for this second option by tapping the Settings charm and then tapping Accounts. Not all albums are included in a Music Pass subscription.

Acquire Music

1. Select the Xbox Music Store category and then tap the album you'd like to acquire.

2. Tap Preview to try before you buy. If you have a Music Pass, this button will be labeled Play, instead.

3. If you want to purchase the album, Tap Buy Album.

4. Review the cost and then tap Confirm.

5. Tap Done to complete the process; the downloads will appear in your music app.

6. If you have a music pass and want to download the album to listen offline, tap Add To My Music.

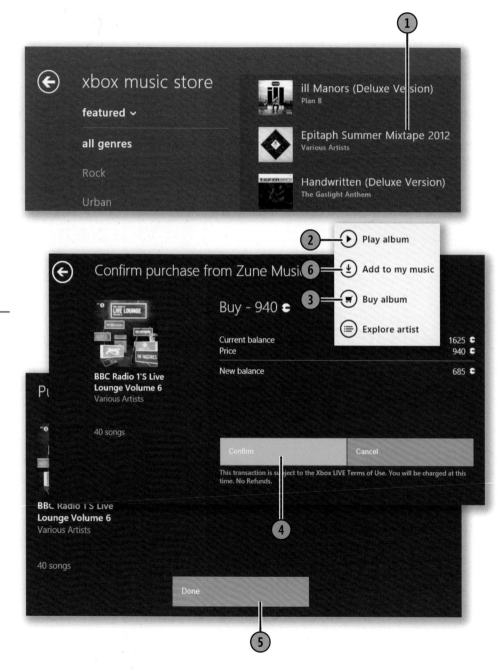

Introducing Video with Xbox Video

The Xbox Video App in Windows 8 makes it easy to watch movie releases and to download videos to your tablet. It's very similar to the Xbox Music app. You access the Xbox Video App on the Start screen.

Browse Video Categories

1. Tap and hold to pan left and right or flick in either direction.

2. Tap a movie to jump directly to it.

3. Tap a category title to view more movies in that category.

4. Tap to view movies in different groupings.

5. Tap to view information about a movie and to rent, buy, or start it playing. If you have an Xbox, you can play the movie directly to your Xbox, as well.

Buying or Renting Videos

You can take advantage of the movie market place in the Xbox Video app to either rent or buy a movie. You can start watching rentals immediately or download and watch them offline, but you can watch the movie all the way through only once. Buying a movie means you can watch it offline or stream it as often as you like.

Rent a Video

① Browse the marketplace for a movie you want to watch and then tap the movie.

② Tap Rent or Buy.

See Also

You'll need Microsoft Points (the currency of Xbox Live) to buy or rent movies using Xbox Movies. The advantage of Microsoft Points is that you don't need a credit card to watch movies. Points can be purchased when you attempt to buy or rent a movie using a credit card or you can buy them from any store that sells Microsoft Points gift cards. See page 276 for more information on adding Microsoft Points and managing your account.

(3) Tap one of the rental methods or purchasing options to select it, and tap Continue. (SD and HD indicate quality—HD is high definition.)

(4) Tap Next to continue.

(5) Tap Confirm to rent or buy the movie. If you don't have enough points you'll have the opportunity to purchase points before completing the movie rental or purchase.

Playing Music or Videos

Once you have some music or videos in your collection, which you can get from the store or from your own collection of media files, you'll want to start playing them. You can also play music or video by browsing your homegroup.

Play Music or Video from Your Collection

(1) Tap and hold or flick to pan to the right from the Music or Video app to find My Music.

(2) If the album or video you want to play is listed, tap the album and skip to step 7. If the app tells you, "It's lonely here," you need to acquire some music or videos.

(3) Tap the My Music or My Video title to browse your entire collection.

(4) In the Music app, tap to view albums, songs, or artists. In the Video app, tap to view movies or other.

(5) Tap to change how to view your selections; for example, from A to Z, by artist, or by some other grouping or category.

(6) Tap to open the track or video.

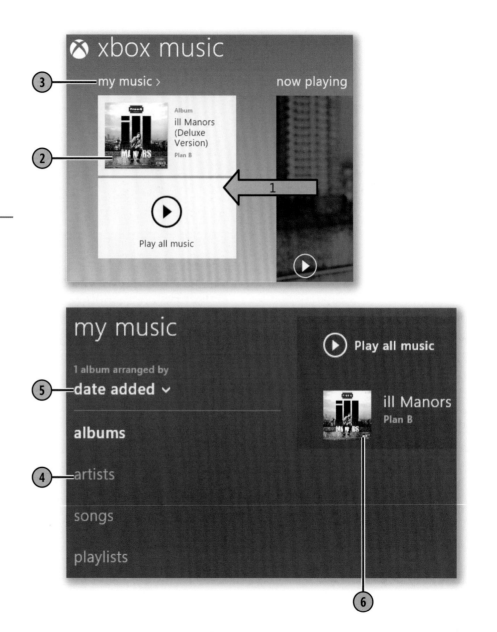

⑦ Tap Play to play the album or video.

⑧ Tap Add To Now Playing to add to the music queue if something is already playing.

⑨ Tap to find out more about the artist or about the movie.

⑩ Swipe upward from the bottom of the screen to show the App Bar for music or video control options.

Currently playing track

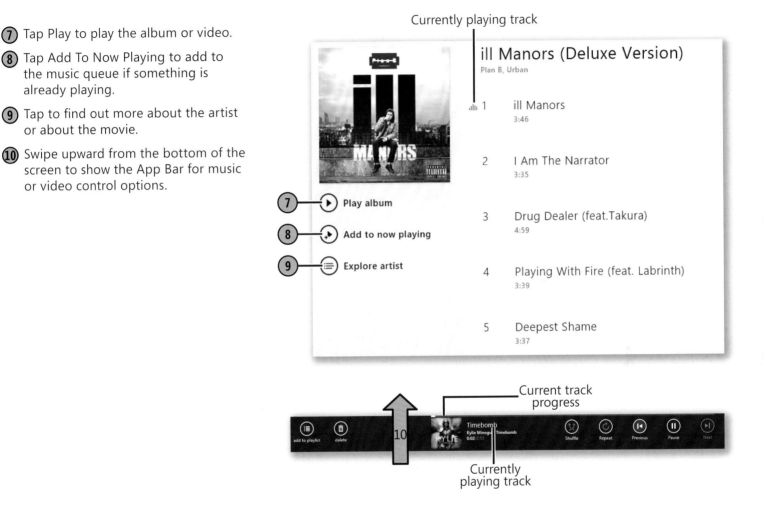

ill Manors (Deluxe Version)
Plan B, Urban

1   ill Manors
3:46

2   I Am The Narrator
3:35

3   Drug Dealer (feat.Takura)
4:59

4   Playing With Fire (feat. Labrinth)
3:39

5   Deepest Shame
3:37

⑦ ▶ Play album

⑧ ▪▶ Add to now playing

⑨ ☰ Explore artist

Current track progress

Timebomb
Kylie Minogue Timebomb
0:02/2:57

add to playlist   delete   10   Shuffle   Repeat   Previous   Pause   Next

Currently playing track

Play Music or Video from Homegroup Computers

① Swipe upward from the bottom of the screen to show the app bar in either the Music or Video app and tap Open File.

② Tap Files and then then tap Homegroup.

Files ˅   Videos

Music

Videos

Desktop

Downloads

Homegroup

Computer

Network

Camera

Photos

SkyDrive

s in this view.

Tip

This same process works for opening music or videos stored in places other than the music and video libraries on your tablet.

Tip

You can also play music or video stored directly on your SkyDrive by selecting SkyDrive on the Files menu.

③ Tap the computer or user whose files you want to access. (The computer must be on.) Then, continue to tap into folders to browse until you find the media to play.

④ Tap the video or music to play. Note that you can select multiple files by swiping down on each.

⑤ Tap Open to play the file.

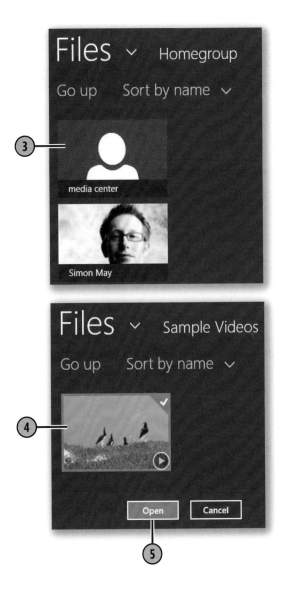

 Tip

When browsing for files, you can use "semantic zoom" to make navigation a little easier. Pinch to zoom in on the files, just as you would if you were looking for less detail in a photo, and you are shown an alphabetic pick list. Just tap a letter to go directly to files starting with that letter.

Controlling Music and Video Playback

In addition to being on the App Bar, controls are overlaid on video or music playback, making them more intuitive.

Use Full-Screen Controls

(1) Tap to Play when paused, or to Pause when video is playing.

(2) Tap to skip forward a few seconds.

(3) Tap to skip backward.

(4) Tap to exit playback and return to browsing the app.

(5) Tap, hold, and drag to a point to move forward and back in the video.

(6) The marker will move below the line as you move it. Lift your finger when you reach the point in the video from which you want to play it.

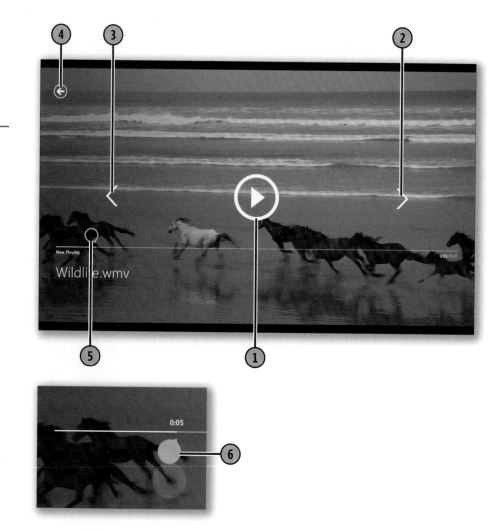

Managing Account Settings

Your Xbox account and Microsoft Account store your billing information, sharing information, and keep track of how many Microsoft Points you have. Both the Video and Music apps bring these settings together in the same way and allow you to purchase Xbox membership levels, a Zune Music Pass, and Microsoft Points.

View Account Settings

(1) With the Music or Video app open, tap the Settings charm.

(2) Tap Account.

From here, you can view more information about each part of your account by tapping the title. For example, tap Microsoft Points to add more Microsoft Points and to see your balance.

At-a-glance information about memberships, passes and points

Each section can be tapped to access more information

Getting an Xbox Music Pass, Xbox LIVE Membership, or Microsoft Points

The process for adding an Xbox Music Pass, buying an Xbox LIVE gold or silver membership, or adding points is the same for each activity. However, there are differences. For example, you select the number of points to add when buying Microsoft points, whereas you select a membership level when adding an Xbox LIVE or an Xbox Music Pass.

Make an Account Purchase

1. In the Music or Video app, display Account Settings and tap Xbox Music Pass, Xbox LIVE Membership, or Microsoft Points, depending on which you want to add.

2. Tap the membership level or number of points to add.

3. Tap Next.

4. If you've not already entered billing information for the account, you'll be asked to provide details such as your billing address and name. When done, tap Next.

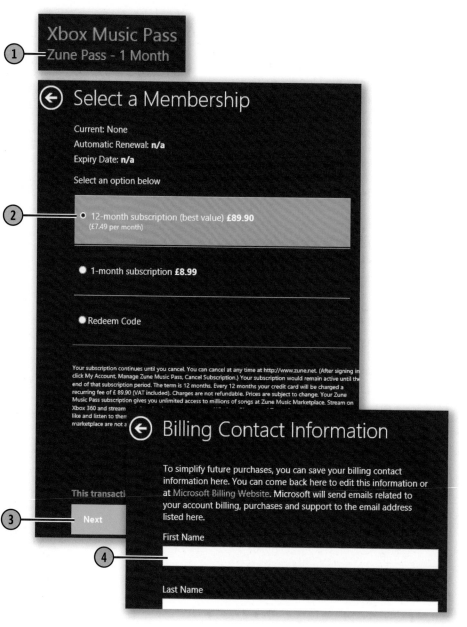

(5) If you don't have a credit card set up or if you want to add a new card, tap Add A New Credit Card.

(6) Ensuring that the correct credit card is selected and then tap Confirm Purchase.

(7) You are asked to enter the CVV number on the back of your card (or the front for American Express) to confirm the transaction.

(8) Tap Submit to make the purchase.

Caution

All purchases are final when you tap the Submit button.

Tip

All billing and account settings can also be managed online at *Xbox.com*, where you can also add Microsoft Points, including to your kids' accounts.

(⬅) Add Microsoft® Points

1000 Microsoft Points - Price: £8.50 Plus Applicable Taxes

1000 Microsoft Points will be deposited into the account associated with your Xbox Live gamertag. Your account will be charged £8.50 VAT Included. Use Microsoft Points to acquire gamer pictures, themes, and game content from Xbox Live Marketplace. For information about changing or canceling your membership and your membership refund policy, go to www.xbox.com/live/accounts.

List of payment options

Add a new Credi...

This transaction is su...
Your payment option...
Validation is required...

Confirm Purchase

(⬅) Enter the CVV of Your Credit Card

To protect your credit card information and transaction, we ask you to enter the Card Verification Value (CVV) of your credit card again as an additional security precaution. We will NOT store your CVV.

Payment Information

Credit card   Name on card
                                MR S J R MAY

Enter Card Verification Value *

Locating Your CVV

MC, Visa, Discover   American Express

Three digit CVV   Four digit CVV

Submit   Cancel

12

Connecting to Cloud Storage with SkyDrive

The cloud seems to be everywhere today, and Windows 8 and your tablet are ready to work with it. "The cloud" is an all-encompassing term for services delivered over the Internet, and the service we're looking at in this section is SkyDrive. SkyDrive is your personal cloud storage area; consider it an extension of your tablet's storage. When you need to save a document, save it to SkyDrive. When you need to save photos, save them to SkyDrive.

There are many advantages to saving files in your SkyDrive, not least of which is that they're accessible everywhere that you have an Internet connection, and you don't even need your tablet. SkyDrive has a web app that allows you to view, edit, upload, delete, and manage the files stored in your SkyDrive from anywhere by using a web browser. Another great advantage of this approach to storage is that if you forget or lose your tablet, or if it breaks or is stolen, you can still access your important files.

It's also really easy to share and collaborate on photos and documents with friends by using SkyDrive and the Microsoft Office Web Apps that are built into SkyDrive. Even without Microsoft Office, you and your coworkers, friends, and family can access your SkyDrive files to view and edit them, if you allow them to.

Connecting to the Cloud with a Microsoft Account

To connect to SkyDrive, you need a Microsoft Account. If you have a Microsoft Account (which you do if you have Hotmail, SkyDrive, or Xbox LIVE) and want to have Windows set up your connection to the cloud for you, you should switch your logon account to a Microsoft Account. Otherwise, you will need to sign up for one when you first use SkyDrive. With a Microsoft account, you can take advantage of Microsoft's cloud services which will automatically integrate throughout Windows seamlessly. When connected, you'll have access to your SkyDrive account for storing pictures, and any other cloud sharing services, such as Flickr, that are associated with your account will be also be connected throughout Windows.

Connect to a Microsoft Account

① On the PC Settings page, tap the Users category.

② Tap Switch To A Microsoft Account.

③ Enter your current password that you used to sign in to the account.

④ Tap Next.

⑤ Enter the email address of your Microsoft Account.

⑥ If you don't have a Microsoft Account, tap the link to sign up.

⑦ Select Next to complete the process.

You are asked to confirm your Microsoft Account password and security information.

PC settings

Personalize

Users

Notifications

Your account

Simon
Local Account

You can use your email address as a Microsoft account to sign in to Windows. You'll be able to access files and photos anywhere, sync settings, and more.

Switch to a Microsoft account

← Sign in with a Microsof

Use your favorite email address to sign to PCs running Windows 8 Consumer P

Email address

Users who sign in to PCs with a Microsc
• Download apps from Windows Store
• Access files and photos anywhere.
• Sync settings online to make PCs look and feel the same–this includes settings like browser favorites and history.

Sign up for a new email address

Sign in with a Microsoft account

First, verify your current password.

Simon

Current password

Next   Cancel

Next   Cancel

Connecting SkyDrive to a Microsoft Account Without Switching

If you don't want to sign into Windows with a Microsoft Account, you can still use SkyDrive on your device. However, if you are using a Microsoft Account to sign into Windows, the following task is done automatically for you.

Sign in to SkyDrive

(1) On the Start screen, tap the SkyDrive icon.

(2) Enter your Microsoft Account email address.

(3) Enter your Microsoft Account password.

(4) If you don't have a Microsoft account, tap Sign Up For A Microsoft Account to establish one.

(5) Tap Save to complete the process.

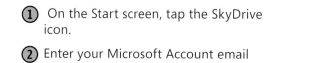

Add your Microsoft account

We'll save this info so you can use your account with SkyDrive.

Email address

Password

Sign up for a Microsoft account

Save   Cancel

Tip

If you don't find SkyDrive on your Start screen, swipe upward and tap All Apps to see all apps installed on your computer. If it's unavailable from there, you will need to install it from the Store.

Introducing SkyDrive

The SkyDrive app is the hub for viewing and managing files on your SkyDrive. SkyDrive differentiates between folders that hold documents and files and those that hold pictures by displaying a thumbnail of a picture on that folder. From here, tap any folder to explore its contents. If you have many folders and need a more compact view, the details view achieves this and also shows more details about the folder's contents.

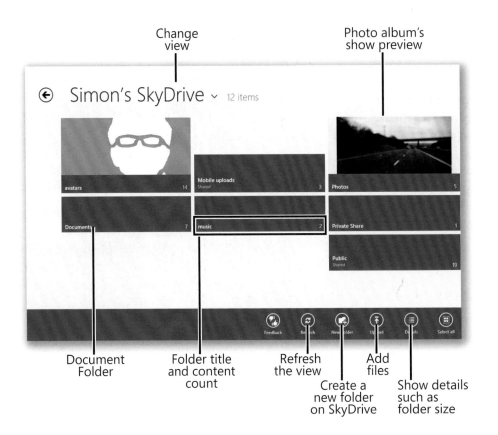

Change view

Photo album's show preview

Document Folder

Folder title and content count

Refresh the view

Add files

Create a new folder on SkyDrive

Show details such as folder size

Adding Files to SkyDrive

SkyDrive is a great place to store files such as documents, photos, and music because they're available to you wherever you go, even without your tablet. You can add files in the SkyDrive app or from any app on your tablet that can save files because SkyDrive is treated like an extended area of your tablet's storage.

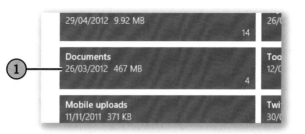

Add Files

(1) In the SkyDrive app, tap to open the folder in which you want to place the files.

(2) Swipe upward from the bottom of the screen to show the App Bar.

(3) Tap Upload.

(4) Tap the Files title and navigate to the location on your tablet that contains the files you want to add.

(5) Tap a file or swipe downward on multiple files to mark them.

(6) Tap the Add To SkyDrive button to add the file to the specified location.

Save Files to SkyDrive from Other Apps

1 Within the application you want to use to save a file, tap the Save button. This might not always be labeled Save; sometimes it might be labeled Export or Save As, depending on the app.

2 Tap the Files title.

3 At the bottom of the locations list, tap SkyDrive. The screen coloring changes to blue to match SkyDrive.

①

New   Open   Export

② Files ∨ Pictures

Documents

Pictures

Music

Videos

Desktop

Downloads

Homegroup

Computer

Network

SkyDrive **③**

④ Tap to open any folders on your Sky-Drive in which you'd like to save the file.

⑤ Enter a file name.

⑥ Tap Save to save the file to SkyDrive.

Viewing SkyDrive Files

SkyDrive has the capability to view specific files, such as photos, and if it doesn't know how to open a file, it prompts you to start an app that can open the type of file you've selected.

View Photos

1. Tap a photo album to view it.

2. Tap and hold or flick to pan left and right to browse photos.

3. Tap a photo to view a larger version of that image.

4. Pinch to zoom out further.

5. Touch the screen with two fingers and spread them to zoom in.

6. Tap Delete to delete the file.

7. Tap Download to select a location on your tablet to which to save the file.

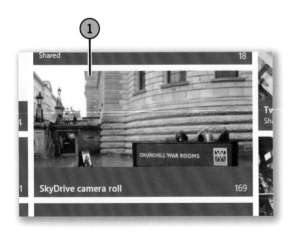

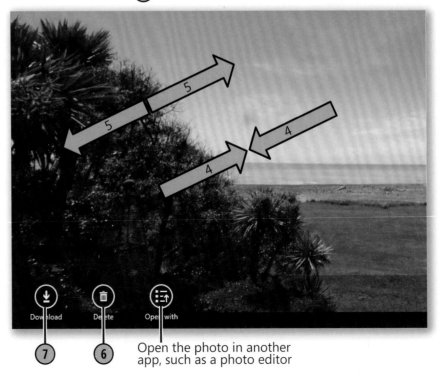

Open the photo in another app, such as a photo editor

View Documents

① Tap to open the folder where the document you want to view is located on your SkyDrive.

② Tap the document you want to open. If an app is installed that can open the document, SkyDrive will start that app.

③ If you don't have Microsoft Office installed and try to open a file created by one of the suite applications (Microsoft Word, Microsoft Excel, Microsoft PowerPoint, and Microsoft OneNote), you'll be taken to the Office Web Apps on SkyDrive.

Tip

You can also delete documents or photos by swiping downward on them when browsing SkyDrive, and then on the Apps Bar, clicking Manage and then Delete.

See Also

See page 303 for more information about the Microsoft Office Web Apps.

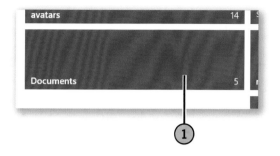

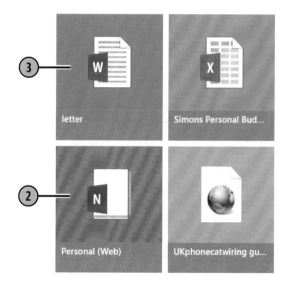

Opening SkyDrive Files in Other Apps

The files you have stored in SkyDrive are available to you in any apps connected to your tablet. So if you want to download a photo editing app from the Store and edit photos on SkyDrive, it's no problem.

Open Files in Other Apps

(1) Within an app that you want to use to work on files in SkyDrive, tap the relevant options to open a file, and then tap the Files title.

(2) Tap SkyDrive. You might need to scroll down. The screen color will change to SkyDrive's blue.

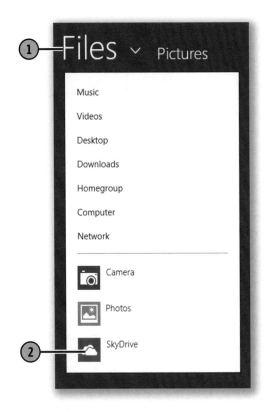

③ Tap to open directories to locate the file you want to open from SkyDrive.

④ If you go too far down, tap the Go Up link to return to the previous folder.

⑤ Tap Open to open the file.

Using SkyDrive on the Web

Interacting with SkyDrive isn't restricted to just your tablet; you can use any computer with Internet access to securely work with your files by using any web browser, such as Internet Explorer 10. By accessing SkyDrive through the website (*skydrive.com*), you can do even more with it; you can share

files with other people and better organize your files. Also, if the right software is installed on your other computers, you can access files not stored in SkyDrive but stored locally on the hard disks of those devices.

Create new documents with Microsoft Office Web Apps

Upload files to SkyDrive

Document folder

Picture folder

Share the folder with friends via email or social networks

Download the folder to your tablet

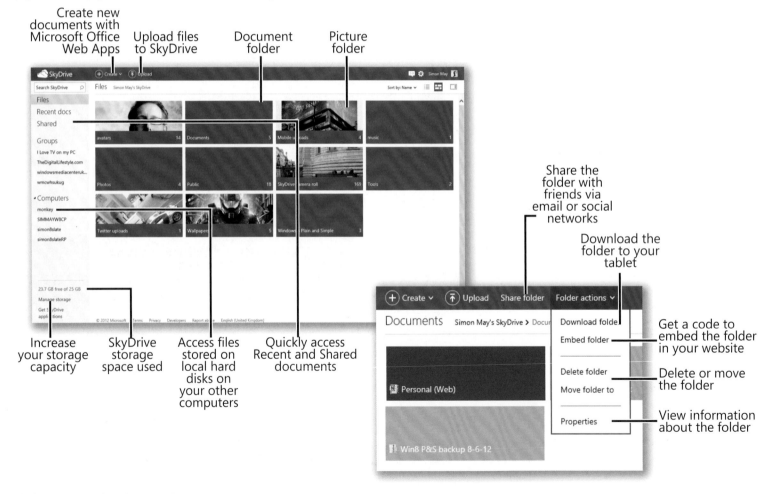

Increase your storage capacity

SkyDrive storage space used

Access files stored on local hard disks on your other computers

Quickly access Recent and Shared documents

Get a code to embed the folder in your website

Delete or move the folder

View information about the folder

Using Microsoft Office Web Apps to View and Edit Documents

SkyDrive includes built-in versions of Microsoft Office apps that are available to you from directly within the SkyDrive app or the SkyDrive web app (*skydrive.com*). Because they are web apps, you do not need Microsoft Office installed on your tablet to use them. Using the web apps feels familiar between apps, so using Word feels similar to Excel.

Open a Document with Word Web App

1 Within the SkyDrive app, tap a Word document.

The document opens in Internet Explorer.

2 Tap File to restore previous versions of the document, translate the document into another language, open editing functions, download a local copy of the document, print the document, or share the document with friends via email or a website.

3 Tap Edit Document to quickly open the document for editing, either in the browser or, if you have Microsoft Office installed, in the full version of Microsoft Office.

4 Tap Share to quickly share and collaborate with friends by email or social media.

5 Tap Find to search for text within the document.

6 Tap Comments to view and make comments to collaborate with friends or coworkers.

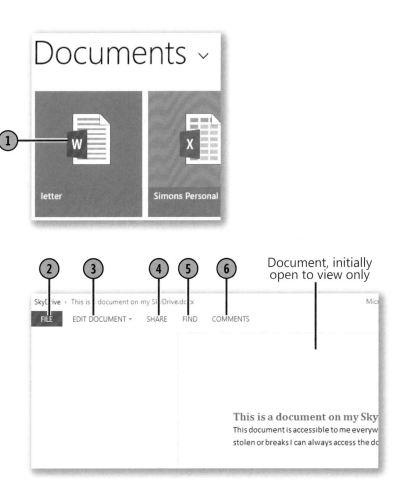

Edit a Document by Using Word Web App

1 When viewing a document, tap Edit in Word Web App.

2 Tap the Save icon to quickly save the document.

3 Tap the Undo and Redo icons to undo and redo recent changes.

4 Tap to switch between mouse and touch-friendly modes.

5 Tap Home for formatting options.

6 Tap Insert to add pictures, clipart, or links.

7 Tap Page Layout to change margins, orientation, page size, and so forth.

8 Tap View to change to reading or editing views.

9 Tap Open In Word to open the document in Microsoft Word on your tablet.

10 Tap within the document body to start editing.

11 When done, in the upper-left corner, tap the Close button (X) to exit the Word Web App.

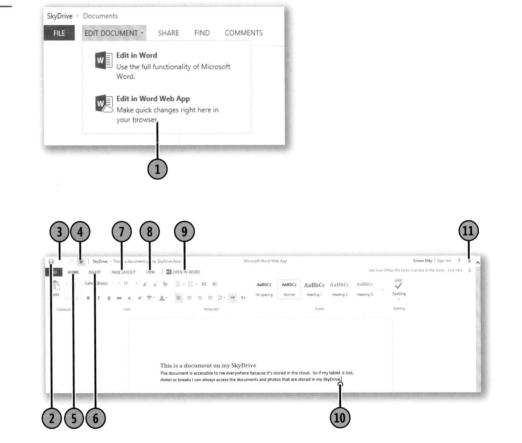

Using Microsoft Office with SkyDrive

If your tablet came with Microsoft Office installed (or if you've bought it since then), you'll be glad to know that your SkyDrive is deeply integrated with Office. Office apps are able to natively save and open documents to your SkyDrive, keeping changes in sync. The process of opening and closing apps is similar in all Office apps, but here we will use Microsoft Excel as the example.

Open a Spreadsheet from SkyDrive by Using Excel

1. Within Excel, tap the File tab.

2. Tap Open.

3. Tap Your SkyDrive (it displays your name).

4. Tap Browse to open a file from your SkyDrive, just as you'd open any other file on the desktop.

Save an Excel Spreadsheet to SkyDrive

1. Within Excel, tap the File tab.

2. Tap Save As.

3. Tap Your SkyDrive (it displays your name).

4. Tap Browse and select the location and file name for your file.

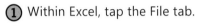

Installing the Desktop SkyDrive App

If you open File Explorer on the Start screen, you probably won't see any sign of your SkyDrive app unless you have the SkyDrive for Windows app installed. This app connects your desktop to SkyDrive and makes it available to desktop apps. The SkyDrive for Windows app also has an extra trick up its sleeve: it can make everything on a computer's local hard disk accessible through your SkyDrive, as long as the computer is on. This +means that even if you don't put the SkyDrive for Windows app on your tablet, you might want it on your other computers.

Download and Install SkyDrive for Windows

1. Go to the SkyDrive web app (*skydrive. com*), and tap the Get SkyDrive Applications link.

2. Tap the download button and follow the download process to get the SkyDrive for Windows app.

3. Tap Run to start the installation process.

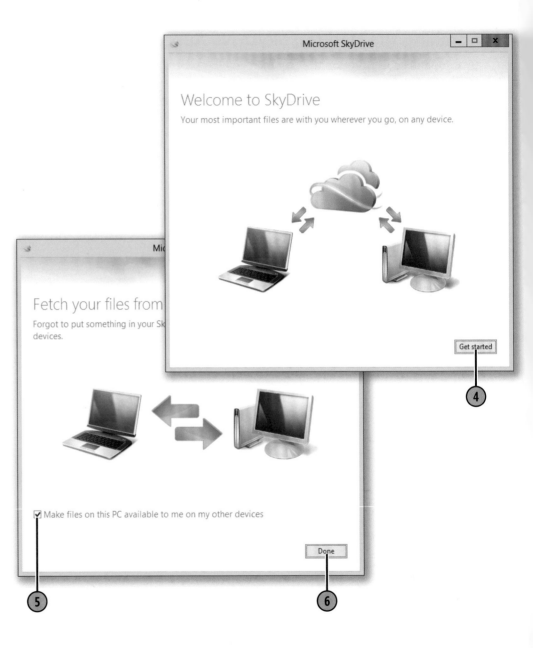

④ Tap Get Started to install the app. Enter your user name and password when prompted, and accept the location to store your SkyDrive sync location.

⑤ Select the Make Files On This PC Available To Me On My Other Devices check box so that your other devices can access files on this tablet from anywhere in the world—with the right security details.

⑥ Tap Done to complete setup.

Access Other Computers

① Open the SkyDrive web app (*skydrive. com*) and find the Computers section. Tap a computer on which you've installed the SkyDrive for Windows software on.

② The first time you attempt to connect from a new computer, tap Sign In With A Security Code. To validate security, Microsoft sends you a special code by email. You need to do this only once; thereafter, everything works just as if you were viewing documents and photos on your Sky-Drive app.

Using SkyDrive in File Explorer

File Explorer is the file manager by which you'll probably do most of your tasks related to creating folders and moving and organizing files. When you've installed the SkyDrive for Windows app, you are able to access your SkyDrive as if it were local to your tablet—in fact, it is local to your tablet. The SkyDrive for Windows app downloads everything from your SkyDrive and keeps it in sync for you, so you can also use SkyDrive at those times when you don't have Internet Access.

Access SkyDrive in File Explorer

1 Open File Explorer.

2 Tap the SkyDrive icon in the Favorites section to view your SkyDrive app.

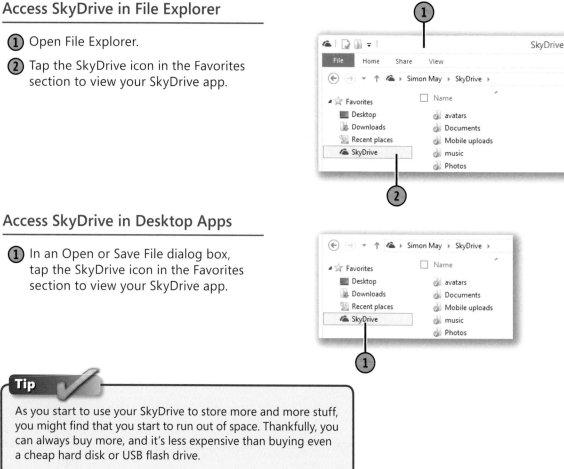

Access SkyDrive in Desktop Apps

1 In an Open or Save File dialog box, tap the SkyDrive icon in the Favorites section to view your SkyDrive app.

> **Tip**
>
> As you start to use your SkyDrive to store more and more stuff, you might find that you start to run out of space. Thankfully, you can always buy more, and it's less expensive than buying even a cheap hard disk or USB flash drive.

Buy More SkyDrive Storage

① While in the SkyDrive app, tap the Settings charm.

② Tap Options.

③ Tap Manage Storage.

④ Tap Get More Storage.

⑤ Tap Select and then complete the authorization process to buy the selected amount of storage.

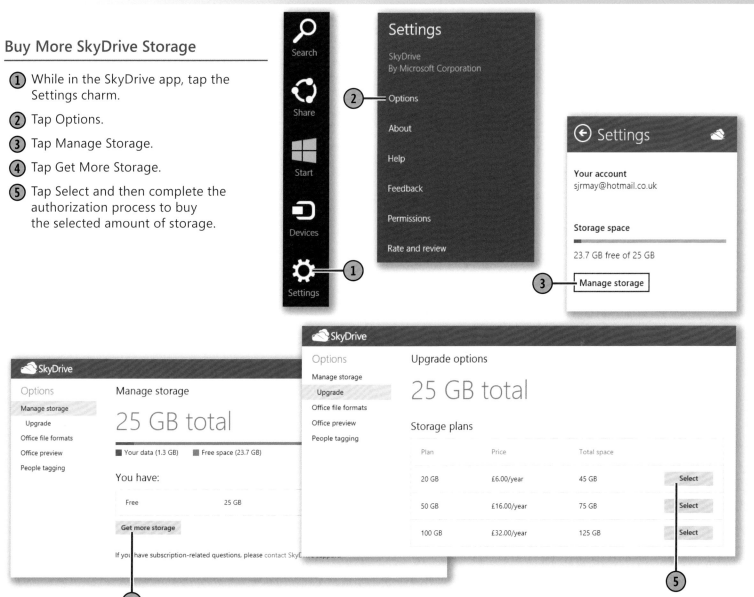

13

Working with Photos

We all have memories recorded in photographs, whether in printed albums, scrapbooks, our hard disks, or shared with friends through social networks. The Photos app makes it easy to view them on your tablet. Flipping through photos is similar to opening a photo album and flipping from page to page.

The Photos app can display photos from your own tablet stored in the Pictures library and can also connect to social networks such as Facebook and Flickr. This connectivity makes it possible to view photos you have stored on those networks as if they're on your tablet. The same is true of your SkyDrive. Storing your photos either privately or publicly online (in the cloud) makes a lot of sense because if something should happen to your tablet, your memories aren't lost. Imagine if the only photos of your newborn were on your tablet, and someone else liked the look of your tablet so much that they stole it. Storing memories in the cloud keeps them in a safe place.

You can also use SkyDrive to fetch photos installed on other Internet-connected computers and view them on your tablet.

Introducing the Photos App

Microsoft has created a Photos app that makes the most of viewing your photos on your tablet. The app makes it fun to flick through your photos, create slide shows, and share those photos with friends. The Photos app not only shows photos from your tablet but also those from other places where you're likely to have them, such as your Facebook account or a photo sharing site such as Flickr. SkyDrive is the perfect place to store your photos, and the Photos app makes the most of viewing them. SkyDrive also has a trick up its sleeve: the Photo app can use SkyDrive to connect to other computers and fetch photos from them, as well.

Your chosen background image

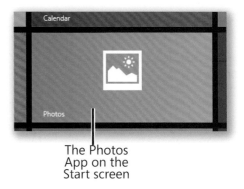

The Photos App on the Start screen

Photos on your tablet

Photos on your SkyDrive

Photos from your Facebook account

Photos from your Flickr account

Photos from other SkyDrive connected devices

Viewing Pictures

The Photos app recognizes many of the same gestures that you'll already be familiar with in Windows 8. You can also use your photos to decorate the Photo app, the lock screen, and the Photos tile on the Start screen.

View Pictures

1. Tap the album to view (Pictures Library in this case).

2. Tap a photo to open it.

3. Pinch two fingers together to zoom out and view thumbnails of the album.

4. Spread two fingers apart to zoom back in on a photo, or tap the photo.

5. Swipe upward from the bottom of the screen to show the App Bar.

6. Tap Set As to apply the displayed photo to the app background, Photos app tile, or lock screen.

7. Tap Delete to delete the photo.

8. To go back, tap the back arrow.

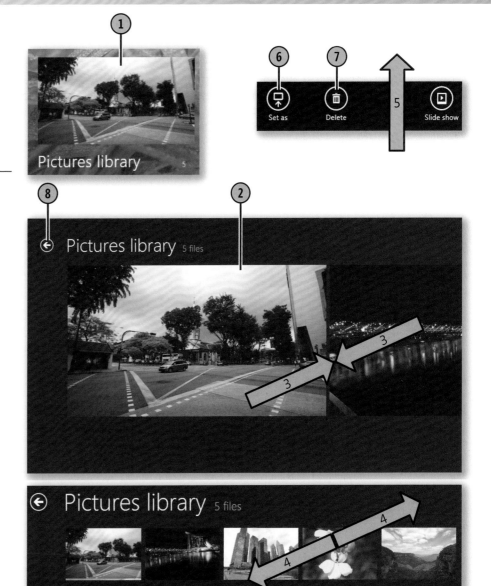

Start a Slide Show

① When viewing a photo or an album, swipe upward from the bottom of the screen to reveal the App bar.

② Tap Slide Show to start a slide show.

If you tap anywhere on the screen, the slide show will stop.

Tip

If you have an Internet-connected Smart TV that has a DLNA logo, you can select the Devices charm and display the photos on your TV.

Connecting Photo Sharing Accounts

If you're like most people, you'll find that you have lots of photos in different places, most likely on other computers and in social network accounts. The Photos app uses your Microsoft Account to store details of these accounts and automatically connects your SkyDrive app. If you are using your Microsoft Account to sign in to your tablet, you can skip the first task in this section. If you have other computers and have installed the SkyDrive for Windows app, you can also view photos on those devices.

Connect to Your Microsoft Account in the Photos App

① Tap any of the album squares to connect to a Microsoft Account.

② Enter your Microsoft Account email address.

③ Enter your Microsoft Account password.

④ Tap Save to complete the process; your SkyDrive app will be automatically connected.

Tip

Don't be alarmed if pictures don't appear immediately. Sometimes they take a few minutes to download if you have a slow connection or lots of photos.

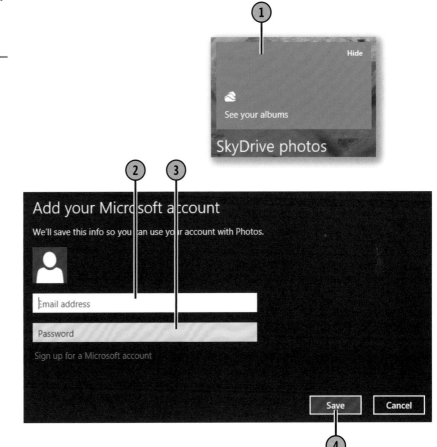

Connect to Other Computers

① Tap the Devices tile. (This tile won't appear if you've already enabled sharing from other devices by installing SkyDrive on another computer; instead you will see the other devices connected to your Microsoft Account.)

② Tap the link for SkyDrive.com, download the SkyDrive for Windows app, and then install this on other computers from which you want to fetch pictures.

③ Tap the back arrow to return to Photos.

Devices 0 files

It's a bit empty in here without any photos.

The Photos app shows you photos and videos from all of your devices in one place.

To see content from other devices go to SkyDrive.com/windows to download and install Microsoft SkyDrive Beta on them. Then sign in with your Microsoft account and ensure that the **Make files on this PC available to me on my other devices** checkbox is selected.

④ When you've installed the app on other computers, a tile appears within the app for each computer; tap the tile to browse photos.

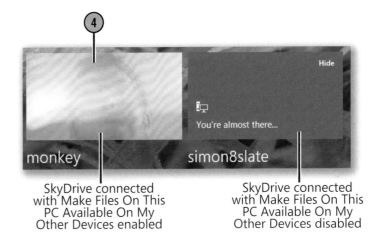

SkyDrive connected with Make Files On This PC Available On My Other Devices enabled

SkyDrive connected with Make Files On This PC Available On My Other Devices disabled

See Also

This functionality requires that the SkyDrive for Windows app to be installed on other computers that you own and that they be connected to your Microsoft Account. For details about how to install SkyDrive for Windows, see page 307.

Connect Facebook or Flickr to Your Microsoft Account

1. In the Photos app, tap either the Facebook Photos or the Flickr Photos tile.

2. If you don't sign in to your tablet with a Microsoft Account, enter your Microsoft Account email address. If you are signed in with a Microsoft Account, skip to step 5.

3. Enter your Microsoft Account password.

4. Tap Save.

5. Tap the Connect button to connect your Facebook or Flickr account to your Microsoft Account.

⑥ Enter the email address you use to log on to Facebook or Flickr. For Flickr, you can also choose to log on with a Facebook account if that's how you normally do it.

⑦ Enter your Facebook or Flickr password.

⑧ Tap Log In.

⑨ Tap Done to complete the process.

⑩ To view your Facebook photo albums or Flickr photos, tap the Facebook or Flickr tile.

⊛ Connecting to a service

f Facebook login

Log in to use your Facebook account with Microsoft.

Email address:

Password:

☐ Keep me logged in

Forgotten your password?

Sign up for Facebook   Log in Cancel

⊛ You're ready to go   f

We're setting things up now, so it might be a few minutes before you see any changes.

⚙ **Add more accounts in settings**
You can add more accounts or change these connection settings at any time in the settings for this app.

Done

Facebook   674

Tip ✓

These settings stay in your Microsoft Account and will be set up automatically if you log on to any Windows 8 computer with your Microsoft Account. You can go to *http://profile.live. com* to change these connections later.

Importing Photos from Cameras and Memory Cards

Your tablet is one of the most mobile computers you've ever owned, and it will probably go everywhere you do, including on vacations, to work, or, if you're a keen photographer, along with you on photo shoots. Windows 8–based tablets have the option of connecting cameras by USB or by using SD or MicroSD cards for photo storage. The Photos app can import pictures to your library from all three sources.

Import Photos

① Swipe upward from the bottom of the screen to show the App Bar.

② Tap Import.

③ Tap the device from which to import.

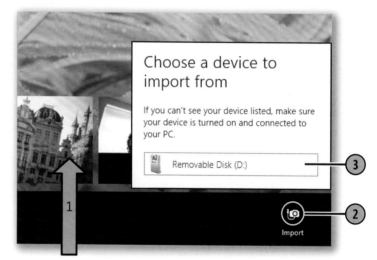

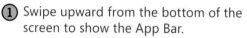

Photos are imported to your Pictures folder on your tablet. As such, you might want to take the time to move them over to your SkyDrive so that you have them in your cloud storage for safe keeping.

④ Swipe downward on any images you want to deselect from the import. By default, all photos on the device will be imported.

⑤ Enter a name for the folder into which you want to import the photos in the local Pictures library; if the name doesn't exist, a new folder will be created.

⑥ Tap Import to start the import process.

⑦ Tap Open Album to go directly to the album into which the photos were imported.

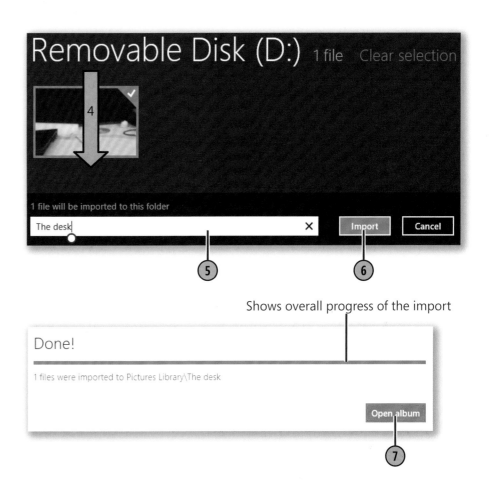

Shows overall progress of the import

Sharing Photos

The Photos app can take advantage of other apps installed on your tablet that support sharing. So, if you have an app installed that supports Facebook sharing, you can use this to share photos. All sharing apps work in the same way, including the Email app.

Share a Photo

① Select a photo that you want to share and then tap the Share charm.

② Tap the app you want to use to share the picture (Mail in this case).

③ Enter any details required to add your personal message to the shared item and tap the icon specific to the sharing app to share the photo. In Mail, this is the Send icon.

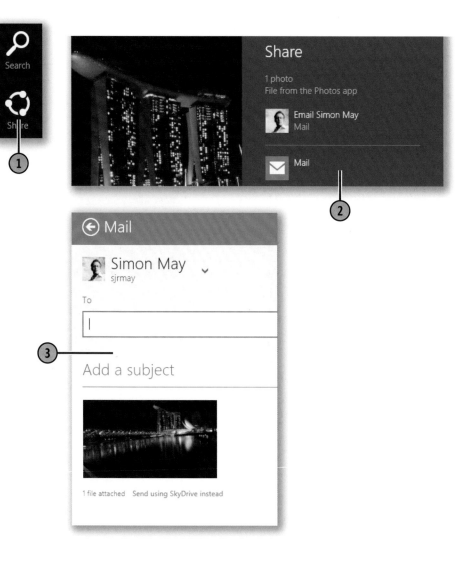

Managing Photos in File Explorer

You can also work with photos on the desktop. The easy way to start working with photos on the desktop is through File Explorer, with which you can view photos and do some very basic editing.

View Photo Libraries

1 On the Start screen, tap All apps view and then tap File Explorer to open it on the desktop.

2 Tap the Pictures library, which is the place to store pictures on your tablet.

3 Tap the Picture Tools Manage tab to access tools for working with Pictures in File Explorer.

4 Zoom out to view more thumbnails by touching two fingers on the screen and pinching them together.

5 Zoom in to view more detail with larger thumbnails by touching two fingers on the screen and spreading them apart.

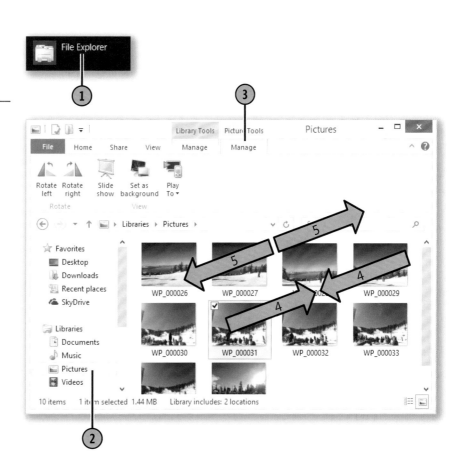

Rotate Photos

① Tap the photo that you want to rotate. You can rotate multiple photos by selecting the check box in the upper-left corner of the photo.

② Tap the Photo Tools Manage tab if it's not already selected.

③ Tap the Rotate Left or Rotate Right buttons to rotate the photo to the correct orientation.

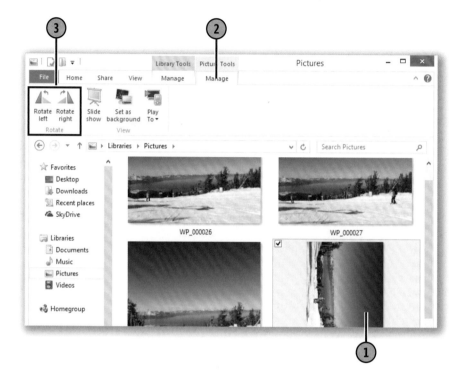

Tip

You can also use these tools to set the background for the desktop. Just tap a photo, and then tap Set As Background. If you use a Microsoft Account, this background will sync across all your devices.

Play a Photo Slide Show from File Explorer

(1) In File Explorer, with either a number of photos selected or no photos selected, on the Picture Tools Manage tab, tap Slide Show.

(2) When the slide show is playing, tap and hold to display an options menu that includes commands to change the speed, pause, or go back in the slide show.

(3) Tap Exit to get out of the slide show.

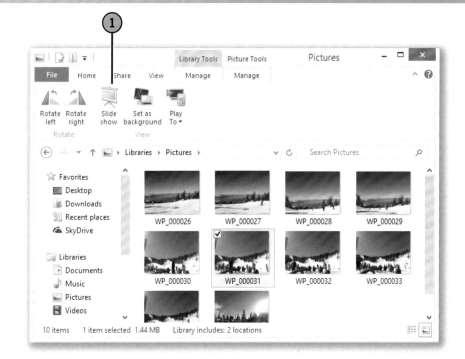

Tip

Unlike in the Photos app slide show, tapping a photo doesn't show a back button. The only way to stop a slide show that was started with File Explorer is to tap Exit or to show the keyboard and then tap the Esc key.

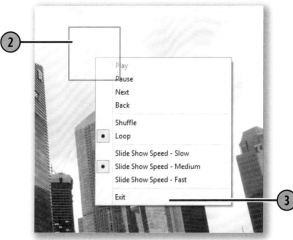

View Photos on Other Devices by Using PlayTo

1. Select one or more photos, and then on the Picture Tools Manage tab, tap Play To.

2. Tap the target device; the device must support the DLNA standard, which is true of most SmartTVs.

3. A slide show starts on the remote device. Use the player controls to control playback on the remote device.

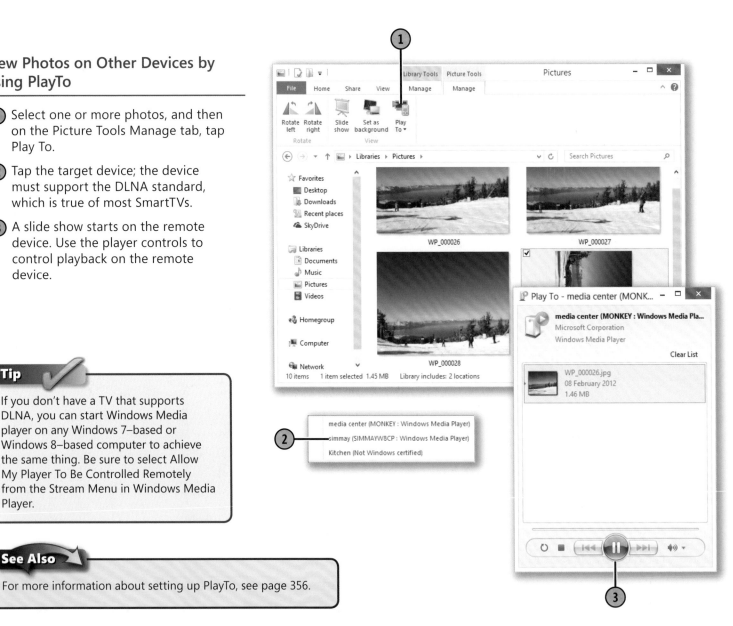

Tip

If you don't have a TV that supports DLNA, you can start Windows Media player on any Windows 7–based or Windows 8–based computer to achieve the same thing. Be sure to select Allow My Player To Be Controlled Remotely from the Stream Menu in Windows Media Player.

See Also

For more information about setting up PlayTo, see page 356.

Using Windows Photo Viewer

You can use Windows Photo Viewer (which is built in to Windows 8) to view photos on the desktop.

Open Photos

(1) Tap and hold a photo.
An options menu appears.

(2) Tap Open With.

(3) Tap Windows Photo Viewer.

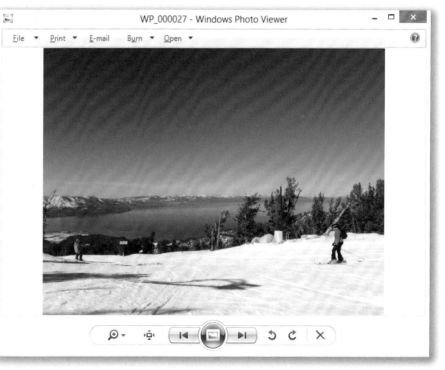

Tip ✔
Windows Photo Viewer can also be started by searching for it on the All Apps Start screen.

Change Picture Properties

① Within Windows Photo Viewer, tap
    File.

② Tap Properties.

③ Enter details about the picture by
    tapping next to an item, in the Value
    column; ratings, comments, and
    tags will help you find pictures with
    search.

④ Click OK.

Tip

Using Picture Properties, you can categorize your photos and determine when and
where they were taken.

Changing the Photos App Settings

The Photos app has settings that control what is displayed within the app and on the tile for the Photos app on the Start screen. It's useful to change them to prevent unwanted images and blank albums from appearing.

Change Photo App Settings

(1) In the Photos app, tap the Settings charm.

(2) Tap Options.

(3) Tap to have the tile for the Photos app display pictures out of order, which can be more interesting.

(4) Tap for each item shown in the Photos app to have photos from that service removed (Off) from the screen.

(5) Tap Options to reconfigure the connection to Facebook or Flickr.

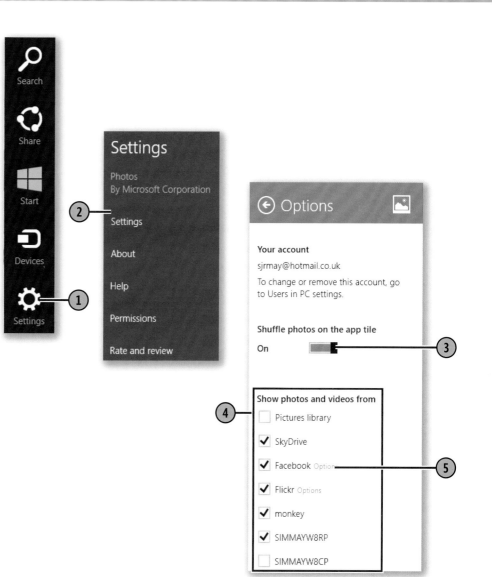

14

Keeping Files Organized

Much of what you'll want to do with your tablet will involve consuming content from the Internet through either Internet Explorer or through apps. Of course, you'll probably also want to save some of that content and even create some of your own, such as documents, music, or photos. Windows makes this really easy, but sometimes you'll need to organize things to make it easier for you to find them.

We all organize things in our own way, and your Windows 8–based tablet has a couple of options to help with that. You can organize your files into folders and then organize those folders in libraries. Those folders and libraries can then be shared with other people and computers on your home network by using HomeGroup.

Managing all of your files is easiest when you use File Explorer, which runs on the desktop and is available on the Start screen. File Explorer can be customized to help you manage your files and to search for items that you can't readily find.

Understanding Files

Files are the most basic items that you work with on your tablet. Files can be music (such as MP3 or WMA); they can be pictures (such as JPG or PNG); they can be video (such as MP4 or WMV); they can be documents (such as DOCX, PPTX, or XLSX); and many other file types.

Essentially, all files contain some type of information that an app on your tablet can do something with. File Explorer is the built-in file management tool for your tablet, and by using this tool, you can move, copy, delete, and do virtually anything you want to organize those files.

Files in Windows are represented by icons that help you recognize what type of content they contain. Files have names (which you often supply) that indicate what the they are. Files also have a file extension (two or three letters after a period at the end of the file name) that, like an icon, indicates the type of file content (such as .docx for a Microsoft Word document).

A picture file with a photo of the kids

A journal file containing notes

Icon

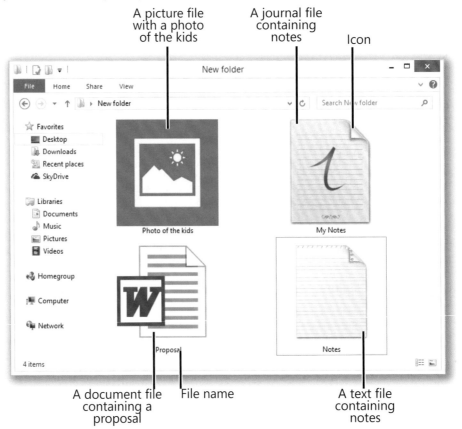

A document file containing a proposal

File name

A text file containing notes

Understanding Folders

Folders are the next step up the ladder from files; they group files into easier-to-manage units. Just like a folder in a filing cabinet, they are containers that group things together in any way you like. Folders can contain any types of files, so you could have a folder for pictures or a folder for documents (which, in fact, you do, as part of your profile). Of course, you don't have to have the same things in a folder; for example, you could have a folder for "wedding planning" that could contain both pictures of wedding cakes and a document detailing the seating plan.

Folders can also contain other folders, often referred to as *sub-folders*, and there is no limit to the number of subfolders you can have within a folder.

All files within Windows "live" inside a series of folders. You own some folders, and some might be owned by other users of your tablet and by apps that run on your tablet.

To make them easier to identify, folders all have a name and an icon, just like files. The icon that is usually associated with them is a manila folder, partly open so that you can see the types of files that it contains.

Icon

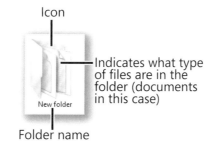

New folder

Indicates what type of files are in the folder (documents in this case)

Folder name

Understanding Libraries

Libraries are groupings of files and folders that have very similar content. By default, Windows 8 provides four libraries on your tablet:

- **Documents**—Containscontains folders that store document files, such as spreadsheets, text documents, presentations, and so forth.

- **Pictures**—Contains folders that store pictures and photos; this is where the Photos app looks for local photographs. This is also where the Camera app saves photos.

- **Music**—Contains music files such as albums you've downloaded by using the Music app.

- **Videos**—Containsvideos files such as those you've downloaded by using the Videos app or that you've taken with your video camera and copied to your tablet. This is also where the Camera app saves videos.

Each of these libraries is made up of a group of folders that have been deemed to be of the type described either by Windows or by you. It's perfectly fine to add your own folders to a library if you don't want to store your files in the default libraries, and they don't even need to reside on your tablet.

Libraries provide a convenient way for you to access files of a specific type on your tablet. By default, your personal Document, Pictures, Video, and Music folders are members of the Document, Pictures, Video, and Music libraries, respectively. In addition, there are "public" versions of the same folders that are available to all users of the tablet. This provides a convenient way to share photos between two people who use the same tablet or who are on a network together.

The various apps on your tablet save the files they create to these libraries, so for the most part, you won't need to go rooting around too much to find where a file is.

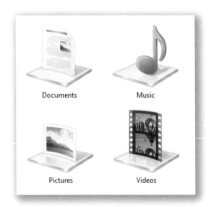

Using File Explorer

File Explorer is the file management tool that opens on the desktop of your tablet. It's a tool that helps you manage files, folders, and libraries so that you can organize your files and folders into meaningful groupings. It's also the tool with which you can copy files on your tablet as well as to and from external storage (such as USB hard disks), and to other computers in your homegroup or home network.

Tour File Explorer

① The navigation pane on the left is where you can quickly get to places, such as libraries, on your computer, on computers in your homegroup, or on other computers in your network. Tap an item to open it.

② Double-tap an icon in the action pane to open that item.

③ Tap the Home tab to access the most common actions for a file, folder, or library.

④ Tap the Share tab to access actions related to sharing files or folders on your network or homegroup.

⑤ Tap View to access settings related to how your files and folders are displayed by File Explorer.

⑥ Tap the arrow to hide or unhide the ribbon.

⑦ Tap in the text box, to type something to search within the current place you're viewing (in this case, Libraries).

⑧ Type the name of a location to get there quickly; for example, **c:**.

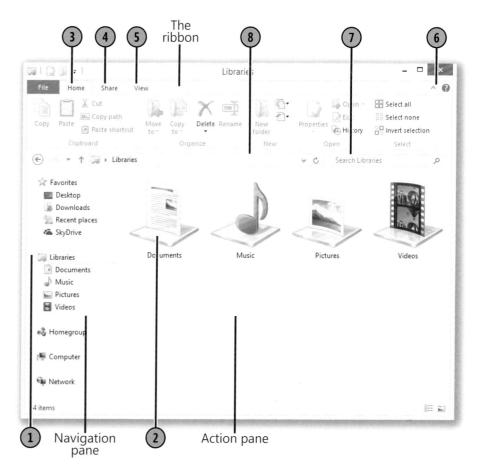

Move or Copy a File or Folder

(1) Tap a file or folder to select it.

(2) Tap the Move To or Copy To buttons.

(3) Tap the location to which to move or copy the item; if the location is listed, tap it and you're done. If the location is unlisted, tap Choose Location.

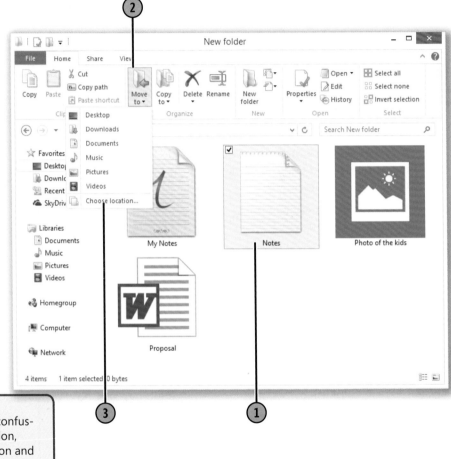

Tip

The difference between move and copy might be confusing. Moving a file removes it from its original location, whereas copying a file leaves it in its original location and creates a new, exact copy in the new location.

④ Tap a location within which you want to place the file or folder.

When browsing, if the small arrow is pointing right, there are more locations within the listed folder; if the arrow is pointing downward, there are no further locations.

⑤ If you want to create a new folder, tap the location within which you want to create the folder and then type a name into the Folder text box.

⑥ Tap Make New Folder to create the new folder in the selected location, using the name you've entered.

⑦ Tap Move to move the file.

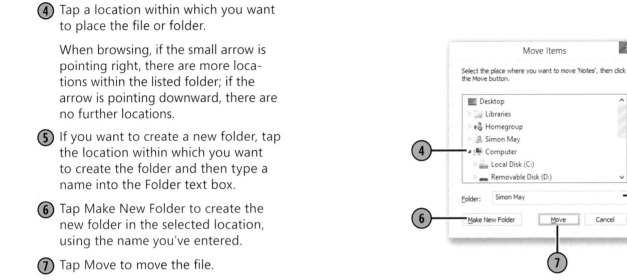

Tip

If you want to move or copy more than one file, tap the check mark in the upper left of the icons. You can also "lasso" them by tapping a blank area and dragging the box that appears around them.

Open a File or Folder by Double-Tapping

1 Double-tap a file to open it by using default app for that type of file.

2 Tap the down arrow next to the Open button on the ribbon.

3 Tap the app you want to open the file with.

Open a File or Folder with a Default Program

4 Tap Choose Default Program to change the default app used to open the type of file.

5 Tap the app you'd like to use as the default app for this file.

Tip ✓

You can do the same thing by tapping and holding a file and then selecting Open With from the options that appear.

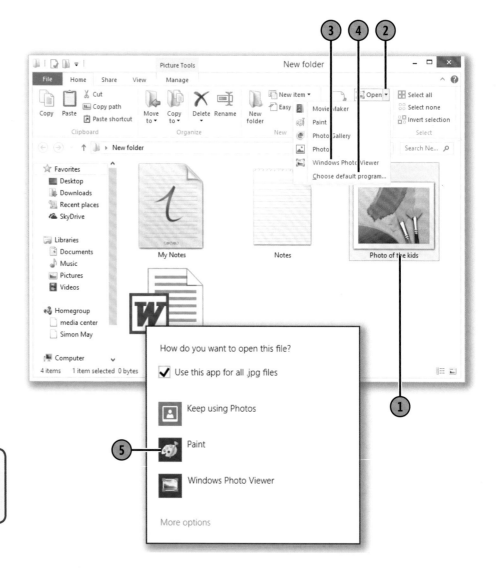

Rename a File or Folder

① Tap a file to select it.

② On the ribbon, tap the Home tab, and then in the Organize group tap the Rename button.

③ Type a new name, and either press Enter or tap elsewhere when done.

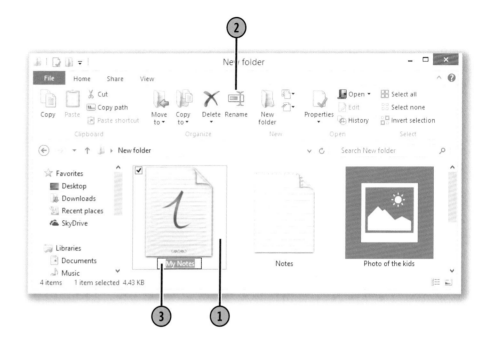

 Tip

An alternative way to change the name of a file is to tap the file and then tap on the name of the file, or if you have a keyboard connected, tap the file and press the F2 key.

Managing Libraries

The Documents, Video, Music, and Pictures libraries on your tablet gather groups of similar content together to make it easy for you to find particular items. Pictures contains pictures, Videos contain videos, and so on, but there are a number of things you can change to make libraries work better for you. For example, you might want to add content from other loca-tions on your tablet to a library. You might also want to change the folder that documents are saved to by default when you save them to the Documents library. You can also control the default location on your tablet to which homegroup users would save a document.

Manage Library Locations

1. In File Explorer, tap Libraries.

2. Select the library with which you want to work.

3. On the ribbon, tap the Library Tools/ Manage tab.

4. Tap Manage Library to change its location by using any of steps 5 through 9.

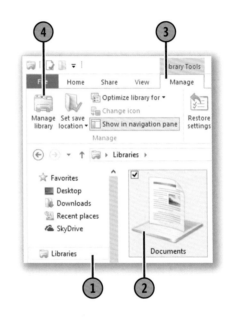

Tip

You can also add folders from other computers in your homegroup to the library in the same way. If you're using the SkyDrive for Windows app, you can add your SkyDrive folders to a library that reflects their content to make them even easier to find.

(5) Tap the Add button to add a new location.

(6) Browse to the folder to add to the library.

(7) Tap Include Folder to include it in the library.

(8) To remove a folder from the library, tap the folder.

(9) To remove a folder, after it's high-lighted, tap Remove.

(10) Tap OK to complete the changes.

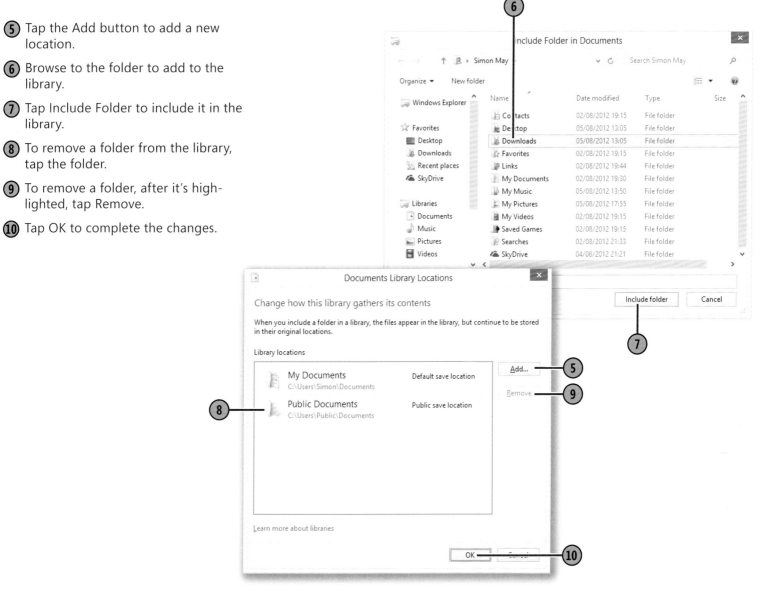

Manage Save Locations

(1) In File Explorer, tap the Libraries location.

(2) Tap the library to change the settings for.

(3) On the ribbon, tap the Library Tools/ Manage tab.

(4) Tap the Set Save Location button.

(5) Tap the location that you want to assign as the default when you save to the library.

(6) Tap Set Public Save Location to set the default location for other people who save files to your library.

(7) Tap the location to which other people save files.

Library Optimization

① With a library selected in File Explorer, on the ribbon, tap the Library Tools/Manage tab, and then in Manage group, tap the Optimize Library For button

② Tap the type of library for which you'd like to optimize. This changes the defaults, such as what tools are visible on the File Explorer ribbon and how apps see the library.

Hide or Show Libraries

① Tap the library you want to hide or show.

② On the ribbon, tap the Library Tools/ Manage tab, and then in Manage group, tap the Show In Navigation Pane button. (This button toggles to show or hide the library.)

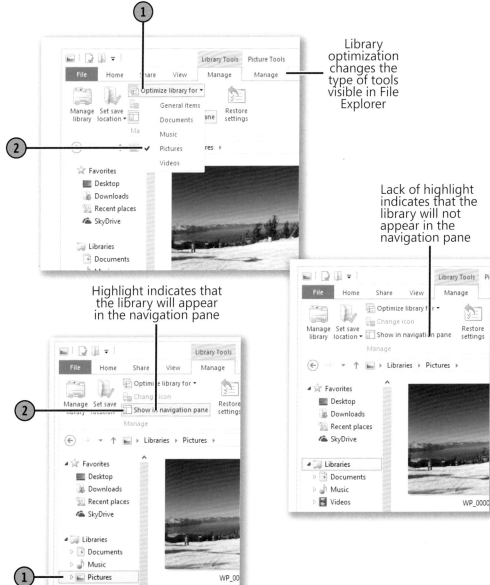

Library optimization changes the type of tools visible in File Explorer

Lack of highlight indicates that the library will not appear in the navigation pane

Highlight indicates that the library will appear in the navigation pane

Restore Library Settings to Defaults

① In the Navigation pane, tap the Libraries section.

② Tap the library to which you want to restore default settings.

③ On the ribbon, tap the Library Tools/ Manage tab and then tap the Restore Settings button to reset all library settings to how they were before you changed them.

This will remove any additional folders you've added to the library and will add back any default folders you removed. It will set default locations back to their original defaults and optimize the library as it originally was.

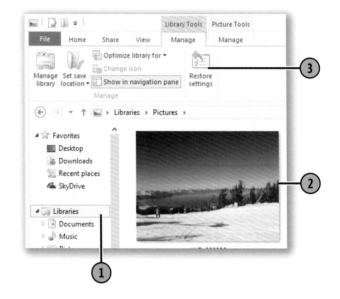

Create a New Library

1. In the navigation pane, tap the Libraries item.

2. Tap and hold a blank area of the action space.

3. In the options panel that appears, tap New.

4. Tap Library to create a new library.

   A new library will appear, waiting to be renamed. Use the steps outlined previously in this section to configure the library to your liking.

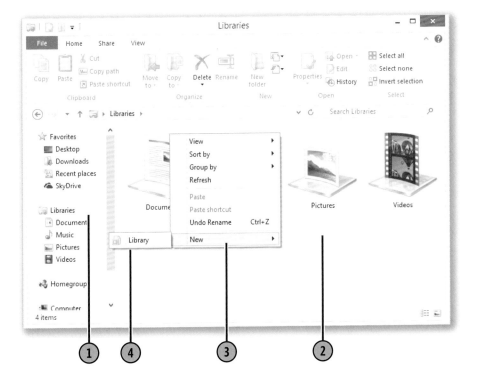

Tip

Create your own libraries to make organization easier. For example, you might want a "Reading" library of all the eBooks you've downloaded.

Viewing Shared Files via HomeGroup

HomeGroup makes it easy and convenient to share your photos, music, video, and documents with family members and for you to transfer your documents and media around the home. For example, you can use HomeGroup on your tablet to listen to music that is stored on another computer in your home. File Explorer is one way to view what is shared with and by other computers in your homegroup and is a simple way to move and copy files throughout it.

Browse Your Homegroup

1. In the navigation pane, tap Homegroup.

2. Double-tap the name of the person or computer sharing files that you'd like to access.

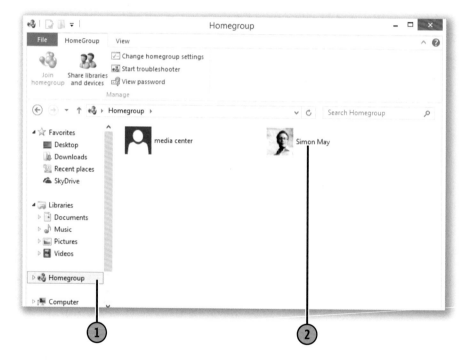

See Also

For information about how to set up your homegroup, see page 138.

See and Change What You're Sharing

(1) In the navigation pane, tap Homegroup.

(2) On the File Explorer ribbon, on the Homegroup tab, tap the Share Librar-ies And Devices button.

Each library that's shared will be shown in the window if the computer where the content resides is turned on and awake.

(3) Tap the Permissions drop-down menu. To enable sharing, tap Shared; to discontinue sharing, tap Not Shared.

(4) Tap Next to complete the process. A message appears to confirm the change.

Sharing Files or Folders via HomeGroup

Although your Documents, Music, Video, and Pictures libraries might be the most obvious locations you will want to share with your homegroup, there might also be other places. Sharing other locations requires just a few taps, and you can use the same process to change the level of access others have to a folder. For example, you could set up a folder within your Documents library to which your daughter copies her homework so that you can check it over—she'd need "edit" access to do that, as opposed to the default, which is "read."

Share Specific Files or Folders

① In File Explorer, navigate to and tap the item that you want to share with the homegroup.

② On the ribbon, tap the Share tab.

③ Tap the person or group with whom you want to share. Each person in your homegroup will be listed, along with Homegroup (View), which applies settings so that everyone in the homegroup can see but not change files. If you select Homegroup (View And Edit), everyone in the homegroup can view and change the files.

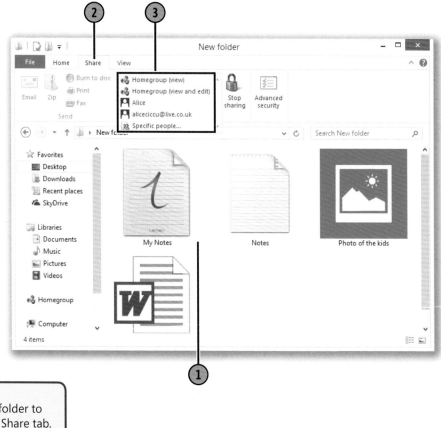

Tip

To quickly stop sharing a file or folder, tap the file or folder to select it, and then on the File Explorer ribbon, on the Share tab, tap Stop Sharing.

Allow Specific People Specific Permissions to Files and Folders

(1) In File Explorer, tap the folder or file to share.

(2) On the ribbon, tap the Share tab.

(3) Tap Specific People to start the File Sharing Wizard.

(4) Tap the drop-down menu to select a person from the homegroup.

(5) Tap Add.

(6) Tap the Permission Level drop-down menu to choose between Read or Read/Write access.

(7) Tap Share to share the file or folder.

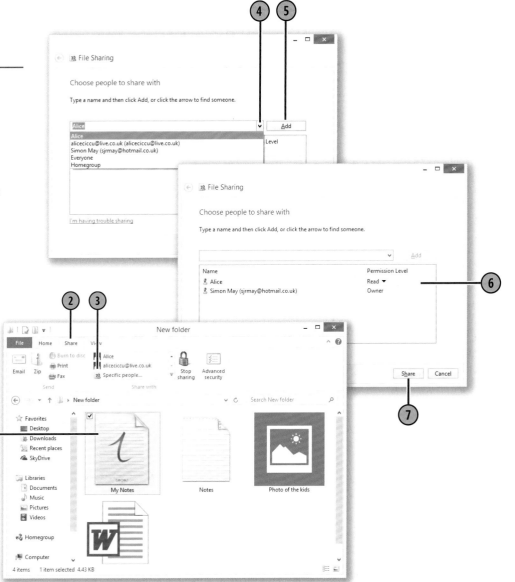

Changing How File Explorer Views Files

File Explorer can be used to view files and folders on your tablet, but the view might not always be what you need. You can change the view to reorder the items in a folder, make icons bigger, hide and unhide items, and much more. The view settings make it easier for you to identify the files and folders you're looking for.

Change View Settings

1 On the File Explorer ribbon, tap the View tab.

2 Tap Navigation Pane to turn the navigation pane on and off and to control what is shown in the navigation pane.

3 Tap to show the preview pane, with which you can preview the contents of the selected file without opening it.

4 Tap to show the details pane, which shows file details, such as size, date, and so on.

5 Tap to change the size of the icons in File Explorer and also the details of files and the window layout.

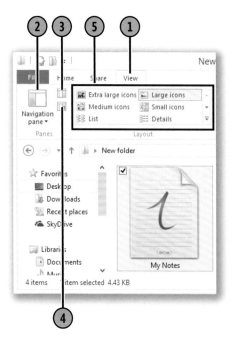

6 Tap to change how items are displayed.

7 Tap to change how many columns are displayed in detail views.

8 Tap to change how items are grouped.

9 Select the Item Check Boxes check box to enable multiple item check boxes in the upper left of each item in File Explorer.

10 Select the File Name Extensions check box to show or hide file extensions (the .jpg or .bmp extension at the end of a file name that indicates what type of file it is).

11 Tap to hide specific items from view or to unhide a hidden item if the Hidden Items check box is selected.

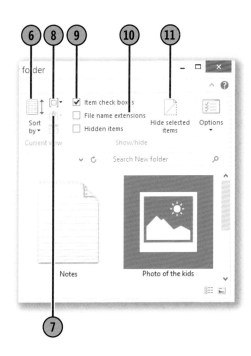

15

Connecting Your Tablet to TV and Display Devices

Tablet devices are fantastic for using on your own, but there comes a time where you want to share some of the fun you're having. For example, you might want to share the experience of watching a video, listening to music, or viewing your family photos with other people in the room. This is when it's handy to be able to connect to an extra display such as a TV, projector, or monitor.

Windows 8 provides the ability to do this in a couple of ways. PlayTo is technology built in to Windows 8 with which you can select some content on your tablet and then play it on another device, such as your TV. This functionality is available for videos, music, and photos in any app on your tablet that makes use of the functionality. Using PlayTo, it's even possible to do things like watch webpage videos on your TV.

Your tablet can also be connected to external displays either physically with a wire, or in some cases with technology proprietary to your tablet. When connected, you can use the extra display to either duplicate what you see on your tablet or to display an additional desktop on which to work.

Using PlayTo Devices

Your Windows 8 tablet is equipped with some very smart new technology to make it possible to play the content you have on your tablet on much larger screens. Using a standard called DLNA, your tablet can connect to a DLNA-compatible receiver and stream music, video, and pictures to that receiver. The content itself doesn't even need to be on your device; for example, you can use your tablet to stream a video that actually resides on another device in your homegroup. To determine the right type of device, look for the DLNA symbol; you'll find it on most Smart TVs.

If you don't have a compatible TV, you can turn any computer running Windows 7 or Windows 8 into a receiver by starting Windows Media Player on that computer. The aim of PlayTo is to make it easy to share your media beyond your tablet.

Discover PlayTo Devices

 Tap the Devices charm.

The Devices menu will list any devices on your network that are capable of receiving the content you'd like to share. If nothing is listed, either a receiver is not on the same network as your tablet or the receiver is unable to receive this type of content.

 Tap the device to connect to it.

③ When you're done enjoying the content on the target device, tap the Devices charm again, and then on the Devices menu, select the target and tap Disconnect.

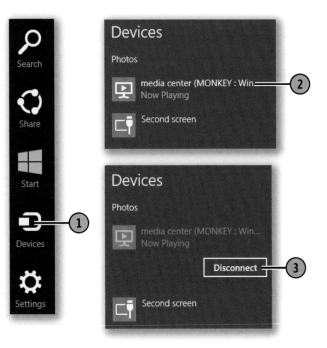

> **Tip**
>
> There are many different types of devices with which you can use PlayTo, including TVs, stereos, home cinema amplifiers, and digital photo frames.

Using PlayTo with Apps

Some of the apps that come with Windows are built for a great PlayTo experience and are a really good way to get accustomed to using and controlling PlayTo.

PlayTo with Videos

① While watching a video in the Video app, tap the Devices charm.

② Tap the device streams on which you want to watch the video; the video streams to that device and stops playing on your tablet.

③ The video controls are still available on your tablet. Tap the screen to use the playback controls just as you would if you were watching the video on your tablet.

See Also

I've shown PlayTo working with the video app here, but I briefly introduced using PlayTo with photos on page 328.

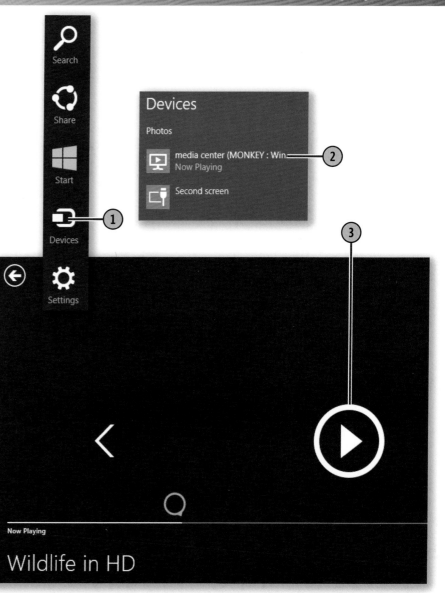

PlayTo with Internet Explorer

(1) While on a webpage in Internet Explorer 10, tap the Devices charm.

(2) Tap the device on which you'd like to play the content.

(3) Use the controls available for media playback for the content you're playing.

Devices

Photos

media center (MONKEY : Win... **(2)**
Now Playing

Second screen

Search

Share

Start

(1)

Devices

Settings

Tip

Not all webpage content can be sent to other devices; however, videos that use HTML5 always work, which includes videos on popular sites such as YouTube.

anning taskbar, and we wanted you to also have access to Metro style apps while you're also using the desktop. A
eloped, and as we see how developers might want to take advantage of multi-monitor configurations in new ways
d full screen apps, we will of course enhance this experience (and APIs) even further.

Building "Windows 8"
Enhancing Windows 8 for multiple monitors

00:00:04   ▮   00:02:25

Download this video to view it in your favorite media player:
High quality MP4 | Lower quality MP4

you enjoy these new multi-monitor features. Thank you for all of your feedback – it has certainly helped us to imp
we moved from Developer Preview, to Consumer Preview, and soon, to the Release Preview

(3)

Progress of play on
target device

Connecting Displays

Connecting your tablet to a TV or monitor is a simple process of plugging in the correct cable between the TV or monitor and the tablet. Windows will detect the new device and either extend or duplicate its display quickly. Duplicating a display means that what's shown on your tablet is exactly the same as what appears on the TV or monitor. Extending the display adds a second screen that you can use to run apps on, thus giving you more workspace. The downside to extending your screen is that you can't control the second screen with touch (unless it also has touch built in), so you'll need a mouse to make the most of this approach.

Your tablet is likely to have an HDMI, micro-HDMI, or mini-HDMI connector, but it could also have a VGA, DVI, or Display port adapter. The adapter might not be on your tablet but might be present only on the dock. Connectivity will vary by device, so check your device manual to see what you have.

Connect to a Display Device

① Tap the Devices charm.

② Tap Second Screen.

③ Tap a mode to use to connect.

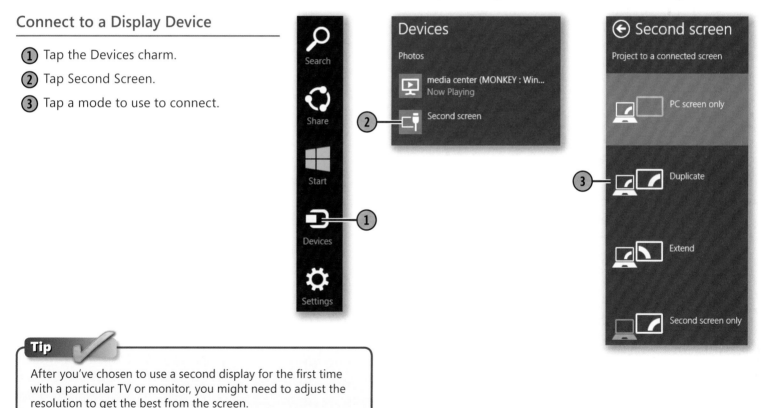

Tip

After you've chosen to use a second display for the first time with a particular TV or monitor, you might need to adjust the resolution to get the best from the screen.

Configure Resolution

1. Tap the Search charm and type **resolution** into the search box. If you're already on the Start screen, just type **resolution** and the search screen will open automatically.

2. Tap Settings to search within settings.

3. Tap Adjust Screen Resolution.

4. Tap the screen you want to change; it should be clear which is the TV or monitor and which is the tablet screen.

5. Tap the correct resolution; this might require some experimentation to get a resolution that looks just right.

6. Tap OK to apply and save the changes.

Tip

If you're unsure which screen is which, tap the Identify button; large numbers will be displayed on each screen to help you work it out.

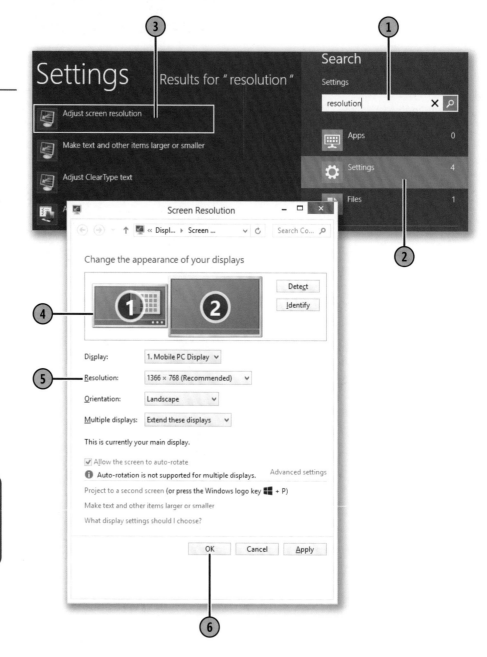

Duplicate Displays

1 Tap the Devices charm.

2 Tap Second Screen.

3 Tap Duplicate; the second screen will display the same images as your tablet.

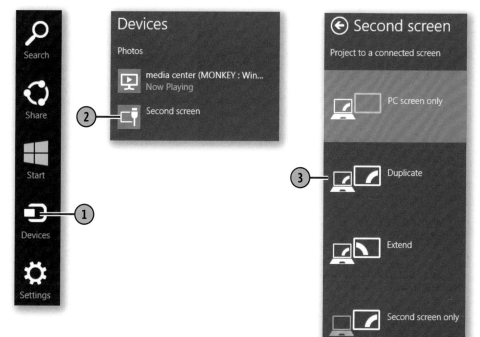

With duplicate screens both screens appear identical

Extend Displays

① Tap the Devices charm.

② Tap Second Screen.

③ Tap Extend; the second screen will display the desktop.

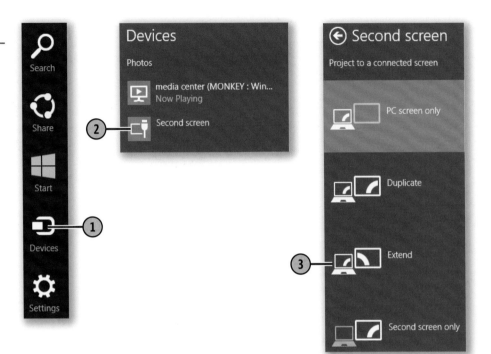

Tip ✓

On the Resolution Settings page, you can change which display shows the desktop by changing the Multiple Displays option to Show Desktop Only On X.

With extended screens, one screen always shows the desktop

Span a Background on Extended Displays

1. In the search box, type **background**.

2. Tap Settings to search settings.

3. Tap Change Desktop Background.

4. Tap the location of the picture you want to use.

5. Tap the picture position list, and select Span to have the wallpaper seamlessly span your displays

6. Tap Save Changes to have your wallpaper applied. If you sign in with a Microsoft Account, this change will ripple across all your Windows 8 devices in a few minutes.

Tip

To make the most of extended displays, you'll want a background image that is wider than it is high; the best images are twice the normal width of a monitor.

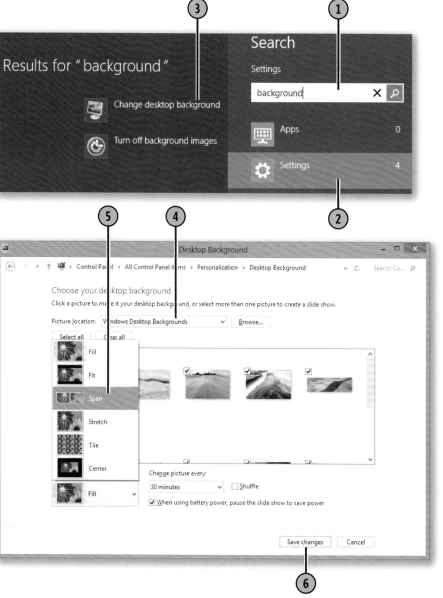

Decide Where the Start Screen and Desktop Appear

1. In the search box, type **resolution**.

2. Tap Settings to search within settings.

3. Tap Adjust Screen Resolution.

4. Tap Make This My Main Display to have the Start menu appear on the selected display.

   If the start menu is already on the selected display, this option will say This Is Currently Your Main Display.

5. Tap Multiple Displays, and select the option to Show Desktop Only On X to have the desktop stay on a specific screen. If you use a desktop app, it will open on this screen.

6. Tap OK to apply and save the changes.

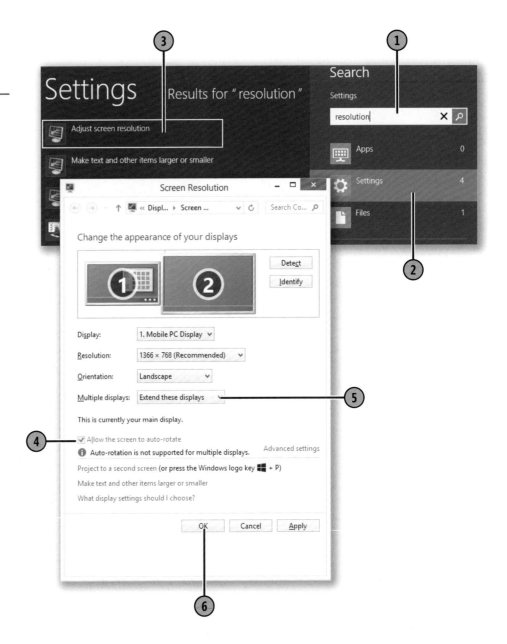

16

Connecting Printers and Devices

Your tablet comes equipped with a USB port so that you can add additional hardware to extend what your device can do. You can add almost any USB device, and you can be sure that any with the Windows 8 logo will be suitable for your tablet. This includes connecting to printers and scanners, adding a higher-quality or more versatile webcam, or connecting extra storage with USB flash drives and hard drives.

Printing is something that we all still need to do fairly regularly; it could be a report or document that you need to print, an email from a friend, or perhaps tickets to the theater that you ordered online. Printing is first class in Windows 8, and you can use the Devices charm to print from almost any app that creates a document. Controlling what happens with your printer is also important; you might need to change paper orientation or the quality of the document. If you print a lot or if other people in your homegroup want to print at the same time, you might need to control some aspects of the print queue (the list of documents waiting to print). Similarly, you might need some control if you get a paper jam or anything similar; Windows 8 provides controls to work with all these things.

Viewing Devices

With all the different devices you can attach to your tablet, you'll want to be able to see what's going on with them.

View Devices

1. On the Start screen, from the right edge of the screen, swipe your finger inward, and then tap the Settings charm.

2. Tap Change PC Settings.

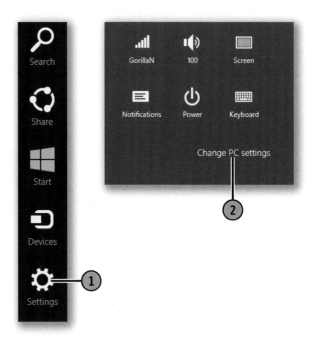

(3) Tap Devices; the right pane shows device options.

Currently attached devices

PC settings

Personalize

Users

Notifications

Search

Share

General

Privacy

Devices

Devices

+ Add a device

home (gibbon)

Kitchen

media center (MONKEY : Windows Media Player)

Microsoft XPS Document Writer

Download over metered connections

To help prevent extra charges, keep this off so device software (drivers, info, and apps) for new devices won't download while you're on metered Internet connections.

Off

(3) Prevent device drivers from downloading on metered connections

Adding Printers

Connecting printers to your tablet is a simple process. Normally, you just connect your printer to your tablet or its dock via a USB cable and Windows will do the rest for you. It will even obtain a driver from the Internet if necessary.

If your printer isn't added by Windows, the first step is to go to the website of your printer manufacturer and obtain the latest Windows 8–based drivers for your printer. These drivers normally come with an install program that will do all the setup work for you.

Add a Printer

① Turn the printer on and connect it to your tablet by using the USB cable supplied with the printer. The printer will begin to install immediately, but if Windows does not recognize the printer, it will prompt you for drivers that you'll need to obtain from the manufacturer's website.

Tip

If your printer isn't available when you insert the USB cable, you might need to use the Add A Printer Wizard to assist Windows in recognizing your printer. Tap the Search charm, tap Settings, and then search for **printers**. In the results pane, tap Devices And Printers and then tap the Add A Printer button. The wizard will guide you through the process of adding a printer.

Tip

Optionally, you can check that your printer is installed correctly by tapping the Search charm, tapping Settings, and then searching for **printers**. In the results pane, tap Devices And Printers. This window will list the printers you have installed.

② You can monitor the installation progress on the desktop. To do so, switch to the desktop, and then on the taskbar, tap the Device Setup icon

A progress window opens. When complete, the Device Setup progress window and icon disappears and the printer is ready to use.

Device Setup ✕

Installing HP Deskjet F4200 series

Please wait while Setup installs necessary files on your system. This may take several minutes.

Shows the install progress
of the printer

Add a Shared or Network Printer

① Tap the Search charm.

② Tap into the search box and enter **printer**.

③ Tap Settings to search within settings.

④ In the results area, tap Advanced Printer Setup.

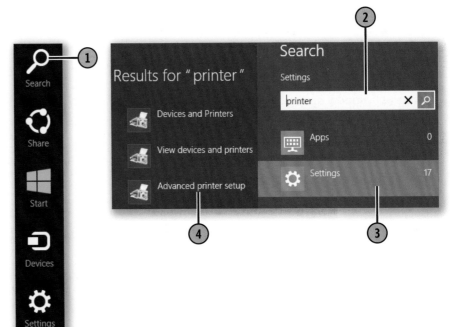

Tip

Printers shared by other computers in your homegroup will be added automatically to your computer, if they aren't, this same process can be used to find them.

Tip

If the printer isn't available on the Add Printer dialog box, follow the steps in the previous task.

(5) Tap the name of the printer to add in the list.

(6) If the printer isn't listed, ensure that both the printer and the computer it's connected to are connected to the network. Then, tap Search again.

(7) Tap Next.

The printer will be added, and if necessary, driver software will be downloaded from the computer sharing the printer with the network, which you are asked to trust. When complete, a confirmation page with the change displays. Print a test page to ensure that the printer works correctly.

⊗ 🖶 Add Printer

Searching for available printers...

Printer Name	Address
🖶 HP Deskjet F4200 series on GIBBON	\\GIBBON\HP Deskjet F4200 series

Stop

⇨ The printer that I want isn't listed

Next   Cancel

Share Printers with your Homegroup

① Tap the Settings charm.

② Tap Change PC Settings.

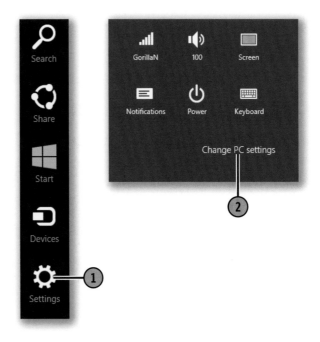

Tip

It's also possible to share individual printers; type **printers** into the Search box and search in the Settings panel, and then select Devices And Printers. From this view, locate the printer to share, tap and hold, and then in the pop-up menu that opens, tap Printer Properties. (Be sure not to select Properties, because this shows hardware settings for the printer.) Finally, tap the Sharing tab to configure sharing settings.

③ Scroll down and select HomeGroup.

④ Tap the switch for Printers And Devices to move it to Shared.

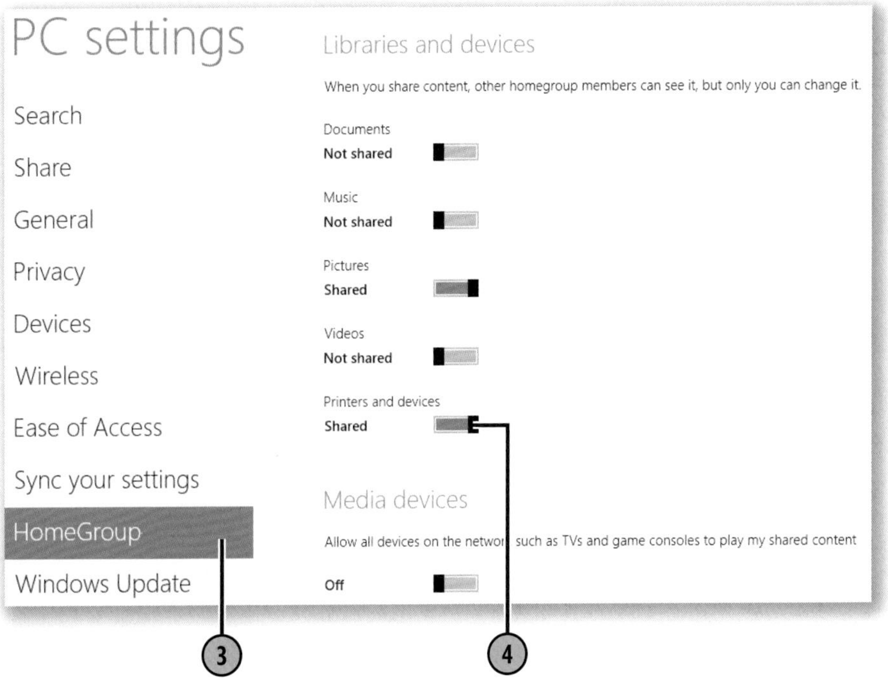

PC settings

Search

Share

General

Privacy

Devices

Wireless

Ease of Access

Sync your settings

HomeGroup

Windows Update

Libraries and devices

When you share content, other homegroup members can see it, but only you can change it.

Documents
Not shared

Music
Not shared

Pictures
Shared

Videos
Not shared

Printers and devices
Shared

Media devices

Allow all devices on the network such as TVs and game consoles to play my shared content

Off

Printing from an App

Printing can be done from any app that enables the facility on your Windows 8–based tablet from the Devices charm.

Print an Email

1. Open the document that you want to print (in this case, email).

2. In the Settings panel, tap Devices.

3. Tap the name of the printer you want to use.

   Note that you must have set up your printer in advance.

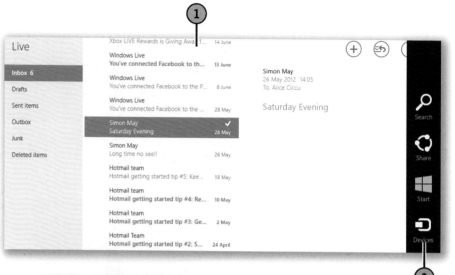

Tip

Some printers have additional printing options, such as paper tray select or the use of duplex printing. These settings will be made available through this print menu.

4 A print preview will be displayed. Optionally, tap to change the current page orientation in which you want to print.

5 Optionally, tap to select the paper size you want to print.

6 Tap Print to send the email to your printer.

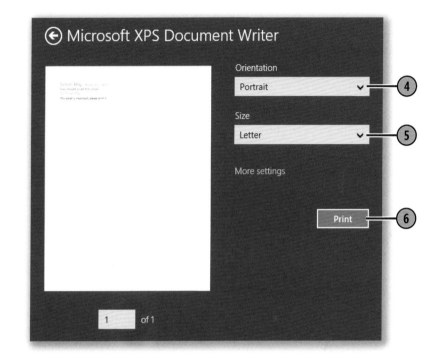

← Microsoft XPS Document Writer

Orientation

Portrait ⌄ — **4**

Size

Letter ⌄ — **5**

More settings

Print — **6**

1 of 1

 Tip

Windows 8 includes the Microsoft XPS Document Writer, which is a special printer that allows you to print to a file (XPS format) rather than to a sheet of paper. This is great if you're mobile and don't have access to a real printer, because you can later print those XPS files to a real printer when you have access to one. To do this, select the Microsoft XPS Document Writer and tap Print. An XPS document is saved to your Documents folder, which you can then open by using the Reader App and print the file as you would any other, by using the Devices charm.

Managing Printers

When you tap Print, your document goes into a queue, and if multiple people are sharing a printer, such as when it's shared by using HomeGroup, everyone shares the queue, too. This allows the printer to produce everyone's documents in turn. You might need to view this queue to understand when your document will print, and you might need to do things such as pause a job to change the paper, restart a job that has gone wrong in some way, or cancel a job that you don't want to print. It's also possible to change preferences, such as the orientation of the page.

See What's Printing

① Tap the Search charm.

② Type **print** into the search box.

③ Tap Settings to search for print settings.

④ In the results area, tap View Devices And Printers.

⑤ Tap and hold the printer for which you want to view the job queue.

⑥ In the options panel that opens, tap See What's Printing.

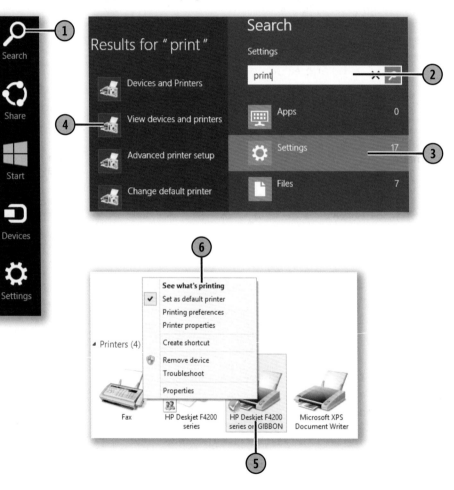

Change Printing Preferences

1 When viewing the print queue, tap Printer.

2 Tap Printing Preferences. The subsequent dialog will allow you to configure preferences for your printer. The specific preferences available will differ printer by printer. Some will allow you to set paper types, print quality, the use of color, and other technologies specific to your printer.

3 Tap OK to save any change you've made.

Tip ✓

The printer used in the images on this page, the Microsoft XPS Document Writer, allows you to print any document to a file rather than to paper. This is especially useful if you're on the move and need to print something but don't have a printer attached. The XPS Document Writer can print to XPS or PDF files, both of which allow for perfect reprints at a later stage, using the Reader app.

Tip ✓

Printing Preferences is usually the place to access tools such as print head cleaning and alignment, for when you change cartridges or refill ink.

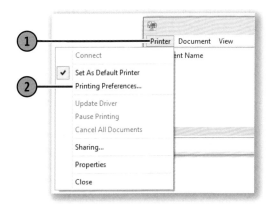

Each type of setting has its own tab

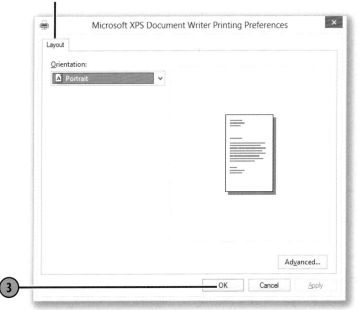

Restart, Cancel, or Pause a Document

1 In the print queue, tap and hold a document you've sent to print from an app.

2 In the options panel that opens, tap Pause to temporarily stop printing. To resume, tap and hold the document again; this time, the option panel displays Resume instead of Pause.

3 Tap Restart to restart a job if something went wrong—for example, if you've had and cleared a paper jam.

4 Tap Cancel to remove the document from the print list before it prints.

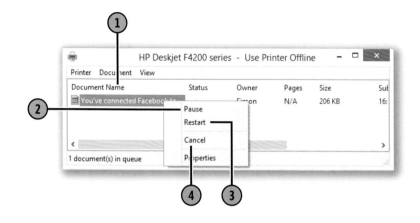

Tip ✓

If you tap Properties, you can access the Printing Preferences for the particular document and thus change the paper type, ink, or any other settings your printer makes available.

Adding a Webcam

Your tablet almost certainly comes with a built-in webcam, but you might want to add a higher-quality external webcam if you dock your tablet with a larger screen so that you can make the most of video calling.

Most webcams install by just inserting its USB connection into your tablet. However, sometimes you'll need to download and run some software from the manufacturer. If you do, follow their installation instructions.

For most webcams, start by inserting the USB cable.

Add a Webcam

① Tap the Settings charm.

② Tap Change PC Settings.

③ Tap Devices.

④ Find your new webcam in the list. There might be some additional steps listed, such as a restart of your tablet.

Tip
You can easily test a webcam in the Camera app to make sure it works.

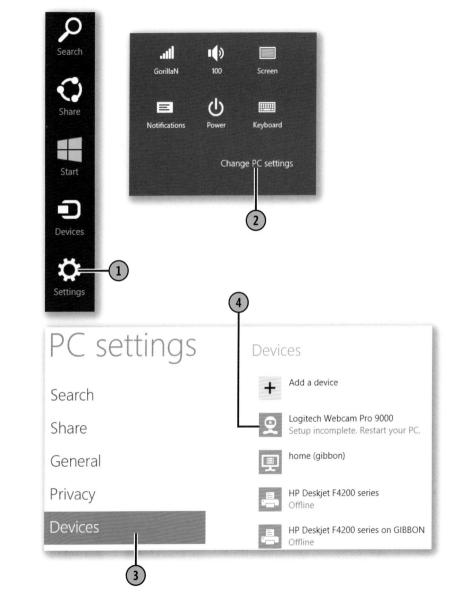

Connecting to Bluetooth Devices

Bluetooth is a wireless way to connect devices to your tablet. It's commonly used with Bluetooth headsets, speakers, and smartphones. There are many things you can do with a Bluetooth connection, including transferring files and making use of audio capabilities.

Connect Bluetooth Devices

1. In the Settings panel, tap the Change PC Settings link, and scroll down to select Devices.

2. Tap Add A Device.

PC settings

Personalize

Users

Notifications

Search

Share

General

Privacy

Devices

Devices

Add a device

DMA2200 (j7jrmhtvrl10)
Offline

Generic PnP Monitor

Kitchen

Lenovo Enhanced USB Port Replicator

LifeCam Cinema

LifeCam Cinema

LifeCam Cinema

③ Wait for your Bluetooth device to be detected; ensure that the Bluetooth device you want to connect is on and set to pairing mode. (You might need to consult the device manual.) When detected, select the device.

④ Depending on the pairing type, you are presented with a code to match with that of your device or you are asked to provide a code for your device. Follow the on-screen instructions to complete the pairing.

Select a device

NOKIA Lumia 800
Phone

Not finding what you are looking for?

Compare the passcodes

Do this passcode and the one on your NOKIA Lumia 800 match?

860092

| Yes | No | Cancel |

Adding a Scanner

You can use scanners to create high-quality digital copies of photos or document pages. Most modern scanners connect to computers by using USB connections. It's quite rare to find a scanner that can be remotely accessed over a network (although they do exist and your tablet can support them). Getting a scanner or camera to work with your tablet should be as simple as connecting it with the USB cable; from there, Windows will attempt to make it work. You might find that you need to take one or two extra steps to make it work if Windows doesn't automatically configure it.

Connecting a digital camera can work in much the same way. However, by default, most digital cameras can also be used like USB hard disks.

Add a Scanner or Camera

① Turn on the scanner and connect it to your tablet by using the USB cable.

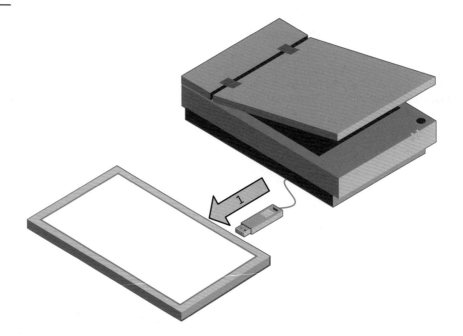

② Windows will begin to install the scanner.

If Windows encounters a problem, such as driver software not being available, it switches to the desktop to ask you for assistance. If this happens, you will need to obtain the driver software for the scanner from the manufacturer. Windows will attempt to do this for you, and just like adding a printer, you can view the status of the install by switching to the desktop and tapping the Device Setup icon on the taskbar. When completely installed, the Device Setup window and taskbar icon will disappear.

②

Device Setup

Installing HP Deskjet F4200 series

Please wait while Setup installs necessary files on your system. This may take several minutes.

Shows the install progress
of the printer

Tip

Many multifunction printers include a scanner; this will be installed by Windows at the same time as the printer is installed.

Tip

If your scanner doesn't install automatically, you can add it manually. Type **scanners and cameras** into the Search box, search within Settings, select View Scanners And Cameras, and then tap the Add A Device button to begin the wizard to add a scanner.

Tip

Scanners, unlike printers, do not show up within the Devices charm. To scan a document, the best option is to use the software that came with your scanner because the manufacturer will have enabled all of its advanced functions through this software. However, if you don't have access to this, you can scan from the Windows Fax And Scan app; just tap the Search charm and type **scan** into the search box.

Adding Hard Disks and USB Flash Drives

Transferring documents and files around on USB flash drives has become second nature to many of us, especially as they've become more and more cost-effective. The same is true of USB hard disks; they're very handy for backup purposes or for storing large amounts of data.

You can plug a USB flash drive or hard disk into your tablet by using the USB port; Windows will just recognize it and get on with the process of making it available to you.

In the past, removing a USB flash drive or hard disk required you to "eject" the drive first. This was to make sure that all your data had been written to the drive to prevent corruption of that data. This is no longer the case. Your tablet will see that a USB drive is being used and will prevent corruption if you just pull the drive out. However, keep in mind that it's still a good idea to avoid removing a flash drive while files are being written to it. (Usually, you'll see a flashing light that indicates this.)

When you insert a USB flash drive or hard disk into your device, Windows applies a default action to it. This will be either to use it as a backup device or to open File Explorer. If you've not yet set a default action, a notification will appear each time a drive is inserted.

Change What Happens by Default to Removable Drives from the Notification

(1) Insert a USB drive and tap the notification if it appears.

(2) Tap Configure This Drive For Backup to have Windows back up to the drive when it's inserted.

(3) Tap Open Folder To View Files to instruct Windows to open File Explorer each time a USB storage device is inserted.

(4) Tap Take No Action to instruct Windows to do nothing for you when you insert a USB storage device.

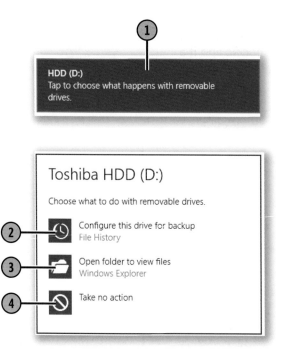

Change What Happens When You Plug In Storage

① Tap the Search charm.

② In the search box, enter **autoplay**.

③ Tap Settings.

④ In the results area, tap AutoPlay.

⑤ Under Removable Drive, tap the drop-down menu to change the default action for removable storage devices.

⑥ Optionally, you can choose to have Windows open a specific app if a specific type of media is found on the removable device.

⑦ For each type of media, select the app you want to use for opening that type of media.

⑧ Tap Save to apply the changes.

Tip

Options for other removable media for cameras, such as SD and microSD cards, are managed in this exact same way.

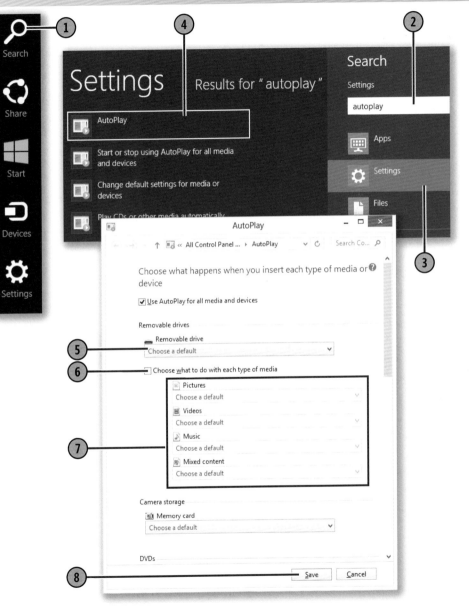

Removing Devices

When you disconnect a device from your tablet, there's a strong chance that you'll want to use that device with your tablet again, so Windows remembers the device. Sometimes, you'll want to disconnect a device permanently, perhaps because you no longer own it, or you might want to remove it for troubleshooting purposes. When you remove a device, Windows forgets about the device and removes the driver software associated with it. If the device is ever connected again, the device driver software has to be added again, although this normally will happen automatically.

Remove a Device

① Tap the Settings charm.

② Tap Change PC Settings.

③ Tap Devices.

④ Tap the device you want to remove.

⑤ Tap the minus sign to the right of the device's listing.

⑥ Tap the Remove button to remove the device.

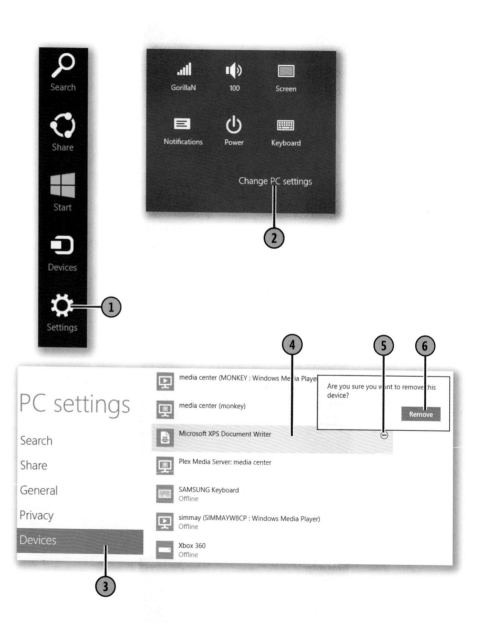

Renaming Devices

Some devices can be renamed to make it easier for you to identify them. A good example is a PlayTo compatible TV. The TV will initially have a generic name, such as the TV model number, but it might make more sense for the TV to be named "Family Room TV" if it's in the family room.

Rename a Device

① Tap the Settings charm.

② Tap Change PC Settings.

③ Tap Devices.

④ Tap the device for which you want to change the name.

If the device can be renamed, the name will change to a text box that can be edited and the keyboard will appear if required.

⑤ Tap the device's name, enter your new name, and then tap anywhere else on screen to make the change.

17

Fixing Common Problems

Your tablet will inevitably experience some problem (or two) over the course of its life. However, there are excellent tools built into Windows 8–based tablets to help you overcome any such problems, whether they are lost files, malware infection, missing device software, or lack of Internet connectivity. In this section, we'll take a look at how Windows tells you that something might not be quite right with your tablet by using Action Center.

Lots of technical knowledge isn't required when troubleshooting issues with Windows 8 because there are a number of very capable automatic troubleshooters built in. These troubleshooters help to solve common problems, such as an inability for the tablet to print, and should be your first ports of call. If all else fails, you might need to revert your tablet back to a time when you know it was working properly. There are simple ways to restore, refresh, and reset your Windows 8–based tablet, depending on the type of problem you're trying to solve.

Knowing When Something Is Wrong

Action Center is a part of Windows that keeps track of the health of your tablet, warning you if you need to apply Windows Updates, if your anti-malware is out of date, or if you're at risk because it's a been a while since a scan ran. Action Center notifies you if you haven't trusted your computer to sync password updates; it also monitors devices in case there's a problem. It's the place to go to find information about problems and to fix them with recovery and troubleshooting options.

Notifications

1 If Action Center has something to tell you, a flag notification icon will appear on the desktop. Tap the flag icon to view more details.

2 The options that appear are actions resulting from specific alerts that Action Center wants to notify you of; tap an action to jump directly to that problem.

3 Tap Open Action Center to view much more detail about the issue.

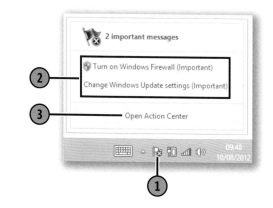

Tip

The flag icon for Action Center will sometimes appear with a warning sign or red X over it. This is normal and indicates the severity of the information that Action Center wants to convey. A red X is most important, a warning sign (exclamation mark) is less urgent, and no overlay means that the Action Center notifications are for information only.

Open Action Center from the Start Screen

1. Tap the Search charm.
2. Type **action** in the search box.
3. Tap Settings.
4. Tap Action Center.

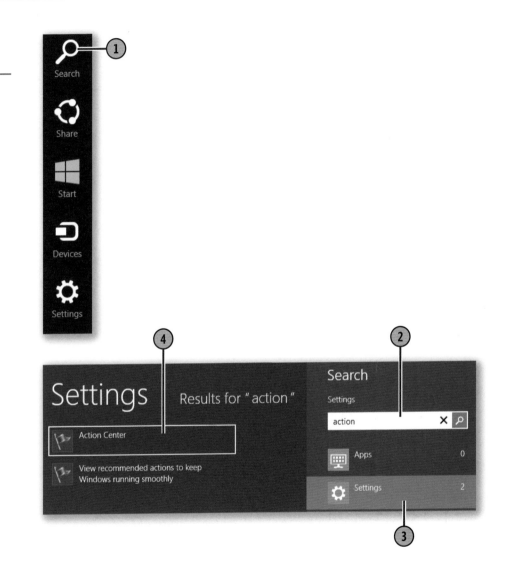

Understanding Action Center

Action Center is the go-to place for understanding the health of your tablet. It displays security and maintenance alerts.

Action pane to allow fast access to settings

Windows Update appears because it's not set to automatically update the tablet and so highlights user actions

Red notifications tell you that the notification represents a potential danger to your tablet

Fast access to automatic troubleshooting

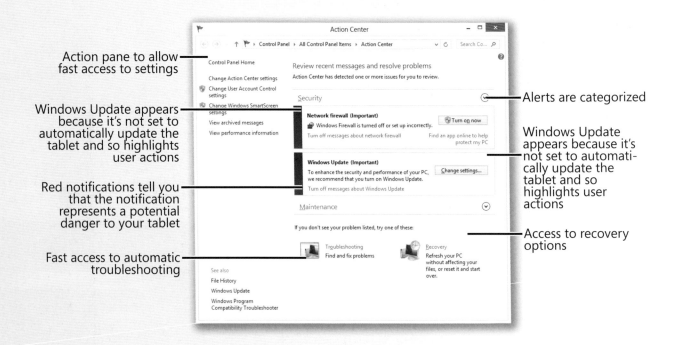

Alerts are categorized

Windows Update appears because it's not set to automatically update the tablet and so highlights user actions

Access to recovery options

Changing Action Center Settings

Although Action Center is the default place for information about problems to be reported, you can turn off reporting of specific types of problems.

Enable and Disable Problems Action Center Reports

(1) In Action Center, in the action list, tap Change Action Center Settings.

(2) Select any items to enable reporting of problems in that area. By default, all items are checked.

(3) Tap a link under Related Settings to open related Control Panel items such as Windows Update.

(4) Tap OK to make the changes.

A User Account Control confirmation will appear. All changes to UAC prompt for UAC permission, to prevent security issues.

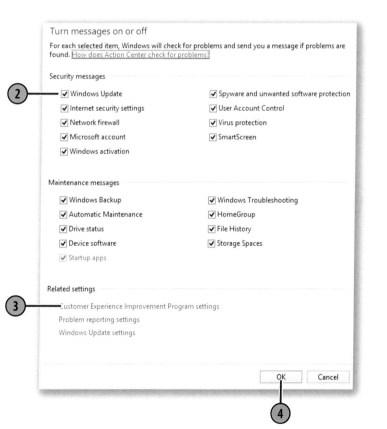

Understanding User Account Control

User Account Control (UAC) is a Windows feature that makes it hard for you to make accidental changes to your tablet and makes it harder for malware to make malicious changes. Each time you need to do something that requires "administrative" access to your tablet, a dialog box appears asking you to either confirm or enter an administrator user name and password. The screen shots on this page show you what messages to look for when using User Account Control.

This type of User Account Control box appears if you are an Administrator and requires you to confirm the request

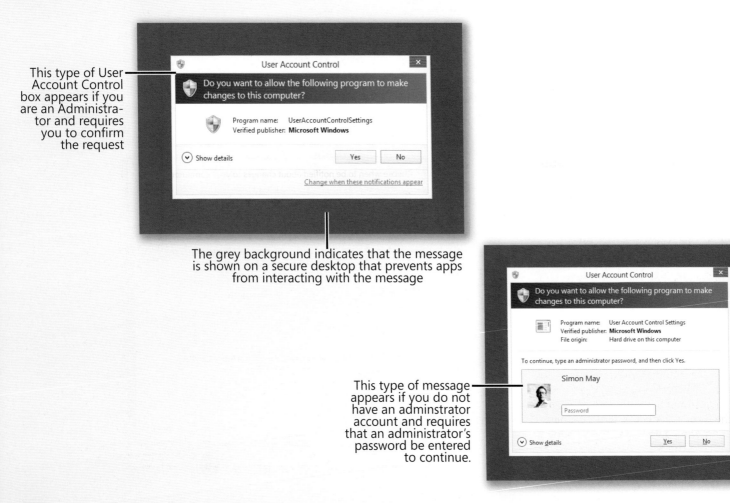

The grey background indicates that the message is shown on a secure desktop that prevents apps from interacting with the message

This type of message appears if you do not have an adminstrator account and requires that an administrator's password be entered to continue.

Adjusting User Account Control Settings

Some people find User Account Control to be too "chatty" for their needs or not quite secure enough in its default state, so it's possible to use Action Center to adjust those settings.

Change User Account Control Settings

① Display the Action Center, and tap Change User Account Control Settings.

② Tap and drag the slider to the level of control you want.

Higher levels notify more, and lower levels notify less. There are four levels: the highest notifies you when apps and you both want to make changes; the next notifies you when only apps want to make changes; the next also notifies you when only apps want to make changes but run in a faster but less secure way; and finally, all notifications are off.

③ Tap OK to save the changes.

Tip

If you see a UAC prompt when you're doing something where you don't expect to need an administrator account (such as browsing the web), think twice before tapping OK or entering details, and use Windows Defender to run an anti-malware scan. Malware might have infected your tablet.

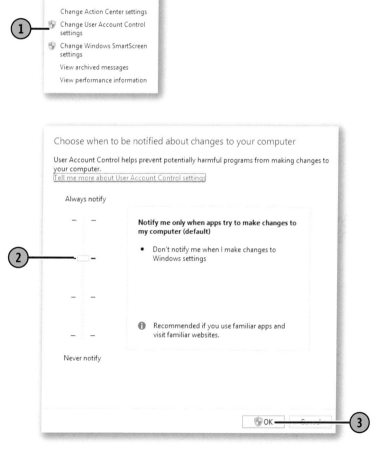

Assessing How Well Your Tablet Can Perform

The performance of your tablet should be pretty good for what you need it for, but it might have one or two weaker points, and if you want to do upgrades, knowing what to upgrade to improve performance is a must. Windows includes a tool for rating your tablet's performance and the performance of its subsystems so that you know what to upgrade.

View Performance Ratings

① In Action Center, tap View Performance Information.

② Tap Rate This Computer if no performance information is displayed, or to update the assessment (such as following an upgrade), tap Re-Run The Assessment.

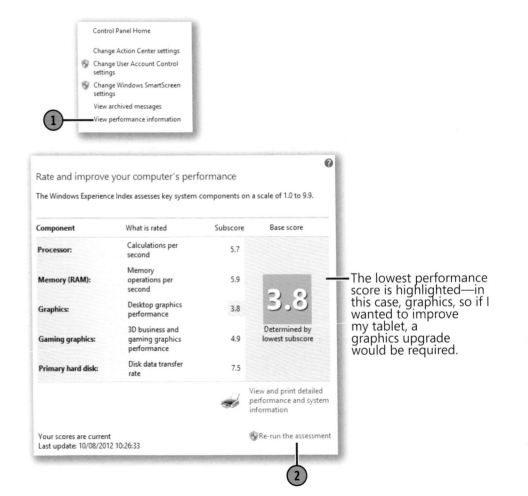

The lowest performance score is highlighted—in this case, graphics, so if I wanted to improve my tablet, a graphics upgrade would be required.

Tip

Tablets are notoriously hard to upgrade, and sometimes it's impossible without voiding the warranty because they include so many custom-built components. However, sometimes it's possible to upgrade the memory and hard disks.

Access Advanced Performance Tools

① Select Advanced Tools from the menu in the left pane.

② If you have any problems that Windows believes are impacting your tablet's performance, there will be an alert here. Tap the alert for more information.

③ Tap Clear All Windows Experience Index Scores and Re-Rate The System to retest your Windows Experience score. This is especially useful if you've upgraded recently.

④ Tap View Performance Details in Event Log to view a detailed log about what may be impacting performance.

⑤ Tap Open Performance Monitor to open a tool that allows you to monitor your performance over time.

⑥ Tap Open Resource Monitor for a tool that allows you to view instance resource use on your tablet.

⑦ Tap Open Disk Defragmenter to recombine all the data on your disk in a way that should make disk access faster.

Caution

Don't run Disk Defragmenter on a Solid State drive, as this will diminish its lifespan.

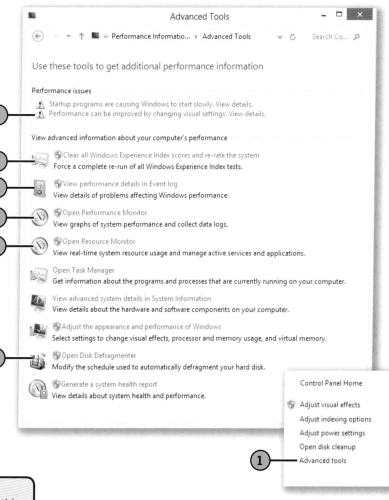

Viewing Real-Time Performance

If you want to know how your tablet is performing right this second you can use the built-in performance monitoring of a tool called Task Manager. Unlike the performance reporting tool in Action Center, Task Manager is designed for understanding how much of your system resources an app is using. This is an advanced area and requires some very deep understanding of what's happening to get the best performance. Typically if resources are reaching near 100% usage it explains slowdowns but there can be many other reasons. If you're experiencing slowdowns, troubleshooting might be a better approach.

View Performance in Task Manager

1 Tap the Search charm.

2 Enter **task** into the search box.

3 Tap Task Manager.

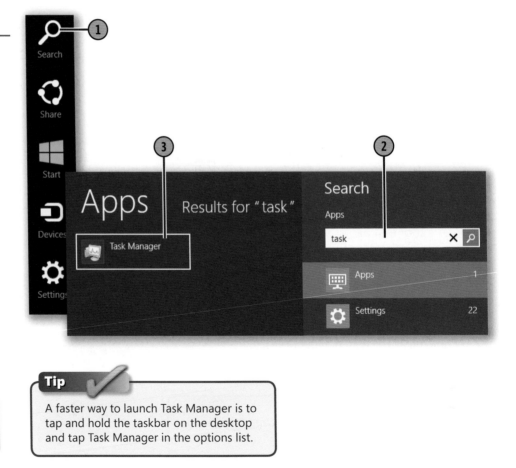

Tip

Task Manager can be used for much more than just viewing the current performance of your tablet. You can use the Processes tab to end apps that have, for some reason, become unresponsive. The App History tab gives you a view on the resources that your open Windows 8 apps have consumed—remember, though, that it's fine to have many "running" as they enter special sleep states. The Startup tab gives you control over what starts when your tablet does—this is a great place to look if your tablet slows down.

Tip

A faster way to launch Task Manager is to tap and hold the taskbar on the desktop and tap Task Manager in the options list.

The graphs show real-time performance of your tablet in each area over the last 60 seconds

(4) Tap More Details.

(5) Tap the Performance tab.

(6) Tap any other system resource to view that resource's utilization.

(7) Tap Open Resource Monitor if you want a very deep view of what's going on.

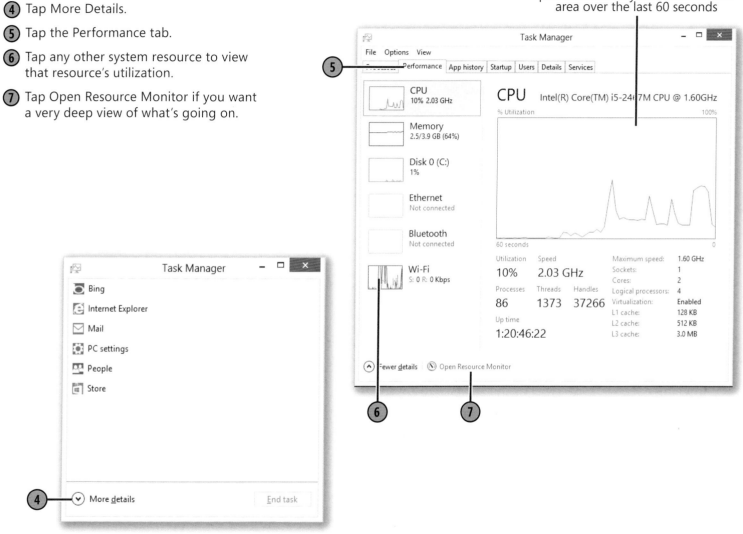

Troubleshooting Problems Automatically

If you've ever used a PC, you will have almost certainly had some sort of problem, and these problems can be very tricky to fix. It could be that you've lost access to the Internet; that your printer has stopped printing; that you can't hear sound from your computer; or that you have an app that ran on a previous version of Windows but won't run on your new tablet. Your

Windows 8–based tablet includes built-in troubleshooting to help resolve some of these very same issues. In the next few pages, we'll take a look at running the Program Compatibility Troubleshooter so that you can understand the process for running all troubleshooters.

Start Troubleshooting

1. In Action Center, tap Troubleshooting at the bottom of the window.

2. Tap the type of problem you want help with; each will list a variety of troubleshooters.

Tip ✓

Another way to get to the troubleshooters is to search for "trouble," using the Settings search box.

If you don't see your problem listed, try one of these:

Troubleshooting
Find and fix problems

Recovery
Refresh your PC without affecting your files, or reset it and start over.

Troubleshooting

← → ↑ ▸ Control Panel ▸ All Control Panel Items ▸ Troubleshooting   ∨ Ç   Search Tro... ₽

Control Panel Home

View all

View history

Change settings

Get help from a friend

Troubleshoot computer problems

Click on a task to automatically troubleshoot and fix common computer problems. To view more troubleshooters, click on a category or use the Search box.

Programs
Run programs made for previous versions of Windows

Hardware and Sound
Configure a device | Use a printer | Troubleshoot audio recording
Troubleshoot audio playback

Network and Internet
Connect to the Internet | Access shared files and folders on other computers

System and Security
Fix problems with Windows Update | Run maintenance tasks
Improve power usage

See also

Action Center

Help and Support

Recovery

Run Old Apps

(1) From the Program Troubleshooting page of the Troubleshooting tool, tap Program Compatibility Troubleshooter.

(2) On the Welcome screen of the troubleshooter, tap Next.

(3) Tap the app you want to troubleshoot. If it's not listed, tap Not Listed; after step 4, the wizard will let you browse to the location of the app on your tablet.

(4) Tap Next with the app selected.

Programs

(1) Program Compatibility Troubleshooter
Find and fix problems with running older programs on this version of Windows.

Program Compatibility Troubleshooter

Troubleshoot and help prevent computer problems

Program Compatibility Troubleshooter
Find and fix problems with running older programs on this version of Windows.

Advanced

Publisher: Microsoft Corporation
Privacy statement

Next   Cancel

(2)

Program Compatibility Troubleshooter

Select the program you're having problems with

If you don't see your program, select Not Listed to browse to the program file

(3)

Not Listed
Access 2013
Database Compare 2013
Digital Certificate for VBA Projects
Excel 2013
InfoPath Designer 2013
Intel(R) WiDi
Lync 2013
Lync Recording Manager
Mouse without Borders
Movie Maker
MyDi

C:\Program Files (x86)\Edge

(4)   Next   Cancel

5 Tap either Try Recommended Settings, to have Windows use recommended compatibility settings to help you run your app, or Troubleshoot Program to provide specifics about how the app runs. If you select Try Recommended Settings, skip to step 8.

6 Select the problems you notice, and the wizard will ask you how you've seen the app run and about any error messages it's shown you. For example, if you select the first option, you'll be asked what previous version of Windows you've run the app on.

7 Tap Next to continue, and provide details about how the app runs.

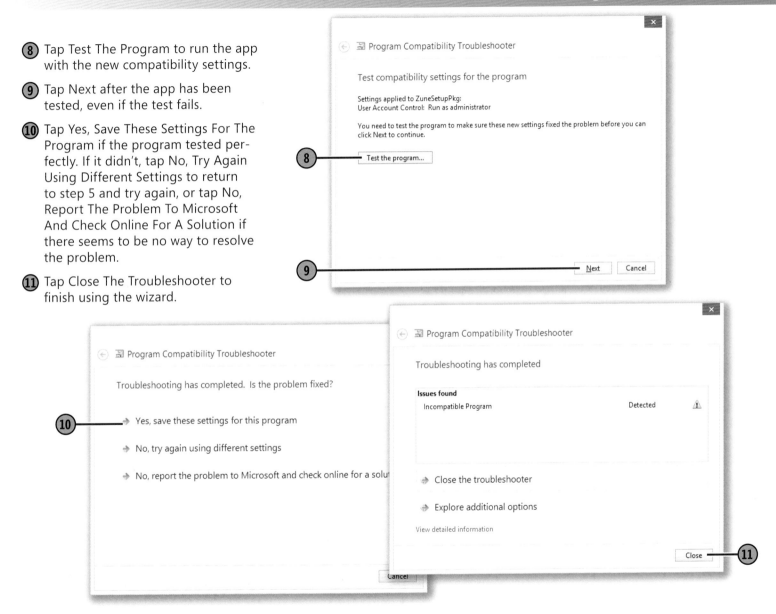

8 Tap Test The Program to run the app with the new compatibility settings.

9 Tap Next after the app has been tested, even if the test fails.

10 Tap Yes, Save These Settings For The Program if the program tested perfectly. If it didn't, tap No, Try Again Using Different Settings to return to step 5 and try again, or tap No, Report The Problem To Microsoft And Check Online For A Solution if there seems to be no way to resolve the problem.

11 Tap Close The Troubleshooter to finish using the wizard.

Program Compatibility Troubleshooter

Test compatibility settings for the program

Settings applied to ZuneSetupPkg:
User Account Control: Run as administrator

You need to test the program to make sure these new settings fixed the problem before you can click Next to continue.

Test the program...

Next   Cancel

Program Compatibility Troubleshooter

Troubleshooting has completed. Is the problem fixed?

→ Yes, save these settings for this program

→ No, try again using different settings

→ No, report the problem to Microsoft and check online for a solut

Cancel

Program Compatibility Troubleshooter

Troubleshooting has completed

Issues found

Incompatible Program   Detected   ⚠

→ Close the troubleshooter

→ Explore additional options

View detailed information

Close

Using Automatic Troubleshooters

The following table lists the automatic troubleshooting tasks available on your Windows 8–based tablet. (Note that some might not be available, depending on the Windows 8 edition you're running on your tablet.)

Problems Solved	Name	Location
Find and fix problems with connecting to the Internet or to websites	Internet Connections	Control Panel\All Control Panel Items\ Troubleshooting\Programs
Find and fix problems with Internet Explorer performance	Internet Explorer Performance	Control Panel\All Control Panel Items\ Troubleshooting\Programs
Find and fix problems with security and privacy features in Internet Explorer	Internet Explorer Safety	Control Panel\All Control Panel Items\ Troubleshooting\Programs
Find and fix problems with running older programs	Program and Compatibility Troubleshooter	Control Panel\All Control Panel Items\ Troubleshooting\Programs
Find and fix problems with printing	Printer	Control Panel\All Control Panel Items\ Troubleshooting\Programs
Find and fix problems with Windows Media Player settings	Windows Media Player Settings	Control Panel\All Control Panel Items\ Troubleshooting\Programs
Find and fix problems with the Windows Media Player Library	Windows Media Player Library	Control Panel\All Control Panel Items\ Troubleshooting\Programs
Find and fix problems with playing DVDs in Windows Media Player	Windows Media Player DVD	Control Panel\All Control Panel Items\ Troubleshooting\Programs
Find and fix problems with playing sound	Playing Audio	Control Panel\All Control Panel Items\ Troubleshooting\Hardware and Sound
Find and fix problems with recording audio	Recording Audio	Control Panel\All Control Panel Items\ Troubleshooting\Hardware and Sound
Find and fix problems with devices and hardware	Hardware and Devices	Control Panel\All Control Panel Items\ Troubleshooting\Hardware and Sound
Find and fix problems with wireless and other network adapters	Network Adapter	Control Panel\All Control Panel Items\ Troubleshooting\Hardware and Sound

Problems Solved	Name	Location
Find and fix problems with accessing files and folders on other computers	Shared Folders	Control Panel\All Control Panel Items\ Troubleshooting\Hardware and Sound
Find and fix problems with viewing computers or files shared using HomeGroup	HomeGroup	Control Panel\All Control Panel Items\ Troubleshooting\Hardware and Sound
Find and fix problems with incoming computer connections and Windows Firewall	Incoming Connections	Control Panel\All Control Panel Items\ Troubleshooting\Hardware and Sound
Find and clean up unused files and shortcuts, and perform maintenance tasks	System Maintenance	Control Panel\All Control Panel Items\ Troubleshooting\Hardware and Sound
Find and fix problems with your computer's power settings to conserve power and extend battery life	Power	Control Panel\All Control Panel Items\ Troubleshooting\Hardware and Sound
Find and fix problems with Windows Search	Search and Indexing	Control Panel\All Control Panel Items\ Troubleshooting\Hardware and Sound
Resolve problems that prevent you from updating Windows	Windows Update	Control Panel\All Control Panel Items\ Troubleshooting\Hardware and Sound

Tip ✓

An easy way to find help with a problem is to just type it into the search box. For example, if you have a problem with the Internet, typing **internet problem** into the search box will reveal the Internet Connections troubleshooter, or typing **hardware** will reveal the Find And Fix Problems With Devices troubleshooter.

Refreshing Your Tablet

If you start to encounter problems with your tablet, there are a couple of ways you can try to get it back to a more pleasing state. Using troubleshooters to resolve specific problems is the first step, but if that doesn't work, you have the option of doing a refresh, which retains your files (photos, music, videos, documents, and other personal files) but removes everything else. Apps not installed from the Windows Store are also removed, so you know that only verified software is on your tablet and you have some reassurance that any such software (which could include malware) has been removed.

Refresh

① Tap the Settings charm.

② Tap Change PC Settings.

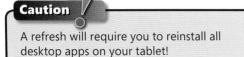

Caution

A refresh will require you to reinstall all desktop apps on your tablet!

Tip

On the desktop you can find a file called Removed Apps that lists all the apps that were removed and couldn't be reinstalled during refresh. Some will have links to websites that you can download the software from again.

(3) Tap the General category.

(4) Scroll down to Refresh Your PC Without Affecting Your Files.

(5) Tap Get Started.

(6) Tap Next after you've reviewed what will happen during a refresh.

(7) Tap Refresh to begin the refresh process.

Your tablet restarts and begins to refresh, showing you the percentage it's completed as it does so. When the process is complete, log in to your tablet normally.

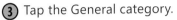

Ensure that you have the license keys for any software you need before you refresh your tablet, if you don't and it's removed during refresh, you might never be able to use the software again.

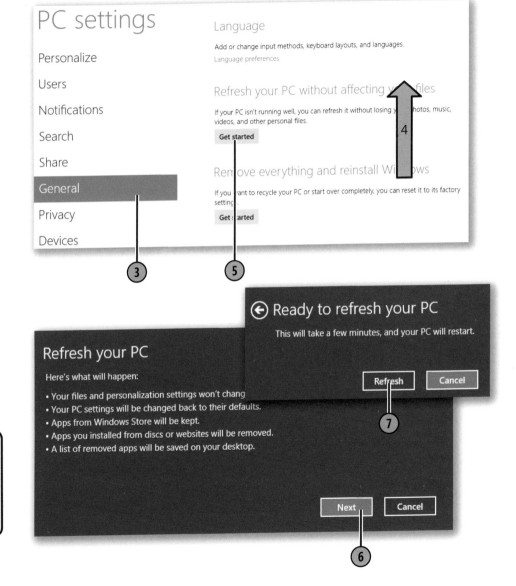

PC settings

Personalize

Users

Notifications

Search

Share

General

Privacy

Devices

Language
Add or change input methods, keyboard layouts, and languages.
Language preferences

Refresh your PC without affecting your files
If your PC isn't running well, you can refresh it without losing your photos, music, videos, and other personal files.
Get started

Remove everything and reinstall Windows
If you want to recycle your PC or start over completely, you can reset it to its factory settings.
Get started

(3) (5) (4)

Refresh your PC

Here's what will happen:

• Your files and personalization settings won't change.
• Your PC settings will be changed back to their defaults.
• Apps from Windows Store will be kept.
• Apps you installed from discs or websites will be removed.
• A list of removed apps will be saved on your desktop.

Next   Cancel

(6)

(←) Ready to refresh your PC
This will take a few minutes, and your PC will restart.

Refresh   Cancel

(7)

Resetting Your Tablet

Resetting your tablet will completely remove all software, all your files, and reinstall Windows. It will be as if your tablet is brand new again. This is great if you are recycling your tablet, but it's a last resort if all you want to do is fix a problem.

Reset Your Tablet

① Tap the Settings charm.

② Tap Change PC Settings.

③ Tap the General category

④ Scroll down the page.

⑤ Tap Get Started under Remove Everything And Reinstall Windows.

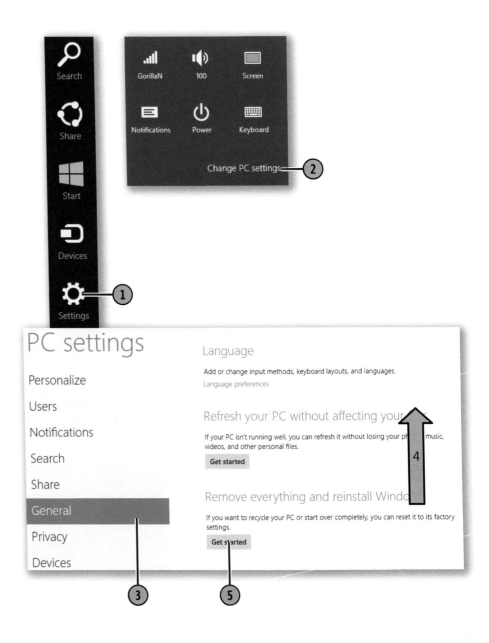

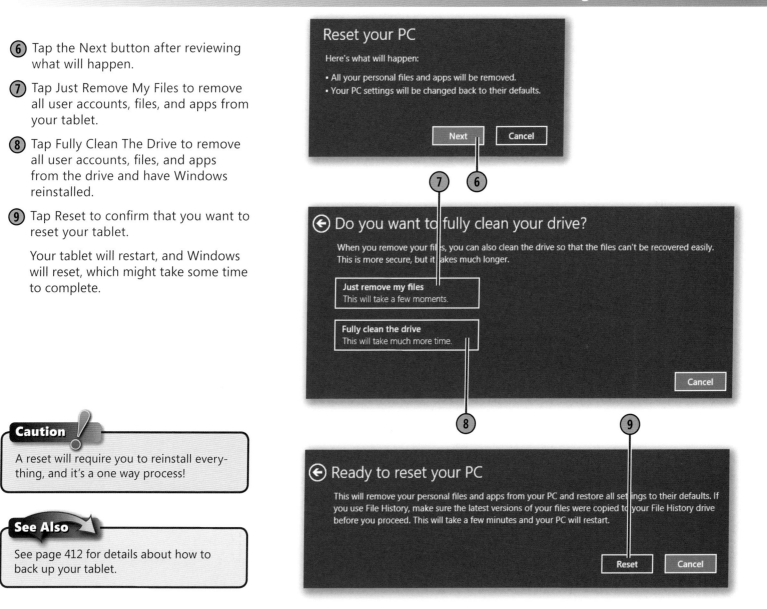

6 Tap the Next button after reviewing what will happen.

7 Tap Just Remove My Files to remove all user accounts, files, and apps from your tablet.

8 Tap Fully Clean The Drive to remove all user accounts, files, and apps from the drive and have Windows reinstalled.

9 Tap Reset to confirm that you want to reset your tablet.

Your tablet will restart, and Windows will reset, which might take some time to complete.

Caution

A reset will require you to reinstall everything, and it's a one way process!

See Also

See page 412 for details about how to back up your tablet.

Reset your PC

Here's what will happen:

• All your personal files and apps will be removed.
• Your PC settings will be changed back to their defaults.

Next   Cancel

⊘ Do you want to fully clean your drive?

When you remove your files, you can also clean the drive so that the files can't be recovered easily. This is more secure, but it takes much longer.

Just remove my files
This will take a few moments.

Fully clean the drive
This will take much more time.

Cancel

⊘ Ready to reset your PC

This will remove your personal files and apps from your PC and restore all settings to their defaults. If you use File History, make sure the latest versions of your files were copied to your File History drive before you proceed. This will take a few minutes and your PC will restart.

Reset   Cancel

Creating a Recovery Drive

Your tablet probably came with Windows 8 preinstalled and might not have come with any installation media, which you need if a computer-life-ending incident occurs, such as a serious virus infection. Your tablet comes with a way to make a recovery drive. You will need at least a 4-GB USB flash drive for this, but this can be reused if you ever need to refresh or reset your tablet. A recovery disk does not back up your personal files, but it can be used to only restore Windows, leaving your personal files unchanged.

Create a Recovery Drive

1. Tap the Search charm.
2. In the search box, type **recovery**.
3. Tap Settings to search within settings.
4. Tap Create A Recovery Drive.
5. Tap Yes.

Caution

This will create a recovery drive, but that drive will not contain your files, just those necessary to restore your existing tablet.

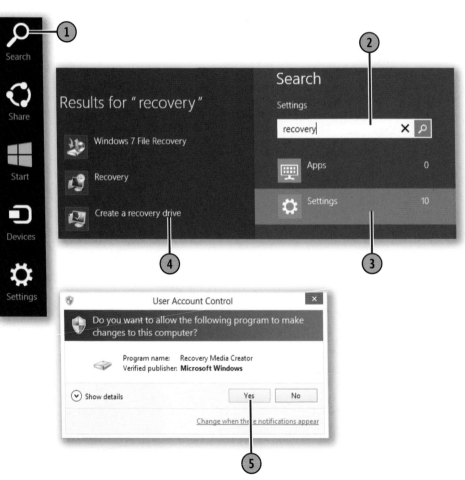

⑥ By default, any recovery partitions on your tablet that your tablet manufacturer might have placed there will be backed up. If you want to stop this, clear the Copy Contents From The Recovery Partition To The Recovery Drive check box. However, it's recommended to leave this selected.

⑦ Tap Next to continue.

⑧ If you have a USB key inserted into your tablet, it will be listed here. If you have more than one, select the one to use as a recovery driver. If you don't have a USB key inserted, insert a USB key and it will show up automatically.

⑨ Tap Next to continue. The recovery drive will be created, and you'll be presented with a results screen; tap Finish on this screen to end the process.

Caution

The recovery drive is a bootable USB key, meaning that if you leave it inserted in your tablet, the next time it reboots it will begin the recovery process again. Remove the USB key until you need it, and keep it somewhere safe.

⊕ 📼 Recovery Drive

Create a recovery drive

You can use a recovery drive to help troubleshoot problems with your PC even if it can't start. If your PC came with a recovery partition, you can also copy it to the recovery drive so you can use it to refresh or reset your PC.

☐ Copy the recovery partition from the PC to the recovery drive.

⑥

Next   Cancel

⑦

⊕ 📼 Recovery Drive

Select the USB flash drive

The drive must be able to hold at least 256 MB, and everything on the drive will be deleted.

Available drive(s)
D:\ (no label)

⑧

Next   Cancel

⑨

Backing Up and Restoring Specific Files on Your Tablet

In addition to creating a recovery drive for your tablet, you might also want to think about keeping a history of your files by using File History, because your personal files aren't included in a recovery image. When configured, File History takes a copy of your individual files every few hours if individual files have changed. That way, if you are editing a photo and accidentally make and save a change that you don't want, you can restore a previous version from File History.

Set Up File History

1. Tap the Search charm.
2. In the search box, type **backup**.
3. Tap Settings to search within settings.
4. Tap Save Backup Copies Of Your Files With File History to launch File History on the desktop.

Tip

You could also type "history" into the search to find the File History app.

Search

Share

Start

Devices

Settings

Settings   Results for " backup "

Save backup copies of your files with File History

Restore your files with File History

Search

Settings

backup

Apps   0

Settings   2

(5) Initially, File History is turned off and will not be able to work until you provide a location. The easiest way to do this is to insert a USB hard disk; this then appears in the Copy Files To section.

(6) Tap Turn On when a backup location is available.

(7) If you're a member of a homegroup, you'll be asked if you'd like to recommend your storage to others in the homegroup.

Because you're doing this on a tablet, you might not want other computers backing up to a drive on your tablet, in case your tablet is away from the homegroup.

(8) When set up, File History will run by default every hour. You can tap Run Now at any time to run a copy on demand.

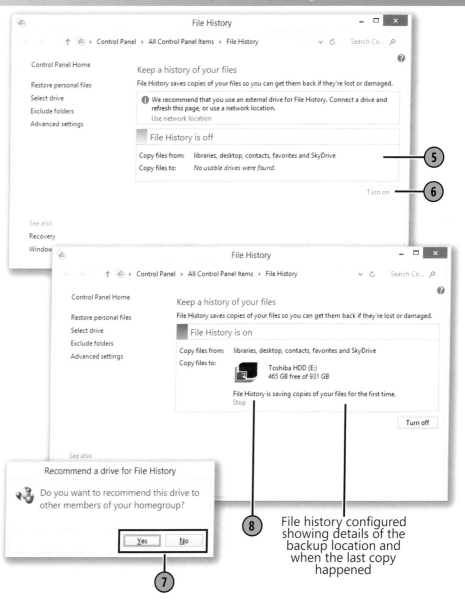

File history configured showing details of the backup location and when the last copy happened

Restore Files from File History

1. Tap the Search charm.

2. In the search box, enter **restore**.

3. Tap Settings to search within Settings.

4. Tap Restore Your Files With File History to begin the restore process.

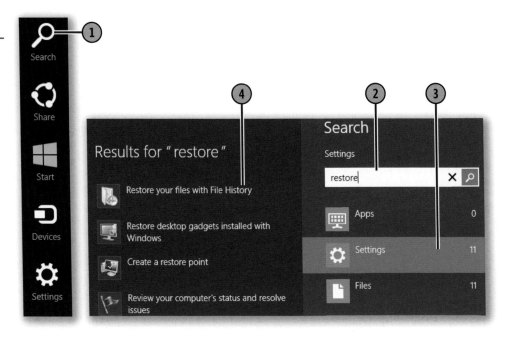

Tip

File History isn't magic; if you haven't set it up in advance, you won't have any files to restore, so your file history will be empty.

Tip

If your File History backup location is unavailable, you won't be able to restore files. If you save File History to a USB drive, plug it in; if you save files to a network drive or HomeGroup location, connect now.

(5) Each file history is viewed in a left-to-right panorama. Tap to go to a previous file history to find the correct version to restore.

(6) Tap if you go too far back in your File History and need to go forward again.

(7) Tap into Libraries or folders to go down to individual files.

You can restore individual files, all files and folders within a folder, or all files and folders within a library. Select multiple folders by selecting the check box to the left of the item.

(8) Tap the Restore button to restore your selected files.

Note that if you select nothing, all files in the File History that you have open will be restored.

(9) If files already exist in the location you're restoring, you'll be asked whether you want to replace them or skip them.

You can get specific about what to keep for each file by tapping Let Me Decide For Each File.

Creating a System Image

Another option for backing up your tablet is to create a system image to an external location, like a USB hard disk. This takes a complete copy of your tablet so that you can restore it and all your documents to the point in time that you created that backup. Unlike a recovery image, your files are also restored to the point at which the image was taken, so any changes since this will be lost.

Create a System Image

1. Tap the Search charm.

2. In the search box, type **windows 7 recovery**.

3. Tap Settings.

4. Tap Windows 7 File Recovery to start Windows 7 File Recovery on the desktop.

5. In the left action pane, tap Create System Image to start the wizard.

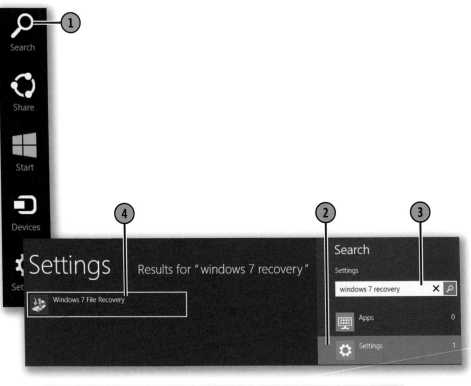

6 Select a location to which to save the backup.

A hard disk is the most efficient; the menu will be populated with any USB hard disks attached to your tablet.

7 Tap Next.

8 Confirm that you're backing up what you want (everything in this case), and tap Start Backup.

The backup will be created.

9 At the end of the backup, you'll be asked whether you want to create a repair disk. If you don't have one, you'll need to provide a USB flash drive before you tap Yes; if you do have one, you can use that.

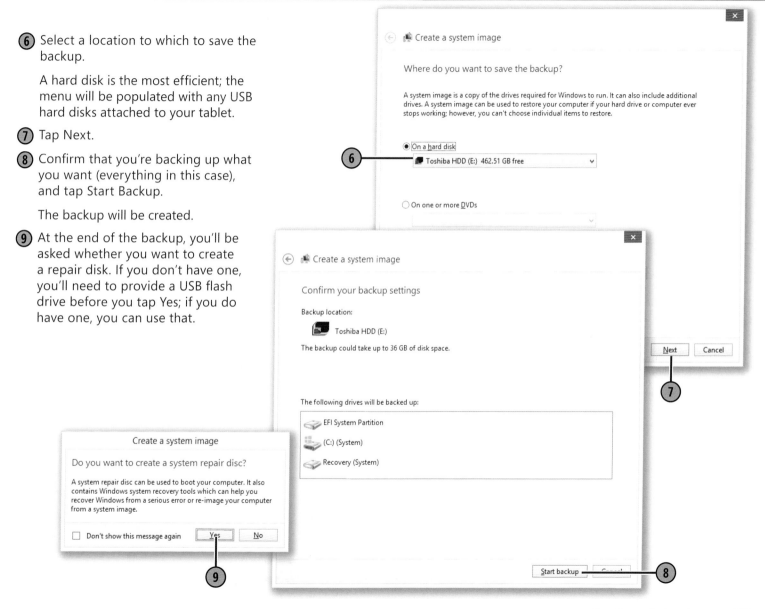

Create a system image

Where do you want to save the backup?

A system image is a copy of the drives required for Windows to run. It can also include additional drives. A system image can be used to restore your computer if your hard drive or computer ever stops working; however, you can't choose individual items to restore.

6

● On a hard disk

⬛ Toshiba HDD (E:) 462.51 GB free

○ On one or more DVDs

Next   Cancel

7

Create a system image

Confirm your backup settings

Backup location:

Toshiba HDD (E:)

The backup could take up to 36 GB of disk space.

The following drives will be backed up:

EFI System Partition

(C:) (System)

Recovery (System)

Start backup   Cancel

8

Create a system image

Do you want to create a system repair disc?

A system repair disc can be used to boot your computer. It also contains Windows system recovery tools which can help you recover Windows from a serious error or re-image your computer from a system image.

☐ Don't show this message again   Yes   No

9

Restoring Files from a Windows 7 Backup

If you have files that you've backed up on Windows 7 and need to restore them to your Windows 8–based tablet, you'll want to use Windows 7 File Recovery. It's also possible to make a backup of your Windows 8–based tablet by using Windows 7 File Recovery, and if you've done that, this task will show you how to recover those files.

Restore Files

1. Tap the Search charm.

2. In the search box, type **windows 7 file**.

3. Tap Settings to search within settings.

4. Tap Windows 7 File Recovery.

5. If you have the drive with the location of your Windows 7 backup attached, File Recovery will recognize it automatically and list it under Backup. If not, tap Select Another Backup To Restore Files From, and browse for the backup you want to use.

6. Tap Restore My Files to begin the restore.

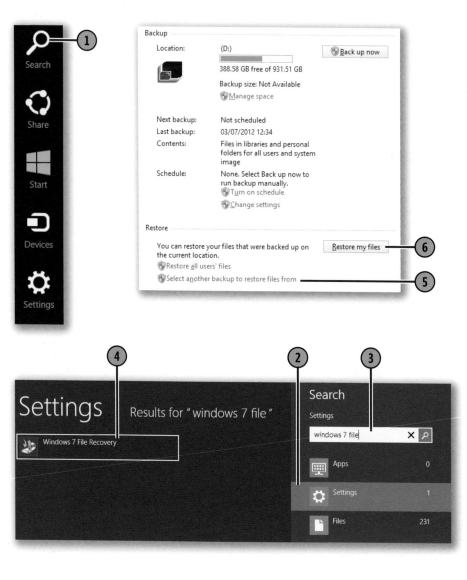

⑦ Tap Browse For Files or Browse For Folders to locate the files or folders to restore.

⑧ Tap the files or folders you want to restore.

⑨ Tap Next to begin the restore process.

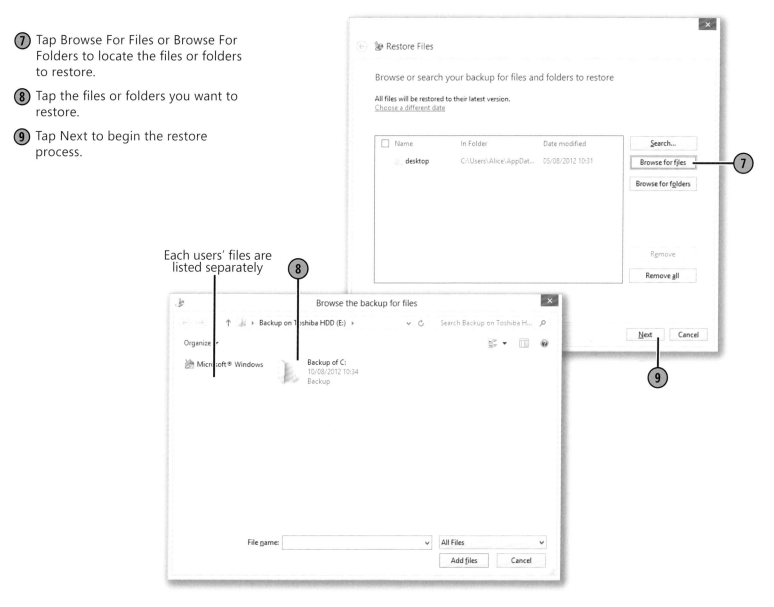

Each users' files are listed separately

10 Tap In The Original Location if you want to restore the files to where they were originally, or tap In The Following Location and browse to a location where you want to restore the files.

This can be useful if you aren't sure that the backup copy you have is correct and you don't want to lose your current copy.

11 Tap Restore to begin the restore process.

If files are being overwritten (you tapped In The Original Location), you'll be asked for confirmation. When complete, a final confirmation screen will appear; tap Finish on this page to close it.

Restoring a System Image

If you've created a system image of your tablet with Windows 7 File Recovery, you might need to restore it. This can be done in a couple of ways. One is to use a recovery disk to initiate the process if you can't start your tablet. However, if you can start your tablet, it's easier to have Windows 8 restart into the recover environment and restore it from there.

Restart to Restore a System Image

① Tap the Settings charm.

② Tap Change PC Settings.

③ Tap the General category.

④ Scroll down to Advanced Startup.

⑤ Tap Restart Now.

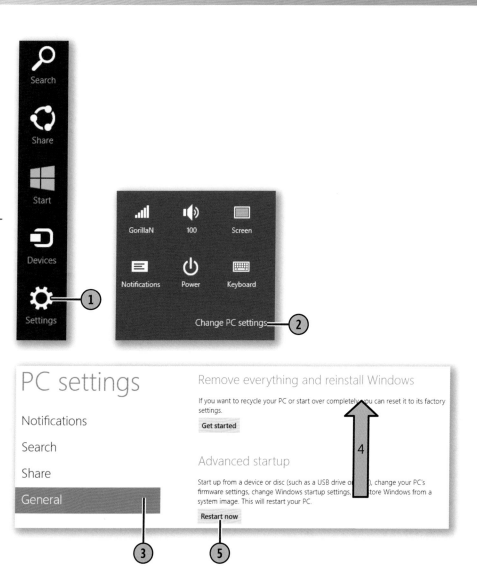

Completing System Image Recovery

When you've started System Image Recovery, whether by booting from a recovery disk or restarting into advanced startup, the process for recovery is the same.

Complete System Image Recovery

1. Your tablet will start a special recovery mode. Tap Troubleshoot on the options screen.

2. Tap Advanced Options.

3. Tap System Image Recovery, which causes your tablet to reboot into a special recover mode.

4. When prompted, select your user account.

5. Enter the password for your account.

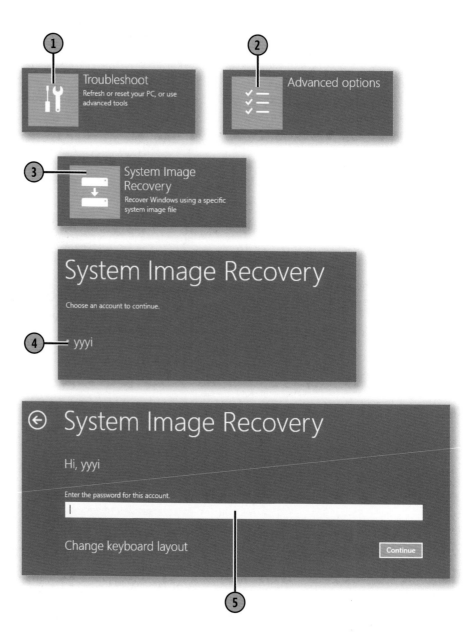

(6) The last created image on your disk should be available and listed; if you want to use another image, tap Select A System Image.

(7) Tap Next to continue.

(8) All available images are listed; select the image to use.

(9) Tap Next to use the image.

(10) Tap Next to continue.

The restore will now occur, and following a reboot, your tablet will be restored to the point in time that the system image was created.

Re-image your computer

Select a system image backup

This computer will be restored using the system image. Everything on this computer will be replaced with the information in the system image.

Troubleshooting information for BMR:
http://go.microsoft.com/fwlink/p/?LinkId=225039

◉ Use the latest available system image(recommended)

Location:	Local Disk (D:)
Date and time:	7/3/2012 3:04:04 AM (GMT-8:00)
Computer:	simon8slateRP

○ Select a system image

< Back   Next >

Re-image your computer

Select the location of the backup for the computer you want to restore
If the system image is on an external device, attach the device to this computer, and then click Refresh.

If the system image is on a DVD, insert the last DVD from the system image backup. Click Advanced to add a network location or install a driver for a backup device if it does not show up in the list below.

Current time zone: GMT-8:00

Location	Most recent system image	Computer
Local Disk (D:)	7/3/2012 3:04:04 AM	simon8slateRP

Advanced...   Refresh

< Back   Next >   Cancel

Re-image your computer

Choose additional restore options

☐ Format and repartition disks
Select this to delete any existing partitions and reformat all disks on this computer to match the layout of the system image.

Exclude dis

If you're unable to select an option above, installing the drivers for the disks you are restoring to might solve the problem.

Install driv

Advanced...

< Back   Next >

Glossary

A

ACTION CENTER. Indicated by the white flag on the Windows desktop taskbar. This feature aggregates system messages and troubleshooting help.

ADMINISTRATOR. A user account level at which a user can make changes to an operating system or programs.

ANTI-MALWARE. Software that can recognize and deal with malware attached to an email, on a webpage, or already installed on your computer.

APP. A software application, especially those accessed via tiles on the Start screen.

APPLICATION. A software program such as Microsoft Word or Microsoft Internet Explorer.

B

BACKUP. Copies of programs or files kept separate from your computer in case the original file becomes corrupt or is deleted.

BANDWIDTH. A measure of the maximum amount of data bits that can be transferred over the Internet or phone system to a computer at any one time.

BLUETOOTH. A technology that uses radio transmissions to allow interaction between a device, such as printer, mouse, or headset, and your computer or tablet.

BOOKMARK. *See also* Favorites. A list of saved sites to make retrieval of those sites easier.

BOOT. To start a computer when the power is turned off.

BROADBAND. High-speed Internet connections such as Cable or ADSL.

BROWSER. Program used to browse the World Wide Web. For example, Internet Explorer, Firefox, Safari, and Chrome.

BUTTON. A graphical representation of a computer command. When you click or tap a button, the command is executed.

C

CHARM. Provides access to Windows features, such as Start, Search, Sharing, Devices, and Settings..

COOKIE. A small text file that is downloaded to your computer by a website. Sites use cookies to remember your logon details and records your activities for future reference. You can block or delete cookies by using settings in Internet Explorer or other browsers.

CD, DVD Disk. Disks provided by software manufacturers to install software on your computer from a CD/DVD drive or used by you to store copies of your files and data.

CHECK BOX. A way to provide on/off input for a feature or setting by selecting or clearing a small box.

CLOUD (The). The practice of hosting programs or services on Internet servers. End users can access these programs or services from their computers without having to install any app locally on their device.

COMPATIBILITY MODE. A special mode in Windows in which programs run in an emulated environment that mimics an earlier version of Windows.

CONTROL PANEL. A set of tools and settings with which you can configure the basic functions of your tablet.

CONTROL KEY. Marked Ctrl on the keyboard. Like Alt and Function keys, this key is used in combination with other keys. Its use can vary from program to program.

CUT or COPY & PASTE. Common tools/menu commands for editing text. With most Windows programs, you can cut or copy a selected item (text or object) and paste it into another place within a document or into another document. Use Ctrl in combination with X, C, and V as shortcuts for cutting, copying, and pasting, respectively.

CYBERCAFE or INTERNET CAFÉ. Public locations where you can get access to the Internet and a cup of coffee.

D

DATABASE. A list of items of data kept on a computer that can be edited, searched, or printed.

DESKTOP. An alternate interface to the Start screen in which users can control settings and programs in an environment similar to previous versions of Windows.

DRIVER. A software program that enables communication between the operating system and a hardware device.

DIALOG BOX. A window that contains sets of commands such as a Font dialog box for formatting text.

DOWNLOAD. The process of transferring files from the web to your computing device. You can download pictures, videos, PDF files, text, and programs.

DRAG-AND-DROP. The facility in most programs to select text or a file and move it to another position or location by using a mouse or finger (on a touchscreen).

DRIVE LETTER. An alphabetical letter from A to Z that Windows assigns to a fixed or removable hard disk.

DVD Player. A disk player for DVD discs. Capable of playing CDs, as well.

E

E-BOOK. Electronic book.

EMAIL. A service by which you can send messages over the Internet.

EMAIL CLIENT. Program used to send and receive emails such as Windows Live Hotmail or AOL Mail.

ENCRYPTION. A cryptographic technique to make data unreadable without an authorized method of unlocking it.

FAMILY SAFETY. A Windows feature with which you can control children's access to certain features and online content.

F

FAVORITES. *See also* Bookmarks. A feature of a web browser by which you add frequently used sites to a list for easy retrieval.

FILE EXPLORER. Used to view files, folders, libraries, and networks on the desktop.

FIREWALL. A program that protects your computer from unauthorized access via the Internet.

FLASH DRIVE. A removable storage device that connects to your computer through a USB port.

FONT. A collection of text characters of a predefined style, such as Times New Roman or Arial, that can be applied to selected text.

FREEWARE. Computer programs that are distributed free of charge.

G

GIGABYTE. 1,073,741,824 bytes.

GPS (Global Positioning System). A technology that uses satellites to establish your computer, tablet, or mobile phone's location.

GRAPHICS. The general term used for illustrations, photographs, and other picture objects.

GRAPHICS CARD. The hardware in a computer that controls the monitor or display.

H

HARD COPY. Printed material.

HARD DISK. A disk or set of disks in a computer that is used to record data such as programs and user files.

HARDWARE. Any piece of computing equipment, such as the tablet itself or a printer.

HOMEGROUP. A networking feature through which Windows 8–based computers and devices can share files and printers within a single network.

HOME PAGE. The first page of a website, usually Index.htm. This is the webpage that loads first when you visit a website.

HOTMAIL. A web-based email service run by Microsoft.

HOT SPOT. A Wi-Fi connection in a location such as a café, airport, or hotel over which Wi-Fi enabled laptops, smartphones, or tablets can access the connection.

HYPERLINK. A segment of text or a graphic on a webpage on which you can click or tap that takes you to another webpage. Text links are often colored and underlined; images and maps can also act as links. When using a mouse, the pointer changes shape to that of a hand when hovering over a link. *See* Surfing.

I

IM (Instant Messaging). An app such as Windows Messaging with which you can send text-based messages to people online in real time.

INTEGRATED SEARCH. A feature of Windows with which you can search apps, files, settings, and a variety of web content from the Start screen.

INTERNET. The worldwide network of computer servers that host the data, including the World Wide Web.

INTERNET EXPLORER. The most common web browser, offered for free download or as part of Windows. Other browsers include Mozilla Firefox and Google Chrome.

ISP (Internet Service Provider). A company that provides you with access to the Internet.

M

MALWARE. Malicious software, such as viruses.

MEMORY. Storage capacity in a computer or tablet that Windows uses to store files and run programs.

MOBILE BROADBAND. High-speed Internet connections that use a cellular service provider to make the connection, usually charged per megabyte of data transferred.

MONITOR. The computer screen. Also called *display*.

MOTHERBOARD. The main circuit board of a computer, to which components such as computer chips and graphics cards are attached.

MP3. A highly compressed form of music, which can be downloaded from the web and played on a computer or a portable device. MP3 stands for Music Program Expert Group Audio Layer 3 (or MPEG3).

N

NET. A nickname for the Internet.

NETWORK. General term for connected computers.

NOTIFICATIONS. Pop-up notices presented by Windows of important information, such as potential virus threats.

O

OFFLINE. Not connected to the Internet.

ONLINE. Connected to the Internet.

OPERATING SYSTEM. A software interface for a computer in which you can run programs and control devices.

P

PC SETTINGS. Common computer or tablet settings that you can access from the Settings charm.

PDF (Portable Document Format). A platform-independent file format developed by Adobe Systems, Inc. for creating documents that can be read across different devices.

PHISHING. This is the name given to a scam by which you receive an email, supposedly from your bank or other source that you are intended to trust, requesting that you confirm your password or other personal data, which the attacker can use in criminal fashion.

PIN. To place a tile for an app on the Start screen.

PIXEL (Picture element). A tiny element that, along with millions of others, makes up the image you see on a computer screen or a photograph. Cameras are often classified in megapixels. A megapixel is one million pixels. The more pixels in an image, the better the detail of the picture. However, more pixels also means more memory is consumed.

PLUG-AND-PLAY. An architecture by which modern computers and hardware (printers, sound cards, DVD players, and so on) are able to recognize when they are connected together, thus enabling easy installation or use.

POINT SIZE. The height of a printed character. A typical email correspondence is usually around 12 points in size.

PORT. Either a physical socket on your computer, such USB, parallel (printer) or Serial communications), or part of the operating system through which communication with your computer takes place (the latter are numbered, for example, Port 110).

PROCESSOR. A physical silicon chip on a motherboard that is the "brain" of a computer or tablet.

R

REFRESH. A way to return a faulty copy of Windows 8 to a properly working copy without losing any files or data.

REGISTRY. A file (one per user on a computer) that contains a database of settings for Windows, user preferences, and installed software and hardware.

REMOTE ASSISTANCE. A feature by which another individual (for example, a Help desk technician) can remotely control a computer over a network or the Internet.

REMOTE DESKTOP. A feature by which you can assume remote control of another computer on a network.

REINSTALL. A way to reset a computer or tablet that is experiencing problems to its original factory settings. All data is lost with this procedure.

S

SAFE MODE. A startup mode that boots Windows in its most basic form, with no background programs in operation. In Safe Mode, the screen displays a very basic (large) layout.

Safe Mode is used to troubleshoot and repair various problems in the operating system, including virus removal and defragmentation. To enter Safe Mode, press Shift+F8 upon startup.

SCANNER. A piece of equipment capable of digitally recording a picture or some text for use on a computer.

SEARCH ENGINE. A program, usually accessed on the Internet, that you use to search for information by entering a few words.

SHAREWARE. Computer programs or software that are free to use, but you are invited to make a contribution toward its development and maintenance costs, typically around $15.

SITE or WEBSITE. An area on the Internet that has its own unique web address (URL). A typical website has a Home page followed by other pages that are linked to the Home page via *hyperlinks*.

SKYDRIVE. Microsoft's online cloud storage solution, found at *http://www.skydrive.com*.

SNAP. A feature that allows you to drag (with a finger or mouse) an open window to the side of the screen to anchor it there.

SOFTWARE. Programs of all kinds which make the computer or tablet act in a particular way to perform certain functions, such as word processing, desktop publishing, and financial calculations.

SPAM. Unsolicited advertising that usually arrives in emails.

SPYWARE. Software that installs itself on your computer without your knowledge which monitors and reports back your activities to its originator.

START SCREEN. The central interface of Windows 8, from which you can access apps and settings.

STREAMING. Receiving sound, video, or pictures over the Internet without having to download the content.

SURFING. Using the hypertext links embedded in a webpage to jump from one website or page to another.

SYSTEM RESTORE. A Windows feature that makes copies of critical system settings and files to be used to restore your system later if required.

T

TAB KEY. Located on the left of the keyboard, you can use this key to jump certain fixed distances across the page when using a word processor, or to jump from one text box to the next when filling out forms, or to move from one table cell to the next when working in a table editor.

TASKBAR. The bar across the bottom of the desktop that contains program and setting icons for quick access.

TEMPORARY FILES. Your Internet browser, some installation programs, and even your own programs can store some files in a part of your hard disk memory. These files are deleted when no longer in use.

TEMPLATE. A standard letter or spreadsheet that forms the basis, or framework, for new documents. Templates can be modified to suit the needs of the current document.

TOOLBAR. An array of icons often found at the top of a program such as a word processor that represent tools and functions you use to carry out tasks.

TOUCHSCREEN. A computer monitor that responds to physical contact by which you provide input to the computer or tablet by touching the screen with a stylus or your finger.

U

USER INTERFACE. A schema to display the user controls for a computer on a monitor. Modern user interfaces are designed to be friendly, intuitive, and usually graphical manner.

UNPIN. To remove a tile from the Windows Start screen.

USER FOLDER. A folder containing a user's files and folders.

URL (Universal Resource Locator). A web address. Web addresses can begin with http:// or www, or both.

USB PORT (Universal Serial Bus). A communication port used to transfer data between your computer and USB devices.

V

VIRUS. A malicious program intended to harm your data or disrupt your computer performance. A virus is spread either from disks or from the Internet.

W

WEB BROWSER. *See* browser.

WEBCAM. A small camera that you can attach to a computer (or is integrated directly in the computer or tablet) with which you can send video images over the Internet.

WEP. An encryption method that provides data security for wireless networks.

WI-FI. A wireless interface that uses radio waves to link computers and other devices.

WINDOW. Part of the Windows interface that allows you to view a program, content, or group of settings in a box that you can shrink, enlarge, or display side by side with other windows.

WINDOWS 8. The very latest edition of the Windows operating system on which this book is based.

WINDOWS STORE. An online store containing apps that work with the Windows operating system.

WINDOWS UPDATE. A feature in Windows for automatically updating the operating system with the latest updates and patches.

WIZARD. A program that helps you through a process such as installing new software or hardware.

WORD PROCESSING. Creating documents on a computer that can easily be edited (processed).

WORM. A virus program that spreads by sending itself to people in your email address book.

WPA. An encryption method for wireless networks.

WWW (World Wide Web). Documents stored on the Internet.

Z

ZIP FILE. A file in which data is compressed to take up less space. Files in zip or compressed files must be extracted to be used.

Touch Gestures Reference

Here's handy reference that shows basic touch gestures.

Show Charms

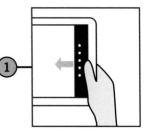

(1) From the right edge of the screen, swipe inward (to the left). Charms allow access to Search, Share, Devices, Settings, and the Start screen at any time.

Switch Apps

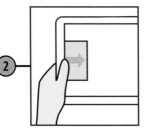

(2) From the left edge of the screen, swipe inward (to the right) to switch between already open apps.

Show Previously Used Apps

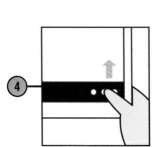

(3) From the left edge of the screen, swipe inward (to the right) and then immediately leftward to display a list of apps previously opened. Tap an app to open it.

Show App Commands

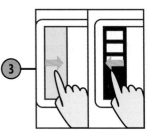

(4) Swipe upward from the bottom of the screen or downward from the top of the screen to show the app bar, which allows access to commands

Close an App

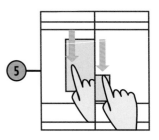

(5) In Windows, apps don't slow your tablet down, so there is no need to close them. However, if you want to close an app, simply swipe downward from the top to the bottom of the screen.

Tap and Hold for Menus

(6) Tap and hold an item to see whether an options menu appears. This mainly happens on the desktop, but some apps, such as Mail, also use this to shortcut actions.

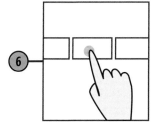

Tap to Do

(7) Tap an item to perform an action such as follow a link, open an app, or press a button.

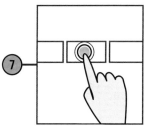

Slide to Pan

(8) Tap the screen and slide either horizontally or vertically to move objects in that direction to pan or scroll.

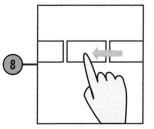

Pinch or Stretch to Zoom Out or In

(9) Touch the screen with two fingers, and move them together to zoom out or apart to zoom in. Pictures can be zoomed to show more or less detail, but many lists of items can be zoomed in to show more or less detail too.

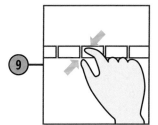

Rotate to Turn

(10) Touch the screen with two fingers and rotate to turn objects such as pictures.

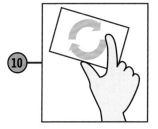

Index

A

About the Author

Simon May is an IT evangelist for Microsoft. He is involved in deploying, managing, and maintaining Windows in large and small corporate environments. Simon spends his time talking to IT professionals around the United Kingdom, explaining how to get the most out of Windows and how IT professionals can encourage smarter use of devices within their organizations. Simon is an author and successful blogger. You can reach him any time through one of his other passions, social media.

10/14 ① 5/13

What do you think of this book?

We want to hear from you!

To participate in a brief online survey, please visit:

microsoft.com/learning/booksurvey

Tell us how well this book meets your needs—what works effectively, and what we can do better. Your feedback will help us continually improve our books and learning resources for you.

Thank you in advance for your input!